# CARING IS EVERYTHING

## Getting to the Heart
## of Humanity, Leadership, and Life

### *By David Irvine*

GONDOLIER

CARING IS EVERYTHING

Copyright © 2016 by David Irvine

Published by
Gondolier, a Division of Bayeux Arts, Inc.
510 – 6th Avenue, SE
Calgary, Canada T2G 1L7
www.bayeux.com

Author: David Irvine
Email: david@davidirvine.com
www.davidirvine.com

Distributed by
Literary Press Group of Canada
University of Chicago Press Distribution

Also available directly from Author

Book set in Adobe Garamond Pro

Cover design by Michael Dangelmaier, Red Pine Design

Edited by Elaine Morin

First published: April 2017
Printed in Canada

**Library and Archives Canada Cataloguing in Publication**
**Irvine, David, 1956-, author**
    **Caring is everything / David Irvine.**

**Includes bibliographical references.**
**ISBN 978-1-988440-00-2 (hardback)**


          **1. Caring.   2. Leadership.   3. Quality of life.   I. Title.**
**BJ1475.I78 2016             177'.7          C2016-905417-9**

The Publisher gratefully acknowledges the financial support of the Canada Council for the Arts, Alberta Culture, Livres Canada Books, and the Government of Canada through the Canada Book Fund.

Canada Council
for the Arts
Conseil des Arts
du Canada
Alberta Culture

LIVRES CANADA BOOKS

Canada
Government of Canada through
the Canada Book Fund

# Praise for
## *Caring is Everything*

David Irvine gives uncommon consideration to a topic common to all of our lives: caring. Accompany him on his own caring journey with some surprising (and enlightening) turns into forgiveness through depression and our shadow selves. You will see what David learned as he followed often uncomfortable paths in caring for others. And you will learn along with him. Well and engagingly presented, this book tests our ability to get beyond ourselves—in order to more fully become ourselves.

Geoff Bellman, Consultant
Author of *Your Signature Path: Gaining New Perspectives on Life and Work*

A buffet of wisdom, a feast for the soul, each page nourishing, but like an appetizer for the next. Thank you, David, for such an eloquent meal.

Dean Beaudry, P. Eng.
Manager, Operations Safety, Syncrude

David is a storyteller. His stories will touch and inspire you. You will grow and learn. Your life will improve.

Don Campbell
Rancher & Holistic Management Practitioner

This is my new Irvine favorite. Courageous, impactful, and so incredibly raw. He shows an insight that left me envious and occasionally in tears.

Ron Campbell
Mental Health Advocate

*Caring is Everything* is a thoughtful, authentic, and engaging read. Dave weaves powerful stories with autobiographical examples to provide deep insights on a timeless topic even more vital in today's me-centered society. This is a book for deep pondering and meditation on its vital lessons.

Jim Clemmer
Leadership Author, Speaker, and Workshop/Retreat Leader

We are all inspired by random acts of kindness, even on a small scale. Why does our caring have to be random? What if we decide to be more intentional in our actions? In *Caring is Everything* David helps illuminate the difference between capriciously floating along and intentionally navigating a more satisfying course through life.

Vincent Deberry, Executive Director
The Center for Public Management at the University of Oklahoma

In this personal, vulnerable documentation of his own experience and development as a human being, David has captured the multiple facets of the caring experience by applying his many years of work with others as a coach, mentor, leadership growth facilitator, and therapist. From caring born of suffering, to caring as a community endeavor, to protecting one's self from "burn out," the reader is taken on a journey with one good man's soul as he grapples with the real nature of what it means to care for each other in a world sometimes filled with fear and aloneness. Offering his focused insight on the caring process and attitudes, David also gives his reader valuable, quickly applied life practices to help us all become better at this elusive behavior we call "caring."

Larry Dick
Retired School Principal

David Irvine's *Caring is Everything* is that rare book capable of tapping into one's personal humanity in the most unexpectedly profound and pervasive ways. David masterfully pulls back the curtain on that one trait that makes us most human ... the act of caring. Caring completes the leader. Caring completes the individual. Caring is the antidote to indifference and personal gain at the expense of others. In these pages, readers will find humility, enlightenment, and hope for a more fulfilling life. It doesn't matter if you are a leader, business owner, employee, or just someone open enough to explore what's really important in life ... *Caring is Everything* will reveal a part of you that will touch the lives of others.

Neil Ducoff, Founder & CEO of Strategies
Author of the award-winning book *No-Compromise Leadership*

David Irvine has always shown caring for me and others who have worked with him. I felt connected and when I read the book I then knew why—because he truly does care about people. He has inspired me to be truly authentic in my own caring for others.

Laurie Gronhovd
General Manager, New Horizon Co-op

David Irvine's most recent book, *Caring is Everything*, provides the reader with an in-depth understanding and perspective of what caring is really all about. A must read for anyone who wants to commit themselves to a life with character and purpose.

Dan Guimond
President and CEO, Manitoba Public Insurance

Here is a very personal story of two brothers reconnecting. Each had gone his own professional way over the years, the younger (the author) as a management consultant and speaker, the older (a highly esteemed rural physician) through his medical practice. In a series of encounters brought about by the older brother's fight with terminal cancer, caring triumphs over careers and the flame of authentic brotherly love is rekindled. A must read.

Warren A. Harbeck, PhD
Linguist, Religious Studies Scholar, and Community Lamplighter

David understands that success in life is an intersection of caring and being authentic in our dealings with others. David's personal journey with his brother is bravely displayed and reminds us all that many of our most rewarding personal journeys with those that we care the most about still await us. *Caring is Everything* reminds us that often we get busy in the day-to-day and don't spend enough time on the relationships that truly reward our soul. David reminds us that our personal success is related to our authenticity and caring toward others.

Ron Hyson
Vice President, Human Resources, Giant Tiger Stores Limited

David Irvine's contribution to humanity continues to evolve intimately; his legacy will be one of healing the world through personal growth, thereby enriching others through his call to be courageous and accountable, to be a better person tomorrow than we were today. David is a rare human treasure of wisdom, and if we listen, he enables us as humans to celebrate our strengths. He challenges us in those areas of our lives that would be enriched with new commitment.

Dale Kelly
President and CEO, POS Group of Companies

David Irvine does a wonderful job of weaving his personal journey of caring through these thought provoking stories … *Caring is Everything* provides plenty of opportunities for the reader to apply David's experiences and those of other respected leaders to his or her own life. I found the book compelling for both my personal and professional situations.

Carol Kitchen
President and CEO, United Farmers of Alberta Ltd.

An inspiring and deeply insightful work that could only be authored by someone with David's profound understanding of the true meaning of caring. You will pick up this book over and over again when you are in need of inspiration that comes from a deeper understanding of what caring really means.

John Knapp
Author of *The Leader's Practice Guide*

The title says it all—*Caring is Everything* is an inspiring and at times emotional read that is as instructive as it is insightful. By letting us into his personal journey and accumulated wisdom, David Irvine challenges the reader, telling us that through genuine caring for those around us, we become a better parent, sibling, spouse, citizen, employee, and leader. It is never too late to enrich your life through caring.

Chief Rod Knecht, Edmonton Police Service
Former Senior Deputy Commissioner of the Royal Canadian
Mounted Police

A truly remarkable and inspirational book! In *Caring is Everything*, David Irvine has been able to capture the Essence of who we ARE. The author demonstrates his authenticity by including himself in this transformational journey of understanding of the Self and the Other. His stories and guided wisdom are simple and powerful, and flow with a grace tying varying concepts of LOVE together in a way very few have been able to achieve. There is something for everyone here! A much needed book at this time in our evolution. Much gratitude, David.

Gerry Labossiere
Former CEO, AIS

David has challenged my thinking with his personal stories, experiences, and very wise words. Caring is everywhere when we choose to see it in others and in ourselves. Caring is what gives me hope and motivates me to do better and to dig deep when challenges get very big. In my work, caring really is everything! Thank you, David!

Della Lastiwka
Principal, Iron Ridge Intermediate School

Another beautiful piece of writing by David. I admire his tremendous ability to take the reader on a journey. Rather than tell the reader what to think, he shares with them his own journey of discovery, and in the process invites you to journey alongside him and discover your own thoughts on the same topic. Pour yourself a relaxing cup of tea and experience this book in its fullness. When you are done, make a list of who you care about and make sure they know it. Today. Caring really is everything.

John Liston
Life and Business Coach, Liston Advisory Group Inc.

As an entrepreneur, leader, speaker, and author, David has yet again put pen to paper to share his experience, knowledge, and insight related to the power of caring. This book is a gift that enables us to reflect and invest in life's many wonders as we seek to find harmony, meaning, wellbeing, and most importantly our own purpose.

Ken MacLeod
President & CEO, TEC Canada

*Caring is Everything* is a journey with David in which he navigates the internal fabric of the power and virtue of caring. David is to be commended for his courage and unwavering conviction in sharing his personal life experiences so we can all have a deeper understanding of the true meaning of *caring*. I unequivocally endorse David's core principles of authentic leadership that resonate and align with my own leadership values.

Superintendent B. K. McLeod (rtd)
K Division (Alberta), Royal Canadian Mounted Police

Acknowledgment, acceptance, and accountability are three powerful words that David Irvine authentically and successfully brings to his storytelling. *Caring is Everything* brilliantly fosters the notion that all of us, regardless of our education, social, or economic status, can sincerely make a difference and bring joy to others, ourselves, and the community in which we serve.

Michael Meloche
Senior Vice President, TMF Foods Ltd

Caring has been at the core of David's work, and his latest book is charged with this ancient wisdom that underpins his life and his writings. *Caring is Everything* is an instructive guide, brimming with a mix of profound stories and practical observations drawn from the author's own journey. David captures the essence of flourishing humanity through the virtue of caring, and invites readers into deep intention to foster these truths. Written with insight, clarity, and passion, this book will inspire, provoke, and challenge you to think anew about your own life, and respond to the call to embrace these higher principles for the good of all.

Marilyn Mahoney
Leadership Consultant, Facilitator, and Coach, Fraser Health

David slowly and surely builds the case for *Caring is Everything* by telling one story at a time. The stories are compelling and certainly lead to a place of self-reflection. This is capped by the Character Inventory and Self-Care Inventory. The *caring* David writes about works to everybody's benefit and you, the reader, are the major beneficiary. What a wonderful read.

Larry Malazdrewicz
Professional Certified Coach

With a decision to focus on caring as the preeminent process for renewing a civil society and the vibrancy of life, David Irvine establishes his credentials as one of the leading thought-practitioners of our time. Whereas other voices call for partial explanations, Irvine leads us to a seminal truth: caring is at the core of all that matters to us as people. Through caring, the inherent value of our life experience is thereby immeasurably enhanced, and David Irvine explains both the why and the how—sustained and supported by the authenticity of his own reflective practice. A great read that offers the possibility for an even greater quality-of-life.

Ronald K. Mitchell, CPA, Ph.D.
Professor of Entrepreneurship, Rawls College of Business, Texas Tech University

Dave's profound compassion for his family and his clients enables him to remind us all that it's time to move forward daily toward this noble goal of truly caring for others in spirit, soul, and body. Dave's many stories bring light and healing. Caring is indeed why we all were born—caring *is* everything.

Dr. Peter Nieman
Marathoner, Physician and Author of *Moving Forward*

Dave's work has always inspired me and made me think more deeply about the meaning and purpose of my life. This book is no different.

Tim O'Connor
CEO, Results Canada Inc.

*Caring is Everything* is a "must read" for anyone committed to personal growth and self-awareness as a way of life. Every page has inspired me to reflect upon how I can be a better me! David Irvine provides practical suggestions and tools that I can and will use to improve the relationships in my life, including with myself. Reading this book has been a rare gift—thank you, David.

Jim Reger
Leadership Author and Family Business Consultant

I've had the distinct pleasure of working with David on a number of projects. His most recent book, *Caring is Everything*, captures the essence of what I believe to be one of the most important components of successful and engaged leadership.

D.W. (Bill) Robinson
President and CEO, AGLC, Asst. Commissioner, RCMP (Rtd)

This book isn't easy. It demands us to stand up and care. David has crafted an important narrative that takes us through some of life's hardest journeys—through the grief of learning his brother is dying, through debilitating depression, sometimes through a failure to do the right thing. Drawing from his own and others' stories, David reveals the joy in caring. The result is an all-encompassing and vital book—for caregivers, for leaders, and for life.

Lance Secretan
Bestselling Author and Advisor to Leaders, The Secretan Center

Once again, David has tapped into a very important but often overlooked aspect of doing business well. Too often we train our business people on the quantitative aspects of success and pay lip service to the human side. Or we tell people to have emotional intelligence and look after the "soft" skills, but it rarely goes deep enough to make a real impact in how they operate as leaders. By shedding new light on the concept of caring and showing how that lives in the hardscrabble world of business, David has made yet another contribution to helping us all understand the practicalities of succeeding not just in business, but in our people.

Mark Szabo, PhD
Executive Director, Strategic Events & Communications,
University of Calgary

In *Caring is Everything*, David narrates his journey and that of his brother Hal, a doctor who became a patient, and is now a model of caring preserved in this book. Through the love shared on this difficult journey, David has been inspired to illuminate the many facets of giving, getting, and being rejuvenated by care. Care is not only an action but also a state of being that we all have the capacity to enjoy and nurture. It is part of what I call our innate nobility.

Ian West
Vice President, Operations, Park Place Seniors Living

David Irvine shines an honest and authentic light on a powerful force that connects us all. A memoir and tribute to those who inspire, this book reminds us of what really matters and leaves me caring that much more—in the workplace, in the community, and close at home.

Brandie Yarish
Caring Leader and Coach

To Hal—who inspired this project

In everybody's life, at some time, our inner fire goes out. It is then burst into flame by an encounter with another human being. We should all be thankful for those people who rekindle the inner spirit.

Albert Schweitzer

One cannot explain the behavior of loving members of families or of soldiers who give their lives for their country, or of many other decent and unselfish acts.

Martha C. Nussbaum

# Contents

# Preface: Caring is a Path to Authenticity

A musician must make music, an artist must paint, a poet must write, if they are to be ultimately at peace with themselves.

Abraham Maslow

## A path to authenticity

Within every person lies a place where, when connected to it, we feel deeply and intensely alive. At such moments there is a quiet voice inside that says, "This is the real me." When we live a life that we are born to live—in alignment with our authentic self—we discover meaning, purpose, and fulfillment in our lives. Living authentically means living with less stress, greater contentment, and more peace. We are comfortable with ourselves. Our worth and security come from within. Discovering and living your authentic self is a journey that is both daring as well as deeply and profoundly gratifying.

Living authentically, however, doesn't just have benefit for one's life. Authenticity, it turns out, also makes you a better leader. From more than a decade of research and observation, we have found that leaders who are authentic are more trusted and better able to influence others. Instinctively, we know this. We are repelled by facades, pretenses, and dishonesty. In our increasingly complex world, we are tired of the gimmicks, fads, and leadership flavors of the month, and are drawn instead to people who are honest, sincere, and real. We no longer just want to be polite. What we seek is *genuineness*. Authenticity impacts the quality of our leadership. It's about becoming a person worth following. We must *be* before we can *do*. It's about our *presence*, not our position.

Measuring authenticity, however, gets difficult. Articulating how someone is authentic is like trying to explain why something is beautiful. Visiting an art gallery can impact me significantly, but trying to describe *why* or *how* a work of art exhibits beauty can actually diminish my experience. If we stop and pay attention, we simply "know" when something is beautiful, just like we "know" when someone is authentic.

Simply put, being an authentic leader is synonymous with being oneself. It is that simple, and it is also that difficult.

My career over the past thirty years has been about guiding leaders—in all walks of life—to their authentic self. This is my reason for being. It is both a challenging and a rewarding journey. A good part of the voyage has been about introspection, self-awareness, and soul-searching. I've learned from writing this book that self-reflection is necessary to discover my authentic self, but going within won't take me all the way. What's also required for living authentically is *caring*. Caring offers us another path to authenticity.

Intentionally learning to care for and about a dying parent, a troubled employee, a cause beyond our own self-interest, or perhaps even learning to care about ourselves, each in our own way, makes us a little more real. The two—authenticity and caring—are inseparable. Learning to care deepens the connection to my authentic self, just as learning to be authentic deepens my caring capacity. You can tell when a leader is worth following, in part, by how much they care—about the work they do, about the people they serve, and about the results they achieve.

For more than three decades, I have put my heart and soul into researching and understanding authenticity and leadership. One simple statement sums up what I have discovered: the road to authenticity is paved with opportunities to demonstrate caring.

# Through the lens of loss

In the midst of a busy, demanding life, it is easy to take too lightly the power of a simple smile, a word of encouragement, a moment to listen to someone in need, or give an honest compliment. The smallest act of caring has the potential to turn a life around.

I don't know if this book will turn a life around or even help anyone. What I do know is that I have benefitted from this undertaking. When I started this project, my motive was simply to honor my good brother and bring forward some words that might someday be valued by our children and grandchildren. I wrote this book because I felt a need to do so and was curious to see if I could adequately convey my feelings about caring. Just as an artist must paint, I must communicate.

I believe the only way to change the world is to change myself. I also know that this project *has* changed me. Writing about caring for the past three years has slowed me down and allowed me to more fully appreciate the people in my life and the beauty of humanity. When life, work, and leadership involve hope and a commitment to caring, the world is better for this.

The book follows my journey with a dying brother. Yet referring to grief as a "journey" implies an ending. And grief isn't like that. It never ends. Instead, I've learned to think of grief as a wound that never completely heals. C.S. Lewis thought of grief as crippling, holding the idea that he *would* learn to walk again—albeit with a limp.

You don't ever "get over" grieving like you get over a bridge. Instead, you find a way to make grief a part of love and you keep walking, even if forevermore you find yourself with a permanent wound, limping.

When the book was sent out for reviews, much of the feedback indicated that the theme dealt a great deal with death and dying, hardship, and illness as a path to learning to care. Caring, I am reminded, is more than responding to adversity. And you can learn to care without having to suffer! Caring can simply be about recognizing and appreciating beauty, creating, playing, being in love, giving birth, encouraging a child, tending to an animal, expressing kindness, and celebrating life.

I recognize that writing a book while walking through the intensity of grief can manifest both strength and weakness. Its strength is that pain was able to open the door to inspiration and allow for a deeper understanding of the human experience. As my friend, the renowned artist Murray Phillips, says, "through grief you see life more clearly." The healing power of grief has been transformative both in my life and in my writing, and has allowed me to find my voice in a way previously unknown to me.

The weakness is that my view of caring is seen through the lens of pain and loss. This journey is skewed toward end-of-life experiences, affliction, and hardship. I make no apology for this. It's where my life is right now. If I were to write a book about caring two years from now, further along this endless journey of grief, I suspect it would be radically different. I know my understanding will evolve as my life evolves, and as I receive wisdom from people who read this. After all, this is why I write: to learn and to give to others.

You will also see in these pages a theme of self-care, learning to say no, stepping back from the arduous work of caring, and setting clear boundaries in the relationships with the people we care about. This emphasis results from my own experience with burnout, exhaustion, learning to set limits, and recognizing my own needs for self-care in the midst of grief. Although I personally need to set limits in my own work of caring, others may need to open their hearts. All I can do is write from my experience and know that, in light of the vast and incomprehensible expression of what it means to be human, it is enough—at least for now. Like caring, this book is done, even though it is incomplete.

David Irvine, July 2016

# Introduction

> Don't aim at success—the more you aim at it and make it a
> target, the more you are going to miss it. For success, like hap-
> piness, cannot be pursued; it must ensue, and it only does so
> as the unintended side-effect of one's personal dedication to a
> cause greater than oneself ... Listen to what your conscience
> commands you to do and go on to carry it out to the best of
> your knowledge.
>
> Viktor E. Frankl

Over the past many months, my brother, Hal Irvine, and his family and caregivers who surround him, have shown me what caring is truly about. In 2013, Hal was diagnosed with an inoperable
brain tumor. Since his illness, the pace in my life has changed. I have
spent more time with him during these past months than in the previous twenty years—and the caring has gone both ways. These quiet
times together have opened up opportunities to share with Hal some
of my own struggles growing up, and my struggles with anxiety and
depression over the years. Stuff Hal and I never talked about before,
things he never knew about me. As a result of these talks, we have
developed a bond I would have never thought possible.

The impact has been far-reaching. My family and work relationships have improved as I've slowed down, and as I've made more
room to be present with those who matter most to me. I have been
given a gift, through it all, of a new perspective and a greater realization of what really matters.

Observing my brother, a hard-working and beloved family physician, and inspired by his caring presence, I knew I wanted to write a book about the power of caring. This book is an investigation into a simple but profound idea: caring is everything. The stories within shine a light on the many dimensions of caring that so often go unnoticed and unacknowledged, but are vital to organizations, relationships, and life itself. This book is for leaders at all levels of organizations and in all walks of life: health care workers, educators, family and community members, and, really, pretty much anyone who wants to offer or receive caring.

Sometimes I've found myself reverting to teacher mode, filling the pages with "shoulds" and "have-tos," when I might simply let the stories speak for themselves. Stories connect us emotionally with each other. It's how we forge relationships. While in my soul I am a teacher, I am doing my best to stand aside and let the stories do their work. "Education is an admirable thing," Oscar Wilde wrote, "but it is well to remember from time to time that nothing worth knowing can be taught." Caring, which is certainly worth knowing, likely cannot be taught. But it can be learned. So instead of teaching how to care, I've decided to scatter seeds. This book is my best effort to spread the seeds of caring into the world.

John Chapman is said to have been a "barefoot wanderer with a tin pot hat and a sack of apples, so he might leave seeds to start trees everywhere he went." I'm a farmer at heart, and feel a bit like John Chapman. People know him better as Johnny Appleseed—a hero of American folklore, pioneer nurseryman, and notorious sower of seeds. I grew up in a farming community and, even now, spend as much time as possible surrounded by people who are close to the earth and who have a love for the land. I realize that, as I may never meet many of the people who read this book, I have no idea if the seeds sown here will take root or be of value to you. Stories cultivate a caring heart by cultivating the soil that allows the seeds to take root. In sharing my ideas and the stories I have gathered over the years, my hope is to leave the world a more caring place.

As difficult as it has been to write about this huge thing that is caring, it is even more difficult to actually *live* what I have learned on this three-year project. I wrote this book because I am deeply part of this struggle and commitment to care. Ever since my early desperate attempts to heal the pain in my family, when I struggled to intervene in my parents troubling relationship—as a way to survive the fear—caring has become a part of my life. In my work, educating and helping to develop leaders around the world, I have learned that caring is integral to good leadership. Caring is central to building great organizations, families, and communities. And caring is essential to a good life. In essence, I've come to believe that caring is everything.

I'm also learning that caring is not without its challenges, paradoxes, and conflicts. How does one care about others while simultaneously caring for oneself? What is the nature of true caring? Is it possible to act caring without actually caring? When can caring become a burden rather than an act of love? How does self-awareness help us care more deeply and more freely? What does it mean to actually care?

Questions like these keep filling my thoughts and so I write this book: to better understand myself, to plant seeds, and, in my own small way, make the world a better place to work and live. Caring is who I am. It's an essential part of me—and I'm still learning its lessons daily.

The writings of Viktor E. Frankl, the Austrian neurologist and psychiatrist, and a Holocaust survivor, have had a foundational influence on my work and life. In *Man's Search for Meaning*, Frankl's groundbreaking memoir, he chronicles his experiences as a concentration camp inmate. His book has challenged me to do what's right, to rise above my own insecurities, to "listen to what your conscience commands."

Creating a more fully human and authentic world has been a cause most dear to my heart. Caring is the only way to make this possible. What follows are stories of caring, along with many of the insights I've gleaned over thirty-odd years as a speaker, family therapist, and advisor to leaders. I hope the stories in this book will inspire you to help make this planet a better place to live and work in, and to listen to what your conscience asks of you. Our future depends on it.

*Caring is Everything* is an investigation into a simple but profound idea: when we take the time to care, to express what is innately within us, we flourish and we enable others to flourish. In caring, we turn our world away from intolerance, indifference, and self-centeredness toward what matters most—to love and to be loved. Rather than instructing readers on how to care, each chapter shines a light on the dimensions of caring that so often go unnoticed and unacknowledged, with stories that illustrate a vital aspect of caring.

Stories are powerful healers. They can enlarge us and provide solace. My hope is that the stories here will knit themselves into the fabric of your life and reveal these essential truths:

- When we care, we live life without regrets.
- Caring connects us to our authentic self, making us a better leader by being a better person.
- Caring—the most noble of all human journeys—has a pervasive and enduring influence on human wellbeing and the wellbeing of the places where we work and live, as well as the survival of our planet.

As you engage with the stories in this book, I hope your vision for your potential will expand, and your many acts of caring will be validated and amplified. This book chronicles my own caring journey and my wish is that it will also add to yours.

*Caring is Everything* is dedicated to my brother, Hal Irvine. I open and close the book by speaking to who Hal was and is, in his living and his dying.

Scattered throughout this book are stories to illuminate what caring looks like and to explore these questions about caring's vital role in our lives. Part I "The Many Dimensions of Caring" explores the many facets of caring and the reasons why caring matters so much. Part II "Anatomy of Caring" speaks to the ways acts of caring have made a profound difference in people's lives. I've tried not to teach or preach too much in these pages, but what teaching I've been compelled to do, I have tried to contain in Part III "Cultivating Caring." Here, I offer practical ideas for giving and accepting care.

Tucked into the back of the book are more practical strategies, useful appendices for the reader to become more caring and authentic—including two inventories to help assess the strength of your character and your practice of self-care. On several occasions in the book, for the sake of privacy, I use pseudonyms for the people whose stories I share.

As a speaker, coach, and therapist, I've long advocated for honesty and the authentic life. I hope that these stories open your heart and carry over into your life: as a leader, caregiver, family or community member, and as a caring global citizen.

# Running out of Time

So it's true, when all is said and done, grief is the price we pay for love.

E. A. Bucchianeri, *Brushstrokes of a Gadfly*

Man was made for Joy & Woe
And when this we rightly know
Thro the World we safely go
Joy & Woe are woven fine
A Clothing for the soul divine
Under every grief & pine
Runs a joy with silken twine

William Blake, "Auguries of Innocence" (1863)

As I write this, my brother is still alive.

His quality of life is poor. Hal cannot get out of bed on his own. He is essentially paralyzed on half of his body, but he remains able to feed himself. Although he is fully cognizant of everything around him and he understands others, his speech is jumbled and mostly incomprehensible. The doctors are working hard to balance his medication to prevent—or lessen—seizures. He sleeps most of the time, and his only remaining pleasures are being with his family, having visitors, getting outside for a stroll in the wheelchair, and watching the birds at the feeder outside the kitchen window. Through the caring presence of his loving and dedicated wife Dianne, his adult children, and his devoted caregiver Val Sarsons, Hal is able to remain at home.

In November 2013, Hal flew to Vancouver, joining his colleagues from every province in the country, to receive the Canada Family Physician of the Year Award for the province of Alberta. Seventy-two hours before the award ceremony, he had a seizure in his hotel room, mere blocks from where he was to be honored. A few days later, the diagnosis was delivered. Grade III Anaplastic Astrocytoma—an aggressive, inoperable tumor intersecting three lobes of his brain. The prognosis was grim. With no treatment, he would live an estimated three to four months. With radiation and chemotherapy, one to three years. With a miracle, perhaps a little longer.

The ensuing months have led me through a journey Hal has called his "Adventure with an Astrocytoma." After the seizure, my normally fluent brother had trouble with speaking and communicating, "a mild but frustrating receptive and expressive dysphasia/aphasia" as he termed it. Because of the aphasia, Hal was forced to quit all committee and clinical work. With the help of family members, he started a blog titled "Adventure with an Astrocytoma" and began chronicling the personal impacts of his diagnosis and treatment. This so-called "adventure" was a grinding mix of aggressive radiation and chemotherapy with accompanying aphasia, memory loss, itching rashes, bloating, dreadful weakness, seizures, headaches, nausea, diarrhea, and so little energy that just putting his feet on the floor in the morning was a measure of success.

In the months since my brother's diagnosis I have discovered just how much, as a healer and leader in his community, Hal has made a difference to many, many hundreds of people.

When I push him in his wheelchair around the neighborhood, the same neighborhood shared by the hospital where he worked for thirty-one years, we inevitably run into one of his patients or a patient's family member who stops and tells a story of the positive impact Hal has made in their life. One afternoon on one of our walks together, we met a young woman pushing a toddler in a stroller. It turned out that Hal had helped give birth to this woman twenty-five years earlier. Two decades later, he also helped give birth to the two-year-old she was pushing beside us. This mom expressed a heartfelt appreciation for Hal's care for her when she was growing up in this community, and for his care for her young son after he was born.

I think it's fair to say that people here have been stricken by Hal's diagnosis. It just makes no sense to anybody.

After his seizures and in emergency care, Hal stayed for periods in the hospital across the street from his home. This was the same hospital where he used to be "the doctor," and there I discovered how absolutely cherished he was—by his colleagues, the nurses, custodial staff, and his patients. Tenderness was obvious in these health care providers as they devoted their attention to him with impeccable dedication and love. Tears would so often fill their eyes.

Hal continues to be adored by his staff and patients, but not because he was "the doctor." He is loved and valued because of who he is as a person. Inside his core, Hal has always cared. About his patients. About his work. He cares about his community. He cares about people. And now all that caring he's given out has been coming back to him. The love that so freely flowed through him in his personal life and in his work, as a husband, a father, friend, and healer in the community, now surrounds him as he faces his difficult prognosis.

In the days spent with Hal during these remaining months, and being inspired by his caring presence and his caring legacy, I was inspired to write a book about the power of caring. It is to my caring brother, Hal Irvine, that I dedicate this book. May the inspiration I received from spending time with Hal during the last months of his life be reflected in the stories I have gathered here.

## The hard part of living and dying

Hal's first MRI following aggressive chemotherapy showed a "stable" tumor, suggesting the chemo and radiation had slowed its growth—at least temporarily. However, two months later the next MRI results presented more sobering news. The tumor in my brother Hal's brain was growing again, which meant he was no longer responding to the chemo. This brought an end to chemo and other aggressive treatments, and it was a door into a new journey—the realization that Hal's death was imminent.

As rain poured outside his kitchen window that June morning, Hal sat across from me at the dining table holding his wife Dianne's hand. Tears filled his eyes. Quietly and courageously, Hal looked directly at me and said, "I'm done with treatments. I have a brain tumor that is killing me and I am going to die."

Unspeakable grief swept through us as we sat and wept together, and as we quietly embraced the horrible reality of his condition. In the midst of our anguish, and after months of determined treatments and trips to Calgary for countless appointments at the Tom Baker Cancer Center, relief was also present. We awakened to the possibility of surrender and acceptance—a release of the burden we'd felt having to contain this aggressive, hostile foreign element living in Hal's head. Unsurprisingly, my brother handled this moment with the same grace and courage he had marshaled through the entire process.

——◆——

At one time or another, all of us may experience the feeling of renewal that comes from a change of pace. Sometimes this pace change can come by traveling to a different culture, learning something new, starting an exercise program, spending time in nature, signing on with a therapist, or simply having an enriching conversation. The change of pace can come as a patch of black ice on a dark winter night, when you skid out of control at a hundred kilometers an hour and are thrown into oncoming traffic, finally coming to an abrupt halt on the wrong side of the highway—and you realize that you need to slow down and pay attention.

For me, the pace change came from spending these months with my brother, contemplating my own mortality and my own reactions to his dying, and reflecting upon why and how my brother has had such a profound impact on the world.

While I wouldn't wish this hell on anyone, I am surprisingly grateful for this change of pace in my own life—a gift from Hal during his cancer adventure. During these past months, we have done some reminiscing. We've laughed about so many childhood experiences. We've made amends for everything that we did to hurt each other in the past. We've said thank you and forgiven each other. Death, dying, and grieving can be strangely and amazingly healing.

Every time we are together, in one way or another, we say that we love each other. And we make time to hang out when he simply can't get out of bed or even utter a word and when I have no clue what to say. This whole imperfect and human experience of being together in an awkward and clumsy way is somehow a blessing. My marriage and my relationships with my daughters have improved as I've slowed down and made more room to be a bit more present, a little more often, with those who matter the most to me. The quality of my life has deepened and has been nourished through this experience of profound reflection and love.

Facing death squarely and honestly helps us see what is fully around us. Paradoxically, the realization that the life we have today won't last forever enables us to appreciate and grasp it more deeply. During the Middle Ages, Christian monks greeted one another with the salutation *memento mori*. It means "remember you must die." Thus, with every encounter, the monks reminded themselves and each other about the impermanence of life and the precious value of each moment.

## Open to precious moments

When I first learned of Hal's brain tumor, and after I worked through the shock of it, I made a commitment to be there in whatever way I could with him for his final journey. In the summer of 2014, while he was still able to walk and speak in complete sentences, I asked him where in the world I could take him. "We can go anywhere you want. This will be our last trip together."

Without a second thought, he mentioned a place in the backcountry deep in the mountain range not far from our home. We spoke of this breathtakingly beautiful wilderness area where Hal and Dianne would often hike with their kids when they were young. Park access is extremely limited in this popular backcountry area, and that helps to reduce tourist numbers and preserve its fragile alpine ecosystem. The valley we wanted to visit is only accessible by hiking up a long road, or via a restricted bus service run by Parks Canada, or by taking the shuttle operated by the lodge. Backpackers must reserve months in advance to obtain a campsite, and reservations at the lodge are even more difficult to secure, with typically a year or more advance notice required.

Knowing that Hal could not possibly handle camping or backpacking, I called to make a reservation at the lodge. After explaining carefully my plight and the conditions under which I was calling, a most caring helper on the other end of the phone said that the lodge was completely booked for the summer, but she would put us on the waiting list and see what she could do.

The next day, she called me back to say she had a reservation for three weeks hence. A party had cancelled, and she had generously moved us up the waiting list and booked us in.

It was a joyous weekend with my dear brother Hal, his wife Dianne, and my sister Kate who made immediate arrangements to fly up from San Francisco. Together, we were able to make one of Hal's last wishes a reality.

———

Fast forward a year ... the tumor has yet to take over the most vital areas of his brain. The right side of his body is essentially paralyzed. With help, he can still get out of bed, where he spends about eighteen hours a day sleeping. The Dexamethasone that is helping to inhibit brain swelling and seizures has left him bloated, with weakened muscles and periods of depression. He can understand everything, but with his aphasia, he usually can't string more than a few words together before they get jumbled and he gets frustrated. Hal described this once in his blog. "I feel like what I have in my head to say is correct, but what comes out isn't!"

Early on in his treatment, my brother also spoke of boredom. "I think boredom is my current big challenge. I feel limited in so many ways. I can't drive, I can't read or listen except to the simplest stuff because of comprehension issues, I can't talk or write because of expression issues (the blogs are a one to two-day project.) I can't participate in conversations about medical care or policies (which I had planned to do in semi-retirement.) I can't realistically return to part-time work.

My main hobby is photography (motorcycling is out)—but even that is limited by fatigue."

On one visit, we go for a walk. It's a sunny day, a good day to push a wheelchair and be outdoors together. Hal wants to go watch the workmen pave the end of his street. After watching that for a while, we go over to the community garden. Hal wants to show me how well it's growing and what a good idea it is. We're both small town farm kids, so watching a new garden grow is a shared delight. We then walk alongside the hospital across the street from where he lives, where he'd spent more than thirty-one years as a physician. Pushing a wheelchair around Hal's neighborhood has given me a different lens through which to view my life. It helps me see life more slowly. It brings a focus to things that matter.

"It must be so hard for you, Hal, to no longer be the doctor here."

There is no auditory response.

As I gaze down at him in his wheelchair, I can see tears forming in his eyes.

"It sucks, Hal. I'm so sorry."

He nods. It's hard to know how long to stay when a person is touched by grief. I have to remind myself to be patient and just do the best I can.

When we arrive back home he points to his bedroom, indicating that he is ready for his afternoon nap.

"How about a foot massage while you're falling asleep?"

"Sure," he smiles.

By the time I am done rubbing his feet, he is drifting off. I lean over his bloated stomach and swollen neck, as he lays peacefully with his eyes closed. He opens them when he feels my presence. I reach my arms around my older brother's heavy shoulders, now sunk into the soft bed, and notice a smile on his face.

"I love you, Hal," I whisper in his ear. And then I kiss his stubbled cheek.

"— love you too, Dave." He smiles and closes his eyes.

I go out to my Jeep, drive around the block, and park in front of the hospital. Tears run down my face. Nothing to say. Nothing to understand. Nothing to fix. Only tears.

Such is the nature of caring and the nature of grief. Grief is the price we pay for love. I have known Hal longer than I have known anyone else on this planet. We played cowboys together when we were young. We camped together. We fished together and we fought together. And then we became "responsible" adults who went our separate ways and who saw each other only on holidays, at funerals, and at weddings.

As I write this—in the midst of losing Hal, while he is dying and yet still here with us—I have struggled with verb conjugation. Paul Kalanithi speaks of this difficulty in his posthumously published memoir, *When Breath Becomes Air*. Kalanithi died at age 37 from lung cancer. He was a writer and a neurosurgeon on the cusp of a brilliant career. He wrote, "Verb conjugation has become muddled, as well. Which is correct: 'I am a neurosurgeon,' 'I was a neurosurgeon,' or 'I had been neurosurgeon before?' … So what tense am I living in now? … The future tense seems vacant and, on others' lips, jarring. A few months ago, I celebrated my fifteenth college reunion at Stanford and stood on the quad, drinking a whiskey as a pink sun dipped below the horizon; when old friends called out parting promises—'We'll see you at the twenty-fifth!'—it seemed rude to respond with 'Well … probably not.'"

Amidst grief comes immense joy. Grieving is not a sign of weakness. Quite the contrary, grief is an indication that we have loved and loved well. Embracing death fully is what Hal calls "the wild dance of no hope." Incredibly, at these times, we find solace in words, in poetry, and in stories.

As we allow grief to flow through us, we freely create an opportunity for reconciliation and the expression of love. Facing death squarely gives us nothing to fear. Caring enough to allow grief's door to open makes living a full life possible.

# PART I

# The Many Dimensions
# of Caring

He who attempts to act and do things for others or for the world
without deepening his own self-understanding ... will not have
anything to give others.

Thomas Merton, Cistercian monk

The greatest thing you'll ever learn
is just to love and be loved in return

eden ahbez

# It's in Our Bones

We ought to do good to others as simply and naturally as a horse runs, or a bee makes honey, or a vine bears grapes season after season without thinking of the grapes it has borne.

Marcus Aurelius Antonius

## What lies in the heart

As I work on this chapter, more than eighty thousand people have, over the past week, fled a natural inferno that engulfed the city of Fort McMurray, 700 kilometers northeast of where we live. The wildfire ripped through the northern Alberta oil capital, turning more than 2,400 structures to ash and debris. Firefighters from all over the country combated the massive blaze that's resulted in the largest wildfire evacuation in Canada's history. Entire lifetimes have been engulfed and swallowed up in an instant as people's homes go up in flames. In many cases, the evacuees were at work or in transit and were unable to return home to retrieve any of their possessions or even, unthinkably, their pets.

The trauma of their situation is unimaginable. And yet in the midst of it all has been this immediate outpouring of generosity and caring. As the convoy made its way north and south of Fort Mac, men and women drove up and down the convoy with gas for stranded vehicles, food and water, baby supplies, and simple words of comfort.

Within hours, in the communities where the thousands were evacuated, people opened their doors to strangers. Schools, educational institutions, and sport facilities were transformed into shelters. Airplane hangars were filled with donations. Restaurant owners were cooking up a storm. Retail stores offered large discounts to Fort Mac residents.

Just last evening, the restaurant where my daughter works part-time while she gets herself through university got a call. "I would like to reserve a seating for eight," the customer requested over the phone.

"Are you okay?" asked the restaurant manager, obviously picking up something unusual on the other end of the line.

After a brief pause, the customer tearfully explained that she was from Fort McMurray and that this was the first time since the evacuation that they could finally be together since uniting with their parents. "We'll have daughters and parents with us as well. We don't care what time the reservation is. It's just important to be all together."

My daughter had the good fortune to wait on their table. After the meal the family asked for their bill.

"There's no charge," Chandra responded. "Our restaurant will take care of this one for you."

While tragedy crushes the soul, it also inspires the human spirit. There is nothing quite so uplifting as the spontaneous eruption of human goodness and caring that emerges in the midst of a tragic catastrophe. Every decent heart is aroused in the center of tragedy. Whether it is a flood or a fire, a tornado or an earthquake, a school shooting, or the suicide of a person who lives next door, it appears to be the human code that every civil citizen, in times of crisis and calamity, becomes your neighbor. As my TV hero Mr. Rogers said once, "When I was a boy and I saw scary things in the news, my mother would say to me, 'Look for the helpers. You will always find people who are helping.'"

If you want to know what lies in the hearts of people, watch what happens in and to a community following a catastrophe. Regardless of how long it lasts or how it expresses itself in the moment, or whether it lies so deeply within us it cannot immediately be found, caring is, nonetheless, in our bones.

## We are interconnected

Rea is a caring, talented manager who works for a large pharmaceutical company. She came to me for some coaching after she found herself stretched thin following a corporate merger.

Sincerely wanting to contribute in her new role, Rea found herself saying yes to requests without thinking them through. In an effort to try to please everyone and try to get everything done, she was spending her whole day running from meeting to conference call without a clear sense of what was important. Trying to juggle too many urgent balls, her stress increased and she found herself dropping one ball after another on the projects and promises that actually mattered to her. Vital tasks were pushed aside as she became a slave to each new urgency. Her frustration and stress levels were mounting to the breaking point. Too often, she would stay late at work catching up on emails, overlooking the significant relationships in her life, including caring for herself.

"I truly care," she told me in one of our early sessions. "I care about the work I'm doing. I care about the projects that are important. I care about the people I work with and serve. But I'm exhausted from it all. I'm just trying to please too many people."

Rea's initial request in our coaching sessions was some instruction on much needed "time management strategies." This was the tip of the iceberg. In the midst of helping her set priorities, it soon became clear that she didn't have a strong sense of herself. Her inability to set clear personal goals, having no sense of self-purpose, the lack of knowledge of what she distinctly valued and what was most important to her, and her incapacity to make what mattered most a priority in her personal life were the same stumbling blocks that were preventing her from having conversations with her key stakeholders to establish a clear focus in her work.

"If you can't find a focus in your personal life," I asked, "how can you hope to find focus in your work?"

Rea's diminished sense of self was evident as she shared an experience of visiting her mother who was living, at the time, in Florida. Her sister, a troubled, unstable woman who had struggles with alcoholism, wanted to come see Rea while she was at their mother's home. Out of guilt, Rea felt obligated to see her sister, but she didn't know how to set boundaries around the visit. She didn't want the hassle or strain of being around her sister, but she also didn't want the hassle or strain from saying no. It was difficult for her to speak up for what she wanted. What she wanted was time alone with her mother. What she ended up with instead was spending all day with her sister.

Sensing her frustration and anger about the whole situation, I asked Rea to describe her feelings about the visit.

"I hated having to put up with her. She was rude and obnoxious. The first day, she came over at nine in the morning just as we were getting up, and she was already drunk. I was exhausted being around her all day. I didn't know how to ask her to leave. It's not the 'Christian thing' to do when your sister is over, to send her away. The only time I got a break from her was when she would go out for a cigarette, then sit in the car and drink. She left her butts and beer bottles all over the porch, and came back inside swearing and in high drama about everything in her life. My mother and I both felt sorry for her, but we hated putting up with her. It was well after midnight when she left, and she was so drunk she could hardly stand up. We finally called a cab to take her home. Then we drove her car back to her place the next day. She was still in bed when we knocked on the door at noon, so at least we didn't have to stay long."

Caring without a strong sense of self results in *pleasing* rather than real *caring*. Pleasing comes from emptiness, while caring comes from overflow. Pleasing means giving people what they want and what they ask for, hoping it will make them happy, while caring means giving *what* you can *when* you can, knowing you can't rescue people from their own unhappiness. Impulsive pleasing without hesitation comes from insecurity and fear of hurting people's feelings, not wanting to impose, and worrying about retaliation and fear of rejection. Pleasing leads to guilt and obligation, and subsequent resentment and exhaustion.

Caring, on the other hand, comes from self-respect, from an honest desire to be with another person, from clear personal boundaries. Caring increases your energy and self-respect. Pleasing and caring are really more of a spectrum than a dichotomy. All caring probably has an element of pleasing, while within all pleasing lies a caring heart. An indicator that you are operating too far on the pleasing end of the spectrum is when it's easier to know what other people want from you than it is to know what you want for yourself.

———

"A healthy family, a healthy country, a healthy world—all grow outward from a single, strong person," the I Ching or *Book of Changes* says. "Therefore, in order to improve our family, organization, nation, or world community, we must begin by improving ourselves." Becoming a strong, self-aware person sometimes requires more discipline than even the best of us can muster. So often, with the demands that surround us, it's easy to simply get too busy to grow.

Upon reflection, what act of service is not, in some form or another, an act of self-interest? Sustainable caring requires wrestling with the commitment to grow ourselves as we help grow others.

Caring relationships consist of the integration of one's sense of self—the "I"—and the ability to reach out and be connected—the "we". Too much "I" and you end up with self-centeredness, a drive for personal gain and pleasure, and eventual loneliness without meaning in your life. Too much "we" and you become depleted and consumed by the world's demands from trying to meet everyone's expectations. Without a clear sense of self, without the clarity to say no, without clear boundaries that give you the strength to care, you end up burned out and exhausted.

Developing the "we" involves learning to be in a community, putting yourself in the place of another, and practicing empathy, vulnerability, and compassion. Developing a strong sense of self or individuation, in order to bring caring into a relationship, often requires an intentional "self-care system," like the one I write about in the chapter "Cultivating a Practice of Self-Care." The system is based on clear values and disciplined habits such as a consistent meditation practice, regular exercise, disciplined sleep habits, pursuing spiritual development, having a supportive community, and working with a coach or therapist.

Developing a sense of herself, and a self-care system, became the focus of Rea's coaching. She has cultivated an awareness of the patterns in her life, like not setting clear boundaries with her sister that were blocking her sense of identity, and she is learning new ways to change these patterns. She discovered, in our work together, that her inability to say no to her sister stemmed from a belief, developed when she was eight-years old, that if she said no and looked after herself, she would not survive. As an adult, she realized that this belief, while critical to her as an eight-year-old, was not helpful to her as a forty-eight-year-old. This has helped her define a sense of purpose and to shed light on what matters to her. We are simultaneously working on developing strategies for setting clear priorities and boundaries at work and on how to function with a new set of personal beliefs that no longer limit her.

The "I" and the "we" in us are not separate and divisible. While developing a strong sense of self may be the best way to heal a relationship, learning to be in a relationship also helps develop the self. In short, being married may be the best way to learn how to be married—at least if we are conscious in our efforts. We may do well to be alone sometimes too in order to learn to be in a relationship. Because without a "self" we have no relationship. Stepping away from a relationship can also be a path to healing the relationship.

There's a paradox in caring, because sooner or later the "I" may collide with the "we." Eventually self-caring will come in conflict with caring for others. On the way to the gym, your teenaged son comes to you in a crisis over his girlfriend. Your child's concert is scheduled on the same night as your restorative yoga class. Your coffee date with a good friend gets waylaid by a request to care for a sick parent. A fulfilling career takes time away from the important relationships in your life. Or you are faced with a choice between paying for a personal development workshop, or giving to the local food bank that could sure use some financial assistance, or volunteering at a homeless shelter that could use an extra pair of hands. Such is the nature of caring.

One night when I couldn't sleep, I went to my study to read about selfless service in the *Bhagavad Gita*, the Hindu scripture. As profound as it was to expand and reflect on my spiritual nature, after an hour I set the book aside and wandered into the living room where I picked up the L. L. Bean catalogue from the coffee table. "What I really need is a new jacket," I thought.

This tension in caring is part of living in the world. There are no easy answers to these dilemmas. When does caring diminish the self, and the self diminish the caring? How can we care for ourselves while caring for others? The best we can do is appreciate and accept the paradoxes as part of our human experience. What's important on this journey is, rather than to expect answers to the questions, to keep asking the questions. When I'm able to do this, the tension lessens. I can relax and put a little less pressure on myself, knowing that the resolution of these paradoxes is not a destination to be reached, but a journey to be embraced, appreciated, and accepted.

We never leave our humanness behind, and we aren't supposed to. But in the midst of these dilemmas, it does at times make planning a day difficult. I am torn sometimes between whether I should go out and *change* the world, or stay home and simply *enjoy* the world.

The caring journey is an entirely human journey, full of paradox and uncertainty and tension. It isn't a matter of choosing between "I" and "we." Instead, caring calls us to step outside the struggle, to accept the paradox along with the tension. Every caring relationship requires both individuality *and* connection, self *and* other, "I" *and* "we," egoism *and* altruism.

Writes the poet Khalil Gibran, "Let there be spaces in your togetherness ... And stand together yet not too near together: for the pillars of the temple stand apart."

Detachment from another can be caring. Backing off from enabling an addict is often the first step toward their recovery from the addiction. Any action that changes the self will change the world, because world and self are indivisible. Caring is both inward and outward, so to learn to care for others, we must individuate and learn to care for ourselves—and at the same time, in order to learn to care for ourselves, we must learn to care for others. This is the caring path.

Observe a parent caring for young children, a recovering drug addict helping another drug addict get clean and sober, an adult child caring for aging parents, a nurse at the side of a dying patient, or a leader committed to supporting an unengaged employee find their place in an organization. A common thread running through all these vast array of expressions is that caring is not necessarily about immediate gratification. Caring can be hard work. It can be messy. It can be uncomfortable. And yet, caring gives as much as it takes.

As humans, it's in us to give. We feel better when we go beyond ourselves. Caring exposes any delusions that we are separate individuals riding our solitary orbits. We are social beings. We are ineluctably interconnected. Caring is who we are.

## Beyond ordinary

In 2008, we hired a renovation company to refurbish a newly purchased home. It was a unique house designed by an architect, but it was sadly showing its age. Virtually nothing had been done to upgrade it since it was built in 1972. Finding the right contractor, someone who could handle the scope of the project, took a lot of time and consideration. We needed someone with a great deal of expertise, someone who could modernize the place without losing any of the architectural charm that had drawn us to buy it.

What impressed us about the company we ended up hiring was their willingness to listen carefully, and to attentively find out what our goal and needs were. We were inspired by their commitment to maintain the integrity and design of the structure while highlighting its natural elements, its themes of wood and rock, and the central atrium that was a focal point in the house. Over the next year, Garth McDaniel, our general manager, was on site almost daily. He took extra caution and care to understand our requirements. He paid close attention to every detail of every task his workmen performed. He set a tone of caring by being present and available and through his attentive listening and desire to understand. He also hired caring sub-contractors—tradesmen who were true craftsmen. Altogether, the team cared about their work, and they cared about us.

During construction, Garth ensured that his workers did not expose the indoor trees in the atrium to construction dust or freezing outdoor temperatures. He was open to making changes if we weren't comfortable with how things were translating from the blueprints to our expectations. The entire mudroom and pantry shelving unit turned out to be too narrow to fit our needs. Garth readily offered to redo these when he learned we were less than enthused with the results.

Our family's needs were always kept in mind, and the work incorporated personal touches that would make our family—and even our pets—more comfortable. The reno was completed *under* budget, five days before the company promised to be done. And some years later, when we discovered a leak above our patio doors, we called Garth and he came out to see us the next day. With careful diagnosis and intervention, the problem was resolved in a matter of weeks, with no charge to us, seven years later!

The world is just a more decent place to live in when there is caring. We enjoy a visit to the dentist more when we know she cares, rather than when she is simply "performing her job." Returning a purchased item is better when a customer service person takes the time to care. Our friendships and family relationships are better when we know we are cared about. Neighborhoods are better places to live in when the community around us is caring. Workplaces are more enjoyable and more productive when we know the boss cares. When there is caring around us, we are more relaxed. It comes down to trust.

Caring is in our bones. If we obstruct the natural expression of who we are, it can get lost along the way. Pablo Picasso is said to have spoken these wise words: "Every child is an artist. The problem is how to remain an artist once we grow up." The same might be said for caring. Every child is a natural giver of care. The problem is how to remain caring once we grow up.

We never regret being present to a friend, a family member, a dying parent, or a stranger in need. We never regret being present to a setting sun, a flower in bloom, or our heart's desire. Caring is the present we give to ourselves of being present *right now*. Caring is ordinary, and it can also be beyond ordinary.

## It's in us to give

"Philosophers and medical professionals have long debated whether blood donors should be paid. Some claim that blood, like human tissue or organs, is special—that we shouldn't be able to buy and sell it like a barrel of crude oil or a crate of ball bearings. Others argue that we should shelve our squeamishness, because paying for this substance will ensure an ample supply." So writes Daniel Pink in *Drive: The Surprising Truth About What Motivates Us.*

Pink describes a study done by Swedish economists who were testing a twenty-five-year-old theory that claimed that paying citizens to donate blood would actually lessen, rather than increase, the number of donors. The study group consisted of 153 women, and in the absence of compensation ... "52 percent of the women decided to go ahead and donate blood. They were altruistic citizens apparently, willing to do a good deed for their fellow Swedes even in the absence of compensation."

In contrast, when blood donors were offered payment, "only 30 percent of the women decided to give blood." When donors were paid and given the option to donate their payment to a charity ... "much the same as the first group, 53 percent became blood donors."

Offering payment may in fact be a disincentive to care. People would rather, it seems, do good works freely. Regardless of the merits of paying or not paying people to donate blood, or whether the Swedish economists designed a valid experiment, or whether they paid people enough, there lies within each of us a seemingly innate impulse to reach beyond ourselves, do our part to ease suffering in the world, and make the world better.

This could be one reason why voluntary blood donations invariably increase during natural disasters and other calamities. That's why the American Red Cross brochure says that giving blood provides "a feeling that money can't buy." Likewise, in Canada, our blood services motto is: "It's in you to give."

The impulse to care develops early writes Martha C. Nussbaum, an American philosopher and Professor of Law and Ethics at the University of Chicago. "Research on human infants has shown that by the time they are ten months old, they engage in spontaneous helping and consolatory behavior, and by two years old they also display signs of guilt after they harm someone." We are drawn to care instinctively as humans. It's why we make personal sacrifices, in love and in war, and in so many of our relationships.

Caring is an essential part of being human. It takes us to the heart of who we are and who we might best be.

## Studies show ...

Most of us know that if we eat our fruit and vegetables, exercise regularly, get plenty of rest, and avoid smoking, we'll improve our chances of living longer and healthier lives. But what your doctor may not have told you is that caring can possibly be added to that healthy checklist. Many recent studies have found that caring has a positive impact on our health.

- In a June 2013 study from Carnegie Mellon University, adults over 50 who volunteered at least 200 hours in the past year (four hours per week) were 40 percent less likely to develop high blood pressure than non-volunteers.
- Stephen G. Post, founding director of the Center for Medical Humanities, Compassionate Care, and Bioethics at Stony Brook University School of Medicine in New York, reports that giving to others has been shown to increase health benefits in people with chronic illness, including HIV and multiple sclerosis.
- A paper, led by Dr. Suzanne Richards at the University of Exeter Medical School, reviewed 40 studies from the past 20 years on the link between volunteering and health. The article, available in the open access journal *BMC Public Health*, found that volunteering was associated with lower depression, increased wellbeing, and a longer life expectancy.
- A 2012 study by Sara Konrath and a team at the University of Michigan, published in the journal *Health Psychology*, found that volunteers had a lower risk of dying in a four-year period

than non-volunteers, as long as they volunteered for altruistic versus self-oriented reasons. "In order to gain a personal benefit from volunteering, you have to focus on how your giving helps other people," said Konrath, director of the Interdisciplinary Program for Empathy and Altruism Research and assistant professor at the Lilly Family School of Philanthropy at Indiana University. "We have the ability to shift our focus, and many of us do have an other-oriented reason for giving. If we can just focus on that aspect rather than what we can get out of it, chances are it will be better for own health too."

- A recent review of studies published in the November 2014 *Psychological Bulletin* found that among seniors, caring, expressed by volunteering, was likely to reduce the risk of dementia and was associated with reduced symptoms of depression, better self-reported health, fewer functional limitations, and lower mortality.

- Rodlescia Sneed, a postdoctoral research fellow at the University of Pittsburgh, explains that, "volunteerism may boost self-esteem and protect people from social isolation, both of which are linked to better health in older adults. Helping others also gives older adults perspective on their own life struggles, which can help them cope with stress."

- Stephanie Brown at the University of Michigan saw similar results in a 2003 study on elderly couples. She and her colleagues found that those individuals who provided practical help to friends, relatives, or neighbors, or who gave emotional support to their spouses, had a lower risk of dying over a five-year period than those who didn't. Interestingly, receiving help wasn't linked to a reduced death risk.

- In a 2006 study by Rachel Piferi of Johns Hopkins University and Kathleen Lawler of the University of Tennessee, people who provided social support to others had lower blood pressure than participants who didn't, suggesting a direct physiological benefit to those who give of themselves. Even just the thought of giving money to a specific charity has a positive effect on health, their research shows.

- The benefits of giving are seen in younger people too. A recent unpublished study of tenth graders at a Vancouver high school found that students who spent an hour a week helping children in after-school programs over a period of ten weeks had lower levels of inflammation and cholesterol, plus a lower body-mass index.

## Caring can make us healthier

Intuition tells us that giving to ourselves, rather than giving to others, is the best way to be happy. That's not the case according to Dan Ariely, professor of behavioral economics and psychology at Duke University. "If you are a recipient of a good deed, you may have momentary happiness, but your long-term happiness is higher if you are the giver," he says. "For example, if you give people a gift card for a Starbucks cappuccino and call them that evening and ask how happy they are, people say they are not happier than if you hadn't given it to them. If you give another group a gift card and ask them to give it to a random person, when you call them at night, those people are happier."

The *way* we give is important too. Taxes are a form of giving that typically does not make people happy. "If we give directly from our paycheck, we don't pay attention to it. It's the way we give and how we give that makes us happy. The key is to give deliberately and thoughtfully, so that other people benefit from it."

According to many researchers, one explanation for the potential positive health effects on caring is that when people even think about helping others, they activate a part of the brain called the mesolimbic pathway, which is responsible for feelings of gratification. Helping others also may promote the release of stress-buffering hormones that reduce cardiovascular risk. In other words, caring doles out happiness chemicals—including dopamine—endorphins that block pain signals. More specifically, caring releases oxytocin, a hormone that helps us to bond with others, and also helps us handle stress better. "Oxytocin dampens how much stress hormone our body releases," explains University of Portland neuro-psychologist Sarina Rodrigues Saturn.

"It curbs our brain's response to emotional stimuli and even how much our heart freaks out during stress." Oxytocin increases our trust levels and our ability to communicate positively. It has been shown to have positive impacts on our health and wellbeing.

A 2007 study published in the journal *Psychological Science* found that the higher a mom's oxytocin levels in the first trimester of pregnancy, the more likely she was to later engage in bonding behaviors such as singing to or bathing her baby. "Oxytocin is a peptide produced in the brain that was first recognized for its role in the birth process, and also in nursing," says Larry Young, a behavioral neuroscientist at Emory University in Atlanta, Georgia.

Although maternal bonding may not always be hardwired—after all, human females can adopt babies and take care of them—oxytocin released during pregnancy "does seem to have a role in motivation and feelings of connectedness to a baby," Young says. Studies also show that interacting with a baby causes the infant's own oxytocin levels to increase, he adds.

Oxytocin is sometimes known as the "cuddle hormone," because it is released when people snuggle up or bond socially. Even playing with your dog can cause an oxytocin surge, according to a 2009 study published in the journal *Hormones and Behavior*. It would appear that the release of oxytocin is both a cause and an effect of caring.

You'll notice that most of the studies on this topic of caring and its effect on our health compare active volunteers to non-volunteers, following them over time to see how they are doing a few years later. This is a very common method used to understand the health effects of various behaviors, like smoking, taking multivitamins, or eating blueberries. The problem, of course, is that it is likely that people who volunteer also establish other habits in their life that actually are the ones that are making them healthy. It would be ideal to do experimental studies that randomly assign some people to volunteer and others to do something else. However, it would also be obviously odd for researchers to *force* a group of people to "volunteer." How would you possibly isolate the motive and act of caring in your subjects?

Researchers in the Interdisciplinary Program for Empathy and Altruism Research (iPEARlab.org) have done detective work on why volunteering may be beneficial to our health—beyond the release of hormones and chemicals. Here are three of their best guesses: first, any activity is good activity. Volunteering means getting off the couch and out of the house, so it makes us stronger and more physically fit. Physically fit people tend to deal with stress better, which can help them live longer lives. Second, social connections are good for us. We are hard-wired for face-to-face contact that includes a lot of touch, eye contact, and smiles. Volunteering is a good way to meet others, make friends, and bond over common beliefs and goals. Finally, volunteering just feels good. Caring through volunteering can give us joy, which is also associated with longer and healthier lives.

Another challenge with all this research is that caring is more complex than measuring volunteer hours in a controlled research environment. Caring can be hard on us. How can supporting a loved one through a cancer journey, or raising a child with autism, or caring for a parent with multiple sclerosis, or working in a hospital with few resources and high demands be good for our health, when our ability to care is stretched too thin?

From my own personal experience, I can appreciate the claims of research that say caring can improve our health and wellbeing. When I was recently in a self-critical mood, unhappy about not being able to complete a project to the level I was expecting of myself, a call came in from a good friend whose twenty-one-year-old daughter died in a tragic car accident just weeks before. My friend was reaching out for support. Within seconds, I completely forgot my trivial problems. When I got off the phone a half-hour later, I felt a sense of gratitude, completeness, and overall wellbeing. Caring made my whole day better, and with this, I can honestly say I felt healthier.

My decision to put my own wants aside and be there for another human being may well have released some kind of hormonal or chemical lift within my body. Caring is no doubt good for us and for our health. It isn't enough, however, to expect the oxytocin to kick in and carry us through indefinitely. While the length of time we care is surely a factor, more important is the *way* we care. This is what determines if caring will deplete us or sustain us, and how caring will affect our health.

When we are overburdened with caregiving, it's important to seek out the support we need. We can stay on the phone too long with that parent who is in such enormous pain. We can take on the suffering of others and make it our own. We can experience an unspoken compulsion to fix. We can care with fear. In short, we can care to the point that it becomes harmful, both to ourselves and eventually to others. All of these would likely override the effects of the oxytocin, and instead cause anxiety and stress. While the act of caring in itself may seem healthy, there is a line where, when crossed, caring can become destructive. This line is different in all of us. Discovering and knowing that line requires attentiveness and continual investigation and awareness.

Learning to let go at the same time that we care, learning to care about ourselves as we care about others, and learning to find support and clarity in the face of the pain that it takes to care, all are part of the caring journey. Caring for others in a way that is not also caring toward ourselves cannot be healthy. If we find meaning and connection and strength in caring, then it will be sustaining and will help make us healthier. Knowing how to care is the key. We can train ourselves to integrate caring for others with caring for ourselves. Opening up this book is a step to exploring the inner landscape of sustainable caring.

The Dalai Lama says this: "My religion is very simple. My religion is kindness." In the twelve-step programs that originated with Alcoholics Anonymous, the constant thought of others is prescribed as the solution to one's problems. The Christian Bible, the Hebrew Scriptures, and the Koran all contain a wealth of passages espousing a life of caring and loving service. Caring opportunities can be enormously nourishing and rewarding. Science may actually support these views, proving that caring acts—when done in a way that serves both the person we care about as well as our own soul—not only helps us feel better, but will also make us healthier.

# What Caring Looks Like

Teach us to care and not to care
Teach us to sit still
Even among these rocks,
... Sister, mother
And spirit of the river, spirit of the sea
Suffer me not to be separated
And let my cry come unto Thee.

T. S. Eliot, *Ash-Wednesday*

## It's a decision

Maybe the reason to care is simply a habit you make. Maybe it's the way you choose to live your life. You can't always control how you feel about other people, but you can control how you behave toward them. You can influence how much you care as you move forward and build a relationship.

But with all this "care" and "caring" tossed about, what exactly does caring mean? Caring can be a verb, a noun, or an adjective. Care appears in carefree and careworn, and in the word caress. There are so many meanings and variations on the word caring, as any dictionary entry for "care" will prove. I'm more interested in what caring feels and looks like. I'm interested in how we care, and how we *say* we care.

In German, "I don't care" translates as "das ist mir wurst," literally "it's sausage to me." This phrase brilliantly illustrates the dynamics of caring. Many Germans will agree that bratwurst and frankfurters are essential to their cuisine. But sausage is just sausage. It's something you consume, not something you love or cherish or enter into a relationship with.

Sometimes we use caring as an excuse to do very uncaring things. We might say, for example, that we "care" about our work—so much so that we don't attend to our health or the important people in our lives. Or we care about things that are addictions or compulsions. Maybe we care more about our morning double latte than the person who regularly serves us the coffee. I'm not saying it's bad to like coffee, especially good coffee! What I'm saying is that caring is something more profound. It implies a deep sense of intent about how you feel in a relationship. Caring means being present, listening, and opening your heart.

Caring basically says this: you are important, I am important, and *this* is important—this relationship we're in together. Caring is a decision. It's deciding what matters.

## To care or not to care

I know a man who walked away from a relationship with a woman and the infant he had fathered to pursue an adventurous life apart from them, because he was unable to meet the demands of caring. Sadly, when the child was a mere eighteen months old, the mother, who suffered from clinical depression, committed suicide. When contacted by the courts, the man made a decision to re-enter his daughter's life, and he chose to raise her as a single father. He'll tell you today that while his own career aspirations and adventurous passions have been suspended, choosing to be a father is the best thing that's ever happened to him.

There is no easy formula for life, and no prescription for caring. Life throws things at us. There are moments when everything changes, and when we have no choice but to change with it. At certain times, the way we have been living catches up to us, and it's a decision to care that moves us forward.

Whether we admit it or not, caring is a decision. It's not an emotional reaction; it's an approach to life. We can decide to care about someone we don't like. We can make a decision to invest in a relationship for some greater good beyond our own self-interest.

When one of my daughters was an adolescent, she didn't want to try out for the middle school basketball team because she lacked confidence. In response to her fears and self-doubt, I reasoned that confidence is not a prerequisite to playing basketball. Confidence, an emotion, is an *outcome* or *result*, of making the decision to give it a go. "Don't wait for confidence," I told her. "The feeling of confidence will come to you *after* you make the decision to get in the game."

Caring is like that. There is no emotional prerequisite to care for someone. All it takes is a decision, and the emotion of caring, like the emotion of confidence, will be the result, the outcome of taking the action.

Perhaps we've been trapped for years in the progressive disease of addiction, and it's a decision to care enough about ourselves and the people in our lives that moves us forward into a new life of recovery. Or maybe we have "done all we can" for an alcoholic partner or a drug-addicted child, and maybe our presence in their lives is only preventing them from picking themselves up and getting better. Maybe there is honestly nothing left to be done. Choosing to care may mean stepping back, saying no, and closing a door.

Like any decision worth making, it's important to dig deeper. Is caring a compulsion? Does it arise from feelings of insecurity, from an unfulfilled need to be loved and deemed worthy? Does caring develop for fear of what might happen if we go against the other person's wishes? Sometimes we can "care too much." When caring comes from unacknowledged suffering, it can be destructive to ourselves as well as to the person we are trying to care for. Caring doesn't always look like caring. Sometimes caring means going against the other person's requests or wishes. It can be hard and it can hurt to care.

Many women have told me that they are vulnerable to caring too much in a relationship, and caring too little for themselves. Whether it's the culture we live in and the gender roles that go along with it, or by virtue of maternal biology, women tend to carry the blessing—and burden—of caring. It seems to come with the territory. But walking away from a relationship that is hurting us doesn't necessarily mean we don't care. It may mean we are simply learning to take better care of ourselves.

Regardless of who we are, choosing to care can mean a decision to set boundaries, to have the courage to respect ourselves enough to say no in the face of fear and needing to please, to risk the backlash of anger, to stay in a relationship or walk away from something that is destroying us. To care or not to care? The question can change everything.

———

A client recently came to me for coaching. He was having difficulty with his marriage and was seriously contemplating a divorce, but he wanted to explore all his options to be sure it was the right course of action. "I don't seem to care about my wife anymore," he told me. "The passion just isn't there the way it used to be."

His wife wasn't meeting many of his needs, he went on to explain to me, and his resentment was building a wall between them.

What I asked of him was to start thinking about what *his wife* might need to feel loved, and try a simple experiment of giving her what he himself hoped to receive. "What do you have to lose? If you aren't a caring person in this relationship, but desire to be," I explained, "then go out and behave in caring ways. If you want to see how a person wants to be loved, observe how they love. Start paying attention. Regardless of the outcome of the relationship, you will be a better person for it. Go home and act as if you love your wife. Tell her how much she means to you. Look into her eyes, remember why you married her, and tell her how beautiful she is."

He made a decision to make his marriage a priority in his life, not with words but with actions. He read *The Five Love Languages* by Gary Chapman—a book his wife had tried to get him to read years before. From this book, he started to understand what his wife needed from him to feel cared for, and he started to show caring on his wife's terms rather than his own. He took initiative and planned date nights around her interests, and around what she wanted from the relationship. He began including her in his world by sharing what was happening at work and in his life.

As he opened up, he was able to express what was important to him in their relationship, not in a demanding, self-centered way, but in a loving, caring way. Through a series of small actions that began with a simple decision, their marriage slowly returned to a solid footing. After several months, he was astonished to realize how much he actually did care for this woman he had lived with for so many years. He had actually decided and behaved his way back into caring.

If we want to be more caring, then we'd do well to decide to behave in caring ways. This is the power of a decision that can change a life. You can decide to care.

Sometimes our reflexes to care must be countered with reason. My niece Lauryn lives a good part of her life in Afghanistan and sent us an endearing picture of Babur, a two-and-a-half-year old mongrel. A friend found Babur as a puppy, in the middle of a busy Kabul street with cars whizzing around, and he jumped out and grabbed her. Babur soon became his companion.

Lauryn's friend is about to leave Kabul now, but cannot take Babur back to his own country and is looking for a home for her. Lauryn wondered if we could take her in. Nowzad Dogs, the official stray dog shelter in Afghanistan, would pay to ship Babur to Canada.

As we admire the photo of the adorable Babur, our compassionate hearts are opened. That is, until reason takes over and we realize that at this moment we are caring for a brother who is dying of brain cancer, a ninety-year-old mother-in-law who needs extended care while her broken femur mends, a brother-in-law who has suffered a brain injury from a recent stroke and is in need of assisted living, two daughters in university, and a third who could use support with her family. Not to mention we have a business and a household to take care of. As we write back to Lauryn to regretfully decline adopting Babur, I am reminded once again that not only does caring come with limits, but just because our compassionate heart is opened, sometimes we have to make a choice to say no to caring, even if our reflexes say go, go, go. We can continue to love, even as we say no.

Caring is not static. It isn't black and white. We can decide to care about someone, even when we don't "feel" like caring. We can act caring toward a co-worker for whom we have little feeling, such as expressing appreciation or giving a compliment, and the "feeling" of caring is the consequence. When we care, we realize that the things we tend to, tend to grow. If we look deep enough, even in those times that we say no, we can *always* find a reason to care.

## Being present

The man in front of me at the health food store is in a wheelchair. In a moment of impatience, I speed up to get past him. I am, after all, in a hurry to get home to work on my caring book! Suddenly recognizing the irony of this non-caring moment, I slow down. Compassion brushes up against me as I realize this man is a quadriplegic. He has no use of his atrophied limbs. He controls his wheelchair deliberately, slowly, and calmly with his chin.

I pause at the sound of the young woman beside him. "Dad, you can try some of my protein powder at home. Or we can get some of these chia and hemp seeds." There is tenderness and acceptance in the young woman's voice: the voice of caring. Father and daughter, working together on a shopping outing.

As I slowly push my cart toward the cashier, I allow myself to be moved by these gentle interactions. "Please, go ahead," I motion to this man and his daughter who stands patiently behind his wheelchair as they wait to get into the checkout line.

And I smile, full of admiration for this young woman's caring.

Caring is everywhere when we start to be present. Caring transforms grocery shopping into a connection. It transforms a "man in a wheelchair"—a person who is in "in the way"—to a father and a human being. It turns a task into a touch, an obstruction into a person. Caring brings life back into our life, a sense of belonging into an alienating world. Caring gives us a place to call home wherever we happen to be.

You can't care about someone or something in the past or in the future. You can only care about them now. Caring is about being here in the present moment. Caring is the quality of your relationship with the now. Caring is not a destination. Caring is a method of travel. There is no way to caring. Caring *is* the way.

I often get so busy I don't pay attention to all the daily miracles around me. Instead of noticing the dawn, I'm planning my day. Instead of pleasantly conversing with the cashier at the grocery store, I'm thinking about getting home and making supper. Instead of spending time with a brother that I claim to care about, I waited until he was dying to spend time with him. I'm a smart person: efficient, disciplined, and organized. But in my zeal to get things done, it's easy to forget the simple art of living. And that simple art of living is found in the simple act of caring. Writing a book on caring is helping to teach me to be more present in every part of my life.

We live in a fast-paced world, but it's still possible to care—if we call caring a simple smile, or a word of kindness to a stranger, an encouraging expression to a colleague, or a moment of patience with a customer service person—because caring only takes a thoughtful moment. I recall, some years ago, when I got a speeding ticket driving through a playground zone. Not a very caring act on my part toward the children in the community. I did thank the police officer for stopping me. To this day I'm grateful it was a policeman, not a child on a bicycle, that slowed me down. Sometimes caring means leaving early enough, learning to s-l-o-w d-o-w-n, and making room for what surrounds me. Being present and paying attention makes recognizing a caring opportunity that much easier.

## Receiving is an act of generosity

When I visit my brother, he is unable to speak more than a few words at a time. Often sitting for several minutes, surrounded by thoughts of inadequacy, I do not have a clue what to say or what to do. I know these long bouts of unsettling silence are there to teach me the value of imperfect presence and how to simply be there for another human being. However, the silence can still be unnerving.

To break that silence, I asked Hal one time if he would like a foot massage, and he responded with a nod and a smile. I panicked. I never imagined ever giving my big brother a foot massage, or even touching him before his diagnosis. But when someone close to you is dying, it has a way of breaking down barriers and opening your heart. It can actually be healing.

I awkwardly took the bottle of massage oil and started rubbing Hal's pasty, cold, swollen feet. I had no clue what I was doing, but I just kept rubbing.

Those foot massages became our ritual every visit. His openness to being touched by his younger brother was a generous gift to me.

Caring includes giving and receiving, cherishing and being cherished, loving and being loved. Caring, in its purest form, is an act of pure generosity. Receiving, for many caregivers, is not easy. Yet receiving care can be as generous as giving care. Without receiving, there can be no giving. It requires a willingness to somehow, in some way, be exposed. Opening ourselves to another, admitting we are lost, conceding that we are hurting, or simply allowing ourselves to be cared for is a gift to those who care for us.

Theo Van Gogh was a Dutch art dealer whose legacy often gets lost in his older brother's luminance. His brother was Vincent Van Gogh, an artist who painted sunflowers and a swirling starry night, who famously chopped off his own ear one horrible, mad night, and who spent the last decade of his life in terrible poverty, feverishly devoted to painting. When he flooded his canvasses with color, Vincent sought not only to visually capture the landscape, but to exact an emotional response, the essence of what it felt to actually be there.

In a letter to the artist Paul Gauguin, Vincent wrote, "I believe that if one placed this canvas just as it is in a boat, even one full of Icelandic fisherman, there would be some who would feel the lullaby in it."

When Theo was only twenty-three years old, he began supporting his artist brother financially. He would continue to do so for ten years until his brother's death, so that Vincent could devote himself entirely to painting. Almost 700 letters passed between Vincent and Theo during their adult years, letters that reveal their close relationship and the extent of Theo's generosity. Theo died just months after Vincent, unaware of the fame and admiration that would one day erupt over his brother's works of art.

Another instrumental player in Vincent Van Gogh's life and legacy was his sister-in-law, Johanna Van Gogh-Bogner. Born in Amsterdam, she'd trained as a pianist and once worked in the library at the British Museum. After her husband Theo died, she was left with an infant son, an apartment in Paris, and most of Vincent's artworks, which were then unsellable. Over the next few years, she would translate Theo's and Vincent's letters into English, help found a women's socialist movement, and bring Vincent Van Gogh's paintings to the wider art world—all while raising a young son.

Caring in its purest form comes from within us, from a desire to be generous without expecting anything in return. In and of itself, caring inspires, uplifts, and changes lives. Some caring actions are so powerful and unforgettable, or simply gentle and beautiful, they become woven into the fabric of our lives.

## Caring means action

As I drive over the crest of a hill, I see a family of ducks: the mother in front, with her fragile young ducklings imprinted and following dutifully behind. This entire lineup of delicate little beings straddles almost the entire width of the road. Instantly, I feel empathy for this audacious little family, and, as I sense their predicament, I imagine their panic as my vehicle barrels down the road toward them. I feel an outpouring of warmth and love toward these ducks, plus a sense of concern. A feeling of compassion.

My empathy and compassion don't equate to action. Caring does that. Empathy and compassion are outpourings of feeling. Caring is the action that emerges and follows. Empathy and compassion open my heart to the vulnerability of the situation. Caring puts my foot on the brake.

Daniel Lussier, a compassionate health care leader in central Canada, expresses the difference between caring, empathy, and compassion in this way: "Empathy is a precursor to compassion. Empathy becomes compassion when you are able to stay strong with all that is present and, from a source of strength and equanimity, are authentically moved to be of service in what is called for. With empathy, you may be able to relate to someone, and feel what the other is feeling, but there may be many barriers that get in the way of a genuine response or sense of connection."

As I write this, we are helping my dear ninety-year-old mother-in-law Mary make the transition from a house she has lived in since 1951 to an assisted living facility. What I see is a very frightened and fragile human being struggling to come to terms with such a major transition. Suffering a broken femur resulting from a fall when she was alone highlighted the reality that she'd be unable to remain in the only home she has known for so many decades. Compounding the situation is Mary's advancing dementia, with accompanying mood swings, negativity, and forgetfulness.

My caring sister-in-law Sheila has taken Mary into her own home while my mother-in-law's leg heals and until we can find more suitable long-term care. All the actions undertaken to ensure good medical help for Mary—in the acute care of her leg surgery, in helping her find a longer term assisted living facility, and with getting her relocated to my sister-in-law's home—have all been caring actions from a most loving family.

However, as caring as we all try to be, as a family we aren't always compassionate in our visits and our time together. Mary is not easy to be around these days. We all lose patience with her, and, like being around a cranky adolescent, we get annoyed in the midst of caring for her and are not always compassionate. That doesn't mean we're not empathetic. We sense how difficult this transition and loss of freedom must be for her.

It's one thing to be empathetic. But we aren't always compassionate. We don't always carry empathy's momentum into loving kindness. It gets tiring when we are continually bombarded with negativity and irritation, and it's difficult to respond in ways that will lead to a sense of loving warmth and connection. It's hard work to remember to have compassion, to put ourselves in Mary's place, to open our hearts when we are both frustrated and offended. Sometimes we just get impatient and angry in response to *her* impatience and anger. It's all part of the caring journey.

Empathy alone does not give us the strength to care. As David Lussier says, "In the case of empathy, sharing a genuine feeling but going no further ... the caring or "doing" will take a much different path. Or the actions will be different than actions coming from a source of strength, inner peace, and love. People often talk about compassion fatigue, but some argue it is actually 'empathetic distress.'" It's warmth and love—the opening of the heart—that leads to caring action.

## Opening the heart

Not long ago, a young cowboy sauntered into a leadership course I was giving to a group of ranchers. Covered with tattoos, he sat off to one side by himself with his arms folded. The minute I saw him, I had him pegged as a guy who couldn't possibly care about anything or anyone but himself. As I watched him sitting off to the side, I imagined others had the same judgment. Considering that our judgments often mask fear, I think the guy just scared me. I had no idea how I was going to reach him in a course on leadership and learning to connect with people.

Caring is about opening your heart. It means moving toward the things you are afraid of, what you judge or label with preconceived views. These were the principles I was teaching in the workshop, and yet I was judging this rancher dude with tattoos. About an hour into the workshop, he rolled up his sleeves and I noticed the writing on the inside of his forearm. "I'll stand by you forever."

At the break, I asked him about these words. "They're for my mom," he said. "She has MS, and this is my way of showing her my dedication to her through her illness."

I could feel the tears behind my eyelids. They dissolved the judgment that had held me at a distance from this young man. I asked
him to share his story of compassion and commitment. When he did,
the whole group softened and opened up to him. It was one of the
best moments in the course. This tough cowboy became a teacher of
caring to me and to the rest of the workshop participants.

While I personally wouldn't get a tattoo to show my own mother
how much I cared about her, this *was* a reminder that when we make
the effort, we can usually find another story underneath the one we
make up in our first impressions. Caring means being unguarded in
our old views and being receptive to new ways of seeing things. Caring
means being willing to create a new story.

I have a friend who works in a public service agency where the
people she serves are often very nasty to her, yet she is known as a
person who can turn nastiness into courteousness. "I open my heart
to them," she explains.

"I don't take their nastiness personally, because I know it isn't
about me. When I take a moment to see the world through their
lenses, I find that they are nasty because someone, somewhere in
their life, has been nasty to them. They expect nastiness wherever
they go, and that's what they get. But not from me. I certainly
respect myself enough to not be abused or bullied by anyone, but
their nastiness usually softens up with a little dose of empathy and
compassion."

## Listening

I know a family physician who practices his "listening" face at the
gym as a way to hone his ability to tune in to others, much as he uses
gym weights to strengthen his muscles. It's an unusual method, Scott
admits, but he's found it remarkably helpful over his twenty-odd
years of medical practice.

Practicing his listening face sprang from a chance encounter with
another family physician early in Scott's career. Shortly after graduat-
ing, he ran into a colleague he'd been to medical school with, a person
he had always admired for her clinical excellence. Scott explained to

her that his father had died recently, and that the grieving process was slow and difficult. He had lost his mother to cancer thirteen years before, and as the oldest of five siblings, he felt pressure to be the head of the family. With a wife and two young children, and a fledgling medical practice, Scott admitted how much he missed his father's companionship and advice. It was hard, he said.

His colleague listened closely. She had been an exceptional student at school and, to Scott, had always exemplified how he felt a physician should be. When he opened up about his struggles, he anticipated she would be understanding. And he was right. But as he spoke, her face grew strained—as if the listening was hurting her. Was this what it meant to be a good listener? It didn't seem that way. Scott left her feeling more distressed than before.

From then on, he decided he would not be that kind of listener. Instead, he would listen with an open and caring face. He would listen in a way that showed confidence in the other person, without strain and without mirroring their pain. In the gym, whenever Scott lifted weights, he started using this time as an opportunity to practice his listening face, seeking inner calmness and translating it into a calm and confident facial expression.

The surprising result has been that, over the years, this practice has made listening easier. By training himself to appear to be a good listener, he has actually become calmer and more patient. He is more receptive to people at work. Listening has actually become quite a bit easier.

Knowing exactly what caring is can be confusing. We often think we are caring, but it isn't received as caring by the person we care about. An act of kindness to a stranger may be perceived as intrusive. An empathetic and concerned face can be distressing. Sometimes an act of caring involves being attentive to what people we care about *actually* care about—and then behaving accordingly. Which means *listening*.

Sometimes caring is backing off. Sometimes it's moving in. It isn't mechanical or static. It involves tuning in to a changing world around us. Our caring needs are all different, and our caring needs change over time. Caring and listening early on in an important relationship will be different than caring for someone we have been around for thirty years.

A wise businessman once said that in important negotiations he had one rule of thumb for himself: "Shut up, shut up, shut up." Sometimes we are stronger when we just listen.

There's a charming story that reminds me that caring means being attentive—not just to the state of the person we are caring for, but also to our own inner state and our relationship with the present moment.

A woman in a grocery store happens upon a grandfather and his poorly behaved three-year-old grandson. It's obvious that the grandfather has his hands full. The child is sitting in the grocery cart, screaming for candy in the candy aisle, cookies in the cookie aisle. Same goes for fruit, cereal, and soda.

Meanwhile, the grandfather is working his way around, saying in a controlled voice, "Easy, Albert, we won't be long. Easy boy." Another outburst from the child and the woman hears the grandfather say calmly, "It's okay, Albert, just a couple more minutes and we'll be out of here. Hang in there, Albert."

At the checkout, the little terror is throwing items out of the cart and the grandfather, again in a controlled voice, keeps saying, "Albert, relax, buddy. Don't get upset. We'll be home in five minutes. Stay cool, Albert."

Very impressed, the woman goes up to the grandfather as he's loading the child and groceries into his car and says, "You know sir, it's none of my business, but you were amazing in there. I don't know how you did it. The whole time you kept your composure. No matter how loud and disruptive he got, you just kept calmly saying things would be okay. Albert is so fortunate to have you for his grandfather."

"Thanks, ma'am," replied the grandfather. "But I'm Albert. The boy's name is Johnny."

Caring involves caring enough to listen, to understand, and to act accordingly—both for ourselves and with those we care about.

# Leadership

As a person committed to helping leaders be better leaders, I can't help but have a lot to say about leadership. Leadership is not just a title or a position. It's about anyone who works through other people to bring value into the world. Whether you are a CEO building a company, a middle manager leading a division, a teacher in a middle school classroom, a supervisor ensuring results on your team, a front-line salesperson, a customer-service representative, a parent attempting to develop a capable young person, a committed volunteer, or a community activist wanting to make a difference in a non-profit organization or a developing country or your neighborhood, you are a leader—not by your position, but by your decisions.

In the ten years that Doug Conant served as CEO of the Campbell Soup Company, he turned the languishing business around by putting the focus back on the people who worked there. Over the course of his time at Campbell Soup, Conant was said to have written 30,000 handwritten thank you notes to his employees, amounting to about ten notes a week. "I let them know that I am personally paying attention and celebrating their accomplishments," Conant said in an HBR podcast.

One-time interim president of Kentucky State University Raymond Burse gave up $90,000 of his annual salary to give minimum wage workers on campus a raise. The lowest paid workers on campus at the time made $7.25 per hour, the federal minimum. With Burse's contribution they made $10.25 per hour, an increase that stayed in effect after the university hired him to be their full-time president.

After working in the leadership development field for more than thirty years, I have learned that good leadership is fundamentally about making contact, building personal connections, and helping people to grow and flourish. It's fundamentally about caring. Good leadership means you go the extra mile to care about your organization. You care about the people you serve. And you care about the work you do and the contribution you make.

I meet some amazing leaders in my work. People hire me to work with their organization and I end up a better person by spending time with them. One such leader who has become a good friend is John Liston. John, formally a regional director at Great West Life and now the principal of Liston Advisory Group, lives what he leads. He's a person of strong character. He's passionate. He cares. He cares about his people. He cares about the work. He cares about his organization. And his approach to leadership produces financial results. At Great West Life, his was the top region in Canada for three consecutive years, 2010 to 2012.

In a conversation with John about his coaching experience with his daughter's under 19 Ringette team, he explained how he coaches the same as he leads. Same philosophy. Same approach. Same leadership. In Appendix A, you will find John's keys for unleashing success with a team that demonstrates how he cares. You will also find some ways that you can make caring in the workplace real.

———

Many leaders, at some time in their careers, have to downsize their organization and lay people off. Any CEO who has experienced this gut wrenching, sleep depriving, brutal, and messy work knows how horrible it is. While it is never easy, I have seen some CEOs, as well as their managers, do it in a caring way.

Caring CEOs, first and foremost, have the courage to take responsibility for a decision. They don't blame it on the board of directors, economic conditions, competition, or anything else. They simply say, "I made the decision. It is what I believe to be the best for our organization. This is what we are going to do." The courage to take responsibility is an act of caring.

Honesty is also caring. Leaders who care avoid the long, drawn-out state of "considering a layoff," which destroys both morale and productivity. They move fast, cut deep when they have to, and cut once. And they certainly don't ask for pity from their staff or go to any great lengths to show the people they are laying off how hard it is on them as a manager. As hard it is on the manager, the person who suffers is still the employee.

While some CEOs who cut staff actually get a big bonus, true caring leaders would have the guts to share in the pain. They would cut their own salary, take a smaller office, and let go of some of the company perks. They would do everything they possibly could to let their employees know, "I'm in this with you." I know this isn't the norm, and it probably isn't even realistic, but I wonder sometimes what would happen if employees saw their senior managers put their own skin in the game.

Above all, leaders who care provide support. They understand that layoffs aren't just about a job. They are about people's lives. They know, too, that it isn't just the people being laid off who are affected, and that the people who stay in the organization are equally impacted, albeit in different ways. They push back on the natural tendency to handle the layoffs with rigid rules based often on unfounded fears. Instead, they give people an opportunity to say goodbye in ways that respect the dignity and authenticity of everyone involved. After all, people are potentially saying goodbye to friends, to the opportunity to belong, and to what the workplace meant to them beyond simply having a "job." They trust people to say their goodbyes in ways that are true to themselves.

While some employees may want to walk out the back door and not be seen, most simply want an hour or two to say what they need to say to their friends and colleagues. Many who choose to go quietly into the night may still have an intention to follow up with friends and colleagues at a later date.

For the people left behind, they may have the same need to see their colleagues, however briefly, to pass along good wishes and, most important, to sincerely say, "Let's stay in touch."

Caring means taking the moral responsibility—on top of the legal obligation—to provide services like coaching and job-search help. There are firms that specialize in helping employees during such transitions. Caring leaders make certain these resources are in place. They understand that they can't do it alone. The skill set to run a company is not necessarily the same skill set required to support a culture through downsizing. Caring means knowing yourself, being honest with yourself, and knowing when to bring in resources to help you. Such resources can be helpful through the immediate trauma and shock of the layoffs, as well as after the crisis is over, during the recovery process when support can be needed most.

Immediately after a layoff, it's natural for a leader to want to retreat to your office, avoid everyone, and get back to "business as usual." Caring leaders resist this natural inclination and get out where they are needed: in front of people. They understand that employees need to see and be with their leaders. Yes, there is a time and place for people to be with colleagues, with their managers in the background, but they also need leaders who care enough to be close-by and available for questions and connection. The brave face worn by the leaders who have made the decisions may be a pretense, but it's an important one.

The recovery process of any layoff experience also takes time and careful attention. Like recovering from any trauma, a transition is involved. The capacity for organizational healing is in direct proportion to how caring the leaders are through the layoffs and beyond. Caring leaders realize that just because you weren't laid off doesn't mean you don't have your own adjustment to go through. Caring means creating space for people to grieve and heal and be honest about their feelings in responsible, respectful ways. Yes, of course they have work to do, but caring leaders understand and respect people's need to heal before they are ready to get their heart into rebuilding. Layoffs are a process, not an event. The road to organizational recovery after a layoff is paved with opportunities to demonstrate caring.

# The Uncomfortable Part About Caring

Proceed now as if we're utterly needed ... that's what we've got to bring to the challenges at hand, not waiting to be convinced that we're needed but proceeding as if we are. Our insignificance has been horribly overstated.

Stephen Jenkinson

## Showing up and facing your Goliath

When I was eight years old, I gave my first public speech. It was to a church congregation of over two hundred people. I still have the notes from that two-and-a-half-minute talk. I rediscovered them when I helped my mother clean out her basement the summer before she died.

The topic was David and Goliath, the story of the young boy who killed the Philistine giant with a stone and with a power greater than them both. At the top of the paper my mother had printed, LOOK AT YOUR AUDIENCE. I still remember that speech. I remember how, as I looked up, it was me facing Goliath that day. Everyone in the congregation was looking at me, waiting expectantly for me to say something. I didn't have any real qualifications to be up there. But I had my mother's careful instruction and support, and I knew people were waiting and counting on me.

Sometimes you can feel that you're not up to the task of caring. But you don't have to be an expert to care. All you have to do is show up, face your Goliath, and do the best you can.

## Caring is messy

Since the tumor has taken a firm hold on Hal's speech center, aphasia prevents him from uttering much in the way of coherent dialogue. Upon wakening, he calls and gestures to the commode, and Dianne and I gently assist him onto the toilet. Leaving him some privacy, we wait in the kitchen until he calls, the monitor in the dining room our saving grace.

When I return to the room, I slide my arms around Hal's chest and lift him to his feet, an action I have become accustomed to over the past several months. Being able to stand, even with someone to lean on and help hold him up, for Hal, is now a triumph. Helping him to wash and brush his teeth, shaving him, dressing him, and combing his hair are becoming familiar rituals during our times together. That he allows me, his younger brother, to help him with these bodily functions is a sacred endeavor.

The last thing I do before I wheel him into the kitchen is to help him with his glasses as his frail hand moves to push them up his nose and into position. Despite the brain tumor that has disabled this brilliant man from doing almost everything, he still wants to see the world around him. Before his energy runs out, he sits and peacefully watches the sparrows, chickadees, sapsuckers, and woodpeckers pick at the seeds and suet in the feeder outside the window. Hal perks up when the magnificent and colorful Pileated Woodpecker, whom the family has come to call Pierre, comes to the window. It's one of Hal's few remaining pleasures.

I have enormous reverence for Hal's determination, in the midst of both his grace and grumpiness, as we go through these rituals. "You are one amazing dude," I whisper in his ear, as I turn the wheelchair and push him down the hallway.

Once Hal is settled in at the kitchen table, I return to the bathroom to clean up. It's uncomfortable having to deal with such a task.

As I dump out the mess and flush the toilet, I wonder too late if it all will make it through without clogging up the plumbing. It doesn't.

The water keeps rising. I holler for help. The plunger is in the basement. By the time help arrives, a murky mess has overflowed onto the bathroom floor. Amidst my anxiety, I forget how to manage the simplest things, like turning off a running toilet. My efforts to appear like a caring brother have disappeared, and I know Dianne and Hal are in the kitchen listening to my frustrated cries. I swear at the stupid toilet. I swear at the ugly mess on the bathroom floor. I plunge helplessly as the murky water just keeps coming up over the rim of the toilet. After what seems like half an hour, the disruption is dislodged. My beloved wife, Val, brings in old towels and a mop, and together we soak up the putrid water, swab the floor, and disinfect the bathroom.

After the drama and the smell subsides, we all sit together and laugh.

Such is the work and life of caring. Caring isn't dignified, magnificent, or newsworthy. It isn't like a movie that comes to a tidy end, with credits scrolling down the screen. Caring is incomplete. It's messy. But in the mess, we can all come together.

## It isn't always comfortable

Our neighbor is caring for his wife who has Alzheimer's disease. Most days Judy doesn't remember her husband and can't sit still for a minute. Bill has cared so much for her over the past three years and has done everything in his power to prolong the inevitable decision to have her placed in a long-term care facility. Because caring comes from action it involves time, effort, and attention. Caring isn't always easy or comfortable. Sometimes it's damn hard work to care.

There is currently no cure for Alzheimer's disease. It is an irreversible brain disorder that starts with small things, like occasional forgetfulness, and only gets worse over time. As the disease progresses, a person experiences more confusion and memory loss, and in later stages, they gradually lose their ability to perform simple daily tasks such as finding their way around the house, dressing, or feeding themselves. The most distressing aspect of the disease is the patient's inability to retain memories of their loved ones.

Caring for a person with Alzheimer's disease exacts a high cost on family members. As a person's capabilities deteriorate, they require more and more constant attention. At times the patient will be perfectly lucid and capable, while at other times it's as if they've returned to being a toddler. Placement in a long-term care facility may be the only reasonable choice, but it's still a difficult transition, and stressful for everyone involved.

The decision to care isn't always easy. Sometimes caring takes hardly any effort, because it's easy and automatic for us. At other times, caring involves very difficult life choices. Sometimes we can choose to stop and adapt to the situation and find a solution that works. But we are socially and biologically wired to care, and no matter how self-focused we may get, caring about others drives much of who we are.

Years ago, when I was working as a family therapist, I was called on to help with the assessment and therapy of an eight-year-old boy who was living in a residential treatment facility for young offenders. His reason for being placed in long-term care was that he had poured gasoline on a cat and set her on fire. Kids like this are not easy to care about. They are often withdrawn, angry, and usually have an impermeable wall of self-protection surrounding them. Sometimes you reach these kids and sometimes you don't, but you don't stand a chance if you can't get past your own judgments and open your heart to them. To dissolve the preconceived notions and open the door of compassion, understanding their history is a great help in seeing their actions in a broader context. Behind every action there is a story that, when understood, helps us see the positive intent in the behavior, an understandable reason for destructive action: stories of horrendous abuse, neglect, exploitation, and violence, as was the case with this damaged lad. The stories don't justify the result. What the stories do is expose the humanity amidst the insanity, transforming an unlikeable person into a human being. At that moment we are able to *love* them, even if we don't *like* them.

There are times I've been called on to care for someone I don't like, a person who, at least initially, rubs me the wrong way. Maybe they felt foreign to me, or they represented something that was antithetical to my beliefs. But when I took a moment to look beneath the surface of the drug addict or criminal, the abuser or hater, or the abrasive colleague, I found their humanity. In that moment I saw their plea for help—a damaged soul burdened with a painful past. Caring begins when we recognize each other's essential humanness, when we realize that at heart, no matter how different others may appear, we share something in common. More often than not, it requires some sacrifice, a suspension of self-centeredness, a commitment. And although caring isn't always enjoyable, it also asks us to find joy amidst the sacrifice. After all, caring with resentment isn't very caring. Remember to stop and smile—and maybe take a deep breath—the next time caring gets uncomfortable. It may help you care more deeply and with greater ease.

Maybe there's something to the Buddhist practice of cultivating compassion even for our enemies. Studies have shown that a caring attitude changes our brains. It changes our bodies. It makes us more evolved human beings. Even if caring doesn't impact the person we care about in the way we think it should, caring changes us.

## It isn't necessarily lenient

Caring in the workplace or at home means knowing when to not be lenient. It means respecting ourselves enough to know when to say no to disrespectful behavior. Sometimes caring means having the courage to confront. While caring is about opening our hearts to others, it can also require courage, being tough, telling the truth, and setting clear boundaries. When a boss holds an employee accountable for not meeting agreed-upon expectations, and follows through on their agreed-upon consequences, it shows caring to the rest of her team, to the employee, and to the boss herself. All of this, of course, illustrates the stamina it takes to care. These competing directions that call on us to care and that are so often at odds with each other can be, even at the best of times, overwhelming. Caring, with all it entails, can be wearing for any leader in any capacity. There is always a "bottom line" along with our desire to help people grow. Both must be respected.

Caring means respecting yourself and others enough to be intolerant of abuse or bullying relationships—at home or at work. We need to know when to step in. Caring and clear boundaries aren't mutually exclusive. Valerie Cade, the founder of Bully Free at Work, an organization that offers compassionate tips for handling bullies at work, has this to say, "It is the nature of a good person's heart to want to connect, as opposed to creating conflict and dissonance. When anything but harmony exists, most people at best try to modify who they really are in order to cope. On the other hand, we tend to gravitate to people who 'allow us to be ourselves.' So what happens when you feel uncomfortable and guarded around another due to their bullying or difficult behavior? Usually, anything but peace and naturalness. Here's the good news ... You do not have to keep reaching out to a person who is not respectful of your feelings, wants, needs, circumstances or desires."

"Decide to not give into force. Remain calm. Don't fight back," Cade proposes. "Assert one key statement in order to state what you want. Leave if too overpowering ... Begin to notice that, where you used to react to the bully's demand and agenda, you now have your boundaries and you stay firm, and the bully has less wiggle room." In other words, it's about setting consequences and sticking to them.

Paradoxically, the best way to deal with a bully may be to show we don't care, in essence, to withhold the emotional response they are seeking. We can appear respectful and calm, but set a firm boundary—and if necessary, walk away.

Caring shouldn't mean giving in when giving in involves disrespecting ourselves. Caring does not necessarily mean leniency. How is it caring when we allow others freedom from consequence for behaviors that are hurtful? This is true in any relationship where caring involves holding people accountable. What kind of leader or parent are we when we are overly permissive and overindulgent? What are the consequences if we think that caring means letting people off the hook?

Valerie Cade says it's important not to jump to conclusions about a situation, and to differentiate a bully from a person in distress. "Reprimanding is not your first course of action. Leaders should always remain curious to an employee's situation and do some dig-ging. Creating an empathetic understanding for an employee's sit-uation of stress is the first step to gaining back the employee's best efforts. I'm not saying to excuse certain behaviors; but changing them involves empathy and understanding on the leader's part. Discipline without relationship is a dictatorship. Develop a relationship of car-ing and concern for your employees. The more you develop this, the more mileage you will have out of corrective action."

Any parent knows that caring, at times, involves saying no, even when the child says, "You don't care!" and even if we doubt ourselves. The axiom, "Mean what you say; say what you mean, but don't say it mean," is a statement about caring. Spoiled children, children raised by insecure, fearful, or overindulgent adults, in the long run do not feel cared about.

A good friend of mine was telling me a while ago that his son, while at college, said to him, "Well Dad, if things don't work out in this career, at least I can come home and live at your place."

"Son," he replied. "You will always have a place to come home to, but you won't have a place to live. You are out of the nest now."

He said it in a most caring way. And he meant it.

Caring doesn't always look like caring. Sometimes we can choose to be tough and not interfere with the growth of what we call maturity. Caring doesn't mean giving in when it involves disrespect-ing ourselves. It isn't necessarily lenient.

## No easy formula

When my friend expressed caring for his son in college by presenting clear boundaries, he was modeling self-respect. He showed his son that he was not a doormat. And he gave his son the opportunity to stand on his own two feet.

I also know a mother whose son, when in his thirties, found him-self in the midst of a cocaine addiction. He was living on the streets, unemployed, and lost. My friend did what many caring parents would do, except she had the courage to set very clear boundaries. She allowed him back into their home with strict conditions: no sign of the addiction, strict curfews, and he had to stay in the drug rehab program he had just enrolled in. His mother told him that if he violated any of these conditions, he was back out on the street. When he started rehab, she brought him into their home and gave him a place to live for a year. During that year, he adhered to all of their agreed-upon stipulations.

"He never stole anything from me during the time he lived with us," my friend recalls. "He knew that I had too much respect for myself to tolerate him ruining our lives with his addiction. But we helped him get his feet on the ground." Now a loving husband and father, her son will tell you, "My parents loved me in those days when I couldn't love myself. I wouldn't be alive today without their caring."

Sometimes we care by being tough and drawing clear lines in the sand. Sometimes we care by opening our heart and letting people in. Sometimes we care by supporting. Sometimes we care by standing back and taking a stand. Sometimes we care by not caring. Sometimes we have to care enough to walk away and follow through on tough consequences. While in most cases, I would not recommend bringing a crack cocaine addict into one's home, I'd say we have to listen carefully to our own inner wisdom, trust ourselves, be prepared to make mistakes and learn from them, pick ourselves up, and try yet again. There is no formula, no rules, no prescribed method of caring. There is no one response.

A friend recently called me from the hallway outside her father's hospital ward where he was being treated for cancer. She had just spent the past three weeks with him as he began his oncology treatments. She lived three thousand kilometers (nearly two thousand miles) away and it was time for her to leave and return home. She was sobbing on the other end of the phone. "It's so hard to see him in this state of helplessness and pain. I want to do more. I want to take the pain away. Months of treatment lie ahead, and I have a job and a household to get back to. I don't want to catch the flight tomorrow, but I also have a life. I know I can come back here when I need to, but right now I just feel horrible."

Caring does not come with easy answers. It has limits. People who care know that we can never do enough. Being able and willing to care often brings with it a sense of inadequacy and guilt. But to care fully means to care enough about ourselves to accept that limitations are all part of the path of compassion. Just like we can't fix or take away the pain of the people we care about, we can't fix our belief that we'll never do enough. Caring is being imperfect, vulnerable, and at times uncertain. When we can accept this, we'll find a degree of solace.

## Under the guise of caring

Tyrants care about their cause. Genocides and wars are justified under the pretense of caring. But was Adolph Hitler, or any other dictator throughout history, caring? To be caring, a leader must contribute to making the world better, but who defines a "better world"? The Nazis under Hitler cared about creating what they believed would be an improved world through annihilating other races and regarding them as inferior. Hutu extremists within Rwanda's political elite blamed the entire Tutsi minority population for the country's increasing social, economic, and political pressures. Even ISIL is fighting, in their view, for a "better world." Religious wars often originate under the guise of improving the world.

Terrible things have been done under the banner of caring. There are religious institutions and political agendas that have imposed abuse and violence upon others. Hitler did seem to care for his culture. He cared for his people and for his party, but was he a caring man? He made decisions for his people, but those decisions have etched a burden of guilt and shame on the German nation. How many atrocities are committed under the guise of caring? Are caring dictators possible? Perhaps it's an oxymoron.

The trouble starts when we choose sides, when we value the conflict more than a commitment to a solution, when we refuse to see our adversaries as people too. From there it's a slippery slope. A leader's vision can be clouded. I don't mean to vilify here. On every side of a conflict, even as peacemakers and mediators, we can misrepresent ourselves and be selective when it comes to caring. But it's courageous leaders like Mahatma Gandhi and Nelson Mandela who choose non-violence, principles of justice and truth that lie above the conflict, reconciliation over vengeance, substance over sides, and forgiveness over bitterness. These are the leaders, truly moral leaders, we would do well to emulate.

So if caring leadership means moral leadership, what is moral leadership? It means working for the betterment of all constituents. Hitler may have cared about himself and his own culture and people, but he was not a moral leader. As such, I would not call a dictator caring.

What we do in war is as important as how we are in peacetime. How we are in our workplaces is as important as how we are at home and in our communities. That's the true measure of a leader, the true measure of an honorable citizen. Regardless of what we say or how we say it, caring, to be called caring, requires that we are truly committed to work toward the betterment of everyone who may be affected by our decisions. It's as simple as that. Any actions done with a motive to obliterate or harm anyone, or anything in our lives, are not caring.

## Caring versus kindness

Sometimes we choose, or we feel bound, to be kind. But kindness isn't always caring.

While kindness is undoubtedly one expression of caring, caring is more than being nice to a person. You can be nice to your rich grandfather who has written you into his will while you put poison in his tea. You can also be unkind to the people you care about the most, or kind to the people you least care about.

When a mother swears at a driver speeding through her neighborhood, she does so because she cares about her children who are playing on that street. And let's be honest. Caring people get tired and irritable and impatient, and at times just aren't very kind. If a friend or relative seems overbearing or judgmental, perhaps they are going through their own suffering and need caring rather than judgment in return.

Sometimes the people I care most about experience me as a not very kind person when I am preoccupied with other things I care about. However, by caring enough to see the caring intent, and by being forgiving to your own unkindness and the perceived unkindness of others, you can make the world a better, more caring place.

## Beyond self-interest

I have a friend with a passion for climbing mountains who has spoken often of how much he cares about climbing. His last trip up Mount Everest was used as a way to inspire and teach an elementary school class in his community. He used technology to touch the lives of these young children. When he shared the experience of this trip in this way, he expressed how it took his caring for the mountain and for climbing to a whole new level. His passion was transformed into caring about something beyond himself.

A demanding objective like climbing the highest mountain in the world takes a lot of self-interested focus, as does any act of caring. When we raise a child with special needs or care for an aging parent or commit to turning an organization around, unless we ultimately do it for ourselves, we risk placing unrealistic expectations on others and end up resentful and bitter. Any action that goes beyond what's easy or comfortable can bring fulfillment and satisfaction if it is the right thing to do. No one wants to be cared for out of obligation. There is an element of "I" in all caring. This is the paradox. We give of ourselves to discover ourselves.

For my friend, shifting his focus to a classroom of young children entirely changed the climbing experience. There was something higher at stake. He felt connected to these young children in a profound way. And as much as he wanted these children to "experience" how it felt to climb Mount Everest, to understand the months of preparation, the long weeks of acclimatization on the mountain, the many laborious steps to reach the summit and get down again, and the important work of the mountain Sherpas who helped set up camps and climbing ropes, he was also able to experience his journey through their young eyes. A truly caring exchange!

Of course, like most extreme outdoor pursuits, high-altitude mountaineering comes with high risks. Yet many who pursue high adventure will tell you it goes beyond choice. Extreme athletes are driven to push their limits, to see how far they can go, to set up a new route on a mountain, to row across the ocean, to be the first to cross an expanse of desert, to fly a spaceship. Some don't come back, or they come back defeated or badly injured. And even if they do return triumphant, in regular life they are often unhappy and restless, until it's time to prepare for their next big objective, at which point they may become so feverishly immersed in their project everything and everyone else disappears. For friends and family members, living with an extreme adventurer can be challenging and worrying and potentially devastating. There is always that risk their loved one won't return.

How is this a caring life? It's complicated. As humans, we need role models. We need trailblazers and heroines and heroes. We need individuals who are courageous enough to push the limits of what is possible. Who is to say, for example, that the Wright brothers were foolishly reckless and self-serving?

— ⁓ —

The documentary film *Meru* reveals a pure case of climbing obsession. In the film, Conrad Anker speaks of his lifelong dream to summit the elusive Shark's Fin on Meru Peak in the Indian Himalayas. It's a dream that comes at great cost. His mountaineering team is brought to the brink physically, mentally, and emotionally. They willingly take on risks and endure difficulties that are out of the realm of ordinary human experience, tackling a nearly unclimbable route fraught with avalanches, storms, thin air, and crumbling rock. What's remarkable is how Anker, with teammates Jimmy Chin and Renan Ozturk, opt for such a difficult objective—this incredibly dangerous and almost impossible goal—unequivocally. There is no more reason to climb the Fin than that it is there. And if any of them should die—a distinct possibility—they'd leave behind heartbroken family and friends. Yet, as they fight to reach the summit, the team manages to shoot enough film for a full length feature. Watching *Meru* leaves you at the edge of your seat, breathless with the sense of being there with them. It makes you believe in the strength of the human spirit.

Even if the scale of our own passions is much more moderate, we can still ask ourselves, is this what caring means? If we take up a "cause" in the name of our passions and obsessions, is our devotion to the cause really honest, or is it a smokescreen to bolster our egos? Is it a commitment to make the world better or a despairing attempt to fill a hole inside of us? There's a popular undercurrent of skepticism about athletes who pursue their dreams in the name of a "cause." People say that their dreams can only be self-interested and hubristic. There may also be something to be said for channeling one's gifts and drives and demons into a meaningful goal, even if on the surface it appears to serve no one else and amount to nothing productive.

I don't believe we need to hang off the side of a dangerous mountain and make a movie about it to show strength of spirit. Surviving a tsunami and rebuilding a community or a city, or overcoming the devastation of a tornado that kills people and seeing the community circle these families with care and sustenance, or coming back from a business mistake and subsequent bankruptcy and then having four close friends die in less than a year, as a good friend of mine experienced, all demonstrate the transcendent power of the human spirit and the courage of caring. The same goes for the simple yet profound act of devoting ourselves to the raising of children, developing the qualities of a strong character, becoming a contributing member of a community, or recovering from an addiction. Each of these acts expresses both courage and caring, even if they are left unacknowledged by the culture that surrounds us.

Maybe it's a simple matter of sharing the experience of our adventures, of letting others know how much their support means to us. A meaningful hug along with that jubilant photo of us on Facebook. A promise to be present in everyday life along with that text message to a spouse or child or parent.

Take a careful inventory of the things you say you care about. Does what you care about really only amount to hard self-interest? Where is the tenderness in your caring? How is your passion serving the world? How does your caring make the world a better place?

## It's the way we live our lives

It's 2:30 am. A single mother is holding her sick two-year-old son in a rocking chair beside her bed. Just as the child's cries begin lowering to a whimper and both start to nod off, the child spews vomit all over them. He starts to scream. Patiently, the mother lays him down on her bed as she drags her tired body into the bathroom, fills up a bucket of soapy water, and begins cleaning up the mess. By now she realizes that the screaming child has awoken his five-year-old brother who is standing at the bathroom door crying. After attempting to soothe the five-year-old, she feels the screaming toddler's forehead and has some concern about his temperature. Reaching for a thermometer, she finds that her younger son has a high fever. She runs a cool bath and puts the screaming boy into the water with her five-year-old sitting on the bathroom floor crying. After witnessing three episodes of dry heaving, she is concerned that her younger son is dehydrated, but she can't get him to drink anything. Realizing that the strategy for lowering the temperature is not working, she wraps up both children, loads them into the car, and drives them into the emergency care center to have the toddler examined by a doctor. By the time the exhausted mother gets back home with some prescribed medicine for her son, it's 7:30 am.

Caring isn't how we act when life is going the way we want it to or when the world is going as we planned. Caring is how we respond to others when our life is so far from how we want it that we can barely breathe. It's how we choose to act when we are scared to death; it's how we respond to others when we are so exhausted and frustrated and angry that we can hardly keep our head up. Caring is how we choose to be in the world when we have to dig deeply within ourselves to respond to others with dignity and kindness, when we ourselves are too tired to stand on our own two feet.

When caring demands little of us—when those we care about give back as much or more as we give to them—it's easier to care. But when the opposite is true, when caring draws every bit of strength from us that we have, caring is anything but easy. And yet I've watched people time and again, with practice, get better at caring.

What's more, caring fosters caring. It's like tapping into a resource inside us that we've ignored or didn't know was even there.

Caring isn't always so simple and straightforward. Caring is complex. On the surface, it can seem effortless. We care about a friend. We spend time with them. We listen to them. We send them a gift or a funny e-card. We happily spend time with children or volunteer in an organization that we care about.

In reality, while at times caring flows from who we are, it is not necessarily pretty, comfortable, easy, or warm and soft. Caring can be bloody difficult. It means making the best choices we can with the best interest of everyone in mind. A tall order. But this doesn't mean everyone will agree or be happy with us just because of our intent. Sometimes we get stretched in too many directions and we have no more caring to give. Life presents itself in the most inconvenient and uncomfortable ways sometimes, but it's often in these difficult moments that we learn what we are truly made of.

# Allowing for Caring

Let yourself be silently drawn by the stronger pull of what you truly love.

Rumi

## Accepting our imperfect efforts ...

My sister Kate, who lives in San Francisco, has flown up every two months since Hal's diagnosis. She must care mostly from a distance. She never feels that she does enough. And neither do any of us. It doesn't matter how close or far away we are, self-doubt seems to accompany the arduous work of caring. But, we are all doing the best that we can.

The courage and capacity to care lies within all of us. It may be buried, but it is there, nonetheless. The challenge is to open your heart and allow caring to happen, accepting that your imperfect efforts are enough.

## The courage to care

When I was in elementary school, I remember a little girl who got teased a lot and wasn't very popular. She suffered from epileptic seizures and hung out mostly by herself. Being an outsider, she was frequently tormented, harassed, and bullied. On one occasion, a group of boys was teasing this poor girl when another boy, who also wasn't terribly popular, stood in front of the bullies, looked them all in the eyes, and told them to stop bugging her.

The poor kid got punched in the nose for his troubles, and his face bled for the rest of the afternoon. That "poor kid" went on to be the high school student union president and a talented quarterback, and he eventually became a lawyer and one of the best crown prosecutors in the province. To this day, I wish I'd had the courage to stand up to those bullies the way he did.

Caring can be dangerous. Caring, at times, means putting ourselves at risk. It puts us in the path of betrayal, rejection, discomfort, unpopularity, and even our safety.

In 1996, a fourteen-year-old grade nine student became enraged after reading a newspaper article about the Taliban's treatment of women in Afghanistan. Waging a one-woman anti-Taliban movement from her parents' home in West Vancouver, she gathered 400 signatures on a petition and fired it off to Canadian cabinet ministers, human rights groups, and the United Nations. She found a fax number on the Internet for the Taliban and sent them a copy overseas.

Two years later, she called up the national organization, Canadian Women for Women in Afghanistan, and offered to start a Vancouver chapter. Its president, Janice Eisenhauer, gratefully accepted. At the time, Eisenhauer had no idea she was speaking to a sixteen-year-old. And when Lauryn Oates, who is my niece, was an undergraduate at McGill University, she opened another chapter in Montreal.

Currently, Lauryn runs a Canadian aid program that also trains Afghan teachers. It's a mammoth undertaking in a country where most teachers are barely literate themselves. Aid delivery in Afghanistan can be fraught and dangerous. It involves driving for hours on dusty, treacherous roads, confronting hostile bureaucrats, avoiding suicide bombers, and returning to the program's service regions, month after month, to ensure donor-funded programs really are delivering the services they set out to provide.

It isn't a job for the faint of heart. While most aid workers hunker down in Kabul compounds, Lauryn has traveled to every region of the country from Jalalabad to Herat—mainly by car—making contacts with locals who can smooth the path of aid delivery. She has been in hotel lockdowns when the embassy next door was under siege, has known colleagues who were shot soon after sharing a meal with them, and has been nearby when a restaurant she often frequented was blown up by a suicide bomber. These horrific and dramatic events, to name only a few, have not once dampened her dedication to the cause of advocating for the universality of human rights, making public education accessible in a developing region of the world, and protecting liberties, like freedom of thought and expression, that are being denied by groups such the Taliban.

Despite the modest funding provided to her aid group, Lauryn's Afghan staff includes more than a dozen instructors who, to date, have trained thousands of teachers. Education is what gives them the most leverage, she tells me. "You can come in here and fund reconstruction by building roads and buildings. Or you can spend less money teaching Afghans to do this work for themselves."

Lauryn has been "commuting" to Afghanistan regularly from Vancouver, yet her commitment remains strong. "I believe in this place. For all its flaws, it still has a soul. Besides, it isn't a sacrifice. I'm totally, madly in love with this place, and I'd be happy to do what I'm doing here forever."

William Blake, in the poem "A Memorable Fancy," enters into an imaginary conversation with the prophet Isaiah: "Does a firm persuasion that a thing is so, make it so?" the questioner asks. Isaiah replies, "All poets believe that it does, and in ages of imagination this firm persuasion removed mountains." And so my niece, in her conviction that she can shift mountains in Kabul, is doing just that.

The root of the word courage is *cor*—the Latin word for heart. Caring means the courage to follow our heart. It means, at times, the courage to stand alone as we stand up for a something or someone we care about.

## It's sometimes risky and incomplete

I know one dedicated mother who cares deeply about her young children. She also cares about getting exercise. For now, though, her children have taken a higher priority. "My children won't be young forever!" she'll tell you. It isn't easy, though. While she fits in some quiet time for herself, walks with friends that trade off babysitting, and does some yoga whenever she can, she misses the strength and fitness afforded by regular exercise. Yet she understands that caring means some sacrifice somewhere.

In the meantime, being a mother is what she considers to be her "yoga practice," at least while her children are young. Yoga, she will tell you, isn't the fancy outfits you wear or what you do on a mat. Yoga is how you live your life.

Caring means making choices. Maybe, for now, we need to spend time caring for an aging parent and let the weeds in our garden grow above our waist. Or, for today, we choose to take care of a client rather than a friend. Or we make our health a priority and get out to exercise despite the emails in our inbox. There will always be more demands than we have time and resources for. Caring means knowing what truly matters and making what matters a priority.

When an employee is late for a meeting and her colleagues feel slighted and assume that she doesn't care about the project, maybe the employee does care, but she cares more about something else that needs to take a higher priority right now. As leaders and co-workers, it's important to be take the time to understand. People's lives are messy. Sometimes we have to leave some things we care about half-done or not done at all. There is no straight path to caring.

Whether a rational decision or instinct, the choice to care is like arriving at a crossroads and taking a risk to choose one path over another. It's like noticing our impatience emerge while maneuvering our vehicle behind a slow driver. We can irritably pass them or we can see the slow driver as a mindfulness teacher. Allowing for caring means taking a risk that we might get things wrong, that it may hurt, we might be late for a meeting, or it might complicate our lives. But the only way to progress is through practice. Like anything worth doing, with practice we can learn to get better at caring. The first step is to slow down and allow caring to happen.

Lindsay Leigh Kimmett was an athlete, a leader, and a medical student with enormous potential to do great things in the world. She was passionate about life and about making a difference, wholeheartedly giving her gifts of intelligence and compassion to everyone she came across. At age twenty-seven, Lindsay's life was taken far too soon.

As a seat-belted passenger in a single car rollover on a clear dry road, she died seven hundred meters (less than eight hundred yards) from her parents' home gateway. Following this horrific tragedy, Lindsay's loving parents were consumed with unimaginable grief. In an attempt to move forward, they were determined to carry on her legacy.

Her amazing family and friends created the Lindsay Leigh Kimmett Memorial Foundation in honor of her memory. To date, hundreds of thousands of dollars have been invested into our community in Lindsay's name across an array of initiatives, including Valedictorian Scholarships at all three of Cochrane's high schools, the Lindsay Leigh Kimmett Prize in Emergency Medicine at the University of Calgary Medical School, and Lindsay's Kids Minor Hockey & Ringette Sponsorships. Since her death, Lindsay's family has also been very active in supporting Alberta's distracted driving legislation and asks all to drive responsibly without distractions. None of this is a substitute for losing their daughter. Caring isn't always perfect. In fact, it's rarely perfect.

Caring is more often risky and incomplete. We might not get the great reception we expected. Maybe it takes a while to figure out how to care. Or maybe no matter how hard we care, we'll never patch the sorrows that loss and grief bring to us. Instead of putting ourselves out there and exposing ourselves to life's imperfections, we could put on a hard shell and protect ourselves from having to care.

Being impervious to caring can make us feel tough, like one of those movie cowboys or action heroes. But that's not real life. Besides, it takes far more courage to open our hearts enough to care: we have to observe things as they are and acknowledge the truth of what we see—and not just our own truth, but another's truth.

## Recognizing caring

When I was running track at university, my coach Sherald James, who trained several US Olympic athletes in his tenure, cared enough to be honest with me. He told me I had good endurance, but not enough speed to compete at the international level. He advised me to start running more for pure enjoyment and put my focus into my academic studies. Reality can hurt, and I didn't feel particularly cared for by Coach James. My pride took a beating, but over time I realized that he'd said what he'd said because he cared, even though it didn't feel like caring at the time.

When we perceive a rejection and when we don't get what we want, caring can appear hurtful. But it also means facing reality and seeing life from a broader view. Coach James's honesty helped me make changes in my focus and life direction, and I will be forever grateful to this man for taking the time to care about me. Caring isn't always seen as being so.

Imagine a tiny three-year-old with sensitive blood sugar levels who goes to her grandmother's house for a visit. When she arrives, she isn't spoiled with the kinds of baking and cakes and cookies that her friend gets when *she* goes to her grandmother's house. The three-year-old cries when her grandmother doesn't give in to her requests for sweets. She's still a toddler, but the girl has type 1 diabetes, and her grandmother cares enough to help her granddaughter monitor her sugar intake, even though she'd love to spoil her. Being cared about does not always feel pleasant. This is especially true if the person perceives caring from their limited viewpoint. Any parent understands that when we say no, our child may not, at the time, feel that we are very caring. They may find it hurtful and anything but pleasant.

With wisdom and maturity, we see others' caring intentions. We also recognize that we don't have to please others or make them happy to care about them.

## The best way to care?

"I remembered one morning," writes Nikos Kazantzakis, "when I discovered a cocoon in the bark of a tree, just as a butterfly was making a hole in its case and preparing to come out. I waited a while, but it was too long appearing and I was impatient. I bent over it and breathed on it to warm it. I warmed it as quickly as I could and the miracle began to happen before my eyes, faster than life. The case opened, the butterfly started slowly crawling out and I shall never forget my horror when I saw how its wings were folded back and crumpled; the wretched butterfly tried with its whole trembling body to unfold them. Bending over it, I tried to help it with my breath. In vain. It needed to be hatched out patiently and the unfolding of the wings should be a gradual process in the sun. Now it was too late. My breath had forced the butterfly to appear, all crumpled, before its time. It struggled desperately and, a few seconds later, died in the palm of my hand."

"That little body is, I do believe, the greatest weight I have on my conscience. For I realize today that it is a mortal sin to violate the great laws of nature. We should not hurry, we should not be impatient, but we should confidently obey the eternal rhythm."

From this story in Kazantzakis's novel *Zorba the Greek*, it's apparent how efforts to care can actually do harm. Help isn't always helpful. Caring isn't always caring, especially when I think I'm trying to save someone from their own unhappiness. If my limited perception of a situation causes an impulse to rescue someone, it usually ends up as a not very caring act. Caring often means being present for someone through their unhappiness, and trusting that they will make the choices they need to make to be on the path they are meant to take, and knowing that this is enough. I'm not advocating for an unhappy life. I'm merely saying that the key to a happy life may be to learn to accept that problems and unhappiness are not only part and parcel of a good life, they are critically necessary to grow a life worth living. Working through problems develops strength, clarity, and capacity.

## Readiness

During the summer of 2011, East Africa was experiencing a terrible famine. The very difficult choice was made to refuse aid to Somalia. There were many possible factors at play, including not wanting to put aid workers at risk and not wanting the food aid to get into the hands of Al-Shabaab militants. By the end of the famine over a quarter million people had died, many of them elderly or children. These were innocent people. They weren't part of the fighting. They hadn't done anything wrong. And yet the global aid community failed to help them. In retrospect, one wonders if we could have done more.

What keeps us from being able or ready to care? How do we make decisions about who or what to care about? Do we refuse to care when we are afraid, or because we don't believe the recipients deserve our caring? Sometimes we fear others, or we mistrust or feel disgust for certain groups, or maybe we are simply indifferent to someone's plight.

Martha C. Nussbaum writes, "Disgust jeopardizes national projects involving altruistic sacrifice for a common good, for it divides the nation into hierarchically ordered groups that must not meet. What 'common good' could cross those lines? ... Given that the other has already been vividly depicted, in one way, as subhuman, the antidote to that way of imagining must itself come via the imagination ..." In other words, from stories.

What makes us ready to care? It seems the more we hear stories about others who are different from us, and the more we live and love and feel their pain, the more we are free and ready to open our hearts.

———

What happens when we care, but people aren't ready to receive our caring? What happens when we love our children and they push us away? What happens when we extend caring arms to a person who has suffered and they reject our love? What happens when someone commits suicide, even in the face of inexhaustible caring? Sometimes people aren't thrilled to receive our caring gifts in the way our limited expectations feel that person "should." Receiving caring, if it means meeting our anticipated responses, maybe isn't their choice at this time.

Caring involves a choice, for the giver and the receiver. Caring also involves letting go of the results of our caring.

Despite all our efforts and love, some individuals may simply not believe that the universe is caring. Whether it's a psychological limitation or a physical impairment, or simply a decision, caring may not always be received the way we want it to be. Sometimes we care in a way that is not helpful. Sometimes people simply aren't ready to receive our caring, no matter what form it comes in. Sometimes we have to keep on caring, maybe in inventive ways, and perhaps it takes years before a person becomes receptive.

And sometimes the door never opens. But we choose to be patient and keep caring, and do the best we can to not take their lack of response personally.

## Caring won't make the world perfect

A desperate mother sat in front of me as tears were creeping into the corners of her darkened, sunken eyes. "My daughter is dying from anorexia. What can I possibly do?"

"Don't ever underestimate the power of love," was my only possible response.

"But it's not enough!" she replied. "The counseling, the support group, the eating disorder program, the psychiatrist ... they all worked for a time. But now she is turning away from them all."

I had no answer for her. I had absolutely nothing to say that would fix this situation, and nothing I could do would take the pain away or give her any answers. All I could do was to be there. It's a hard thing for a parent to bear, watching their child waste away. It's unimaginably horrible to witness helplessly a daughter's self-destruction. It's agony when we're unable to do a thing for someone we love.

Caring doesn't make the world perfect, not if we have any preconceived ideas of what caring is supposed to accomplish. Caring won't necessarily fix what is broken or take away our problems or save us from unhappiness. It isn't meant to. Caring isn't about curing. People we care about may still suffer, stay sick, and even die. While caring won't make the world a perfect place to live, and it won't take away our pain, what it will do is make the world a *better* place to live. It's about, in the words of Professor of Social Work Brené Brown, "leaning into the discomfort of ambiguity and uncertainty, and holding open an empathic space so people can find their own way. In a word—messy."

Adversity seems to be necessary to human development. It's what gives us our opportunities to grow. Hardship prunes us and makes room. Difficulty strengthens the muscles of our inner capacities. Caring is about loving ourselves and others through adversity in a way that cultivates healing, just as heat and moisture on a seed helps it push against its shell to germinate and grow new shoots.

Caring offers support so that we know we aren't alone. Caring also means letting go. We just don't know what good or hard times are needed to help us or those we care about grow.

Franklin D. Roosevelt, who led the United States through the Great Depression and World War II while transforming the U.S. government, is an example of this. An active, ambitious, and outgoing man, Franklin was diagnosed with polio in 1921 mid-career, finding himself suddenly immobilized, helpless, and isolated, his political ambitions at an apparent end. But he responded to this adversity with a courage and compassion that he may not have known he possessed before, and emerged twelve years later to help restore the faith of a gravely terrified country.

"To some extent," writes historian Doris Kearns Goodwin, "the ease of life before the polio might not have equipped [Franklin] for being the leader that he was. There was an ambition, but not the ambition that accompanied the *substance* that came after the polio. What the polio did was transform him in many ways. He learned by withstanding the adversities that came by a trial by fire and thereby he could help others do the same."

Franklin's polio also opened a door for his wife Eleanor to become a public and political power in her own right. Through her own suffering and horrendously difficult childhood, she possessed wisdom and a unique empathy and ability to connect with people that made her a world leader.

Adversity also serves a purpose if we step back far enough to look at it through the eyes of perspective. Circumstances do not determine a person; they reveal the person.

## Suffering teaches us

One summer day in July 1980, Nisha Zenoff suffered every parent's worst nightmare. She learned that her oldest son Victor had died in a hiking accident in Yosemite National Park, a week shy of his eighteenth birthday. Victor had just graduated from high school, and as he left for his camping trip in the mountains, he'd had the promise of the whole world ahead of him. And then he was gone. For his mother, surviving her son's death felt unimaginable.

Nisha Zenoff, already a therapist and a grief counselor, found none of her professional training prepared her for the devastation and pain she would experience in the months and years that followed. In those early days, Nisha made a vow that if she somehow got through the pain, she would help others survive and heal from their loss. After more than thirty-five years, she still feels her son's absence keenly. "The unspeakable loss," she calls it. Her suffering has been a remarkable gift and a teacher. Over the years, Nisha has helped reach many other families who are dealing with the death of a child.

"Impermanence is life's only promise to us, and she keeps it with ruthless impeccability," writes the poet Jennifer Welwood. Grief can drive us to places that transform us when we allow it to expand and enrich our experience of being human. At first the pain is unbearable. There is no way out, no solace possible. We have no one to turn to on the outside, and we can't face what's going on inside us either. As author Allison Nappi puts it, "You are a character in a story that is over ... You no longer fit in the world, and there is no star that can grant your truest wish."

Yet eventually, we can survive it. Coming to grips with death, injury, or illness, relationships ending, children growing up, losing a job, getting old, betrayal, abandonment, or abuse are parts of what I call "the happenings of humanness." Each of these experiences affords us a choice to harden, to withdraw, to become silent and bitter, or, alternatively, to become more empathetic and to deepen our caring. By opening up and being honest, by reaching out to others and strengthening our empathic capacity, a deeper ability to care can emerge through our pain.

How does suffering do this? When pain touches us—through grief or sorrow, through despair, hunger, or terror—we are changed forever. There is no denying how suffering marks us. Yet it affords us opportunities to grow, to gain a hard-earned wisdom to pass on to others. Somehow, through our own healing, we are better able to be there for others when they too are healing. Paradoxically, experiencing hardship and suffering and pain can teach us how to care. It can make us more empathetic and understanding. And because compassion springs from empathy, these seeds breed acts of caring.

# PART II

# Anatomy of Caring

The Universe is made of stories, not of atoms.

Muriel Rukeyser, American poet and activist

## The power of story ...

I recently concluded a session with a group of executives at a retreat center. After all the participants had left, I was packing up my materials and preparing for the long drive home when I noticed one of the hotel housekeepers. She was standing by a side table, leafing through some of my books.

"You like storytelling, don't you," she said.

"Why yes," I replied. "How did you know?"

"I was not just cleaning today. I was also listening."

A silence fell over our conversation. I was intrigued.

"Seeing as you like to hear stories, would you like to hear mine?" she asked.

In all honesty, I wasn't in the mood for more conversation. I was tired and ready to go home—but something inside me said, "Stop and listen. This woman has something to teach you."

So I sat and nodded politely, and motioned for her to take a seat and continue.

She pulled up a chair next to me. "I came to this country ten years ago from Pakistan. I brought little with me except my children and one set of clothes. I worked hard to support my family as a single parent, since my husband had abused and abandoned me in my homeland and left me with four small children to raise."

"After I came here, I grew very depressed, and I wanted to take my own life. The loneliness of living in a new culture with little support was growing to be unbearable. At a bus stop, I found the number for a distress line, and so I called them."

"The woman on the suicide help line began the conversation by asking me to talk about the depression and what might be causing me to be depressed. 'I don't want to talk about my depression,' I replied. 'Tell me a story. I just want to listen to a story.'"

"'About what?'"

"'Anything. Just tell me about your day. Your life. Your dreams.' The volunteer fumbled through an anecdote of a situation that had happened to her earlier that day, dealing with one of her children. I thanked her and before I hung up, I said I would call again."

"A few days later, I found myself calling the distress line again, and when a volunteer answered, I again requested a story. 'Oh, you are the woman we have been waiting for. Please hold on for a minute. There is person here who wants to talk with you.'"

"She went and got the volunteer who had been there on my first call. This time she was prepared with a story. As I listened, tears filled my eyes. And every few days, I would call and request a story, and each day the volunteer would share a new story. Listening to these stories healed me. They saved my life."

I nodded and smiled. I imagined that telling those stories also undoubtedly healed the volunteer on the other end of the line.

# A More Human World

Government, business, the lives we lead … the way we relate to the natural world around us—it's all become too big and distant and industrialized. Inhuman. It's time to do something about it. It's time to make the world more human.

Steve Hilton, former senior adviser to Prime Minister David Cameron

Don't seek to become a person of success, but rather … to become a person of value.

Albert Einstein

## The prison that locks us away

Darren, an entrepreneur and owner of a mid-size pipeline services company, turned to me for help with his leadership. His problem originated from some feedback he had received from his employees from an anonymous survey he'd had them fill out.

Some of the feedback to Darren was:

- You're not a good listener.
- You don't allow input from others.
- You're impatient.
- You aren't very sensitive to the people who work with you.

- Competent in the technical and operational aspects of your job, but you don't connect well with your employees.
- You don't do a good job of recognizing the strengths in others.

This kind of feedback, I found out, was not new to Darren. "I've never really been very good at the people side of business. My job would be so much easier if it weren't for the people. But I probably need to respond to this negative feedback by learning to better deal with my employees."

"Tell me, how were you able to build such a successful company?"

"A lot of hard work. I'm a poor delegator so I do most everything important around here. We also have a good product."

In the first few sessions, Darren was sensible, level-headed, and practical. He accepted my suggestions in a polite and cordial manner. He came with his computer tablet and took plenty of notes while I helped him find new skills and strategies for dealing with the practical side of working with people. Although it was pleasant enough to work with Darren, it felt like I was reprograming a computer rather than coaching a human being.

That is, until things took an abrupt turn in the fourth session, when he arrived cloaked in a demeanor that was more distant and aloof. His usual polite helpfulness was absent. When I asked, "What's up, Darren?" he seemed tense.

"Nothing, really. Let's just get to work on what we started last week."

"You seem anxious and distracted," I said, in my best effort to give him some support but also to be truthful.

"My father is in the hospital. He had a heart attack two days ago. He's never taken good care of his health. He had it coming," Darren added.

"You sound angry. Do you want to talk about it?"

He shrugged.

"How is your father now?" I asked.

"I don't know. I haven't been by to see him. My sister tells me I should go, and that he may not last more than a few days."

"What's your resistance?"

"I don't see him very often."

Over the next hour, Darren spoke about his father's constant criticism and abuse. While he remained cautious, guarded, and reserved, you could have cut Darren's anger and tension with a knife.

"Would you regret not visiting your father if he died?" I asked.

It took a few moments before he spoke. "I think so. I just wouldn't know what to say."

The rest of the session dealt with some ways he might consider approaching his father.

Darren visited his father later that day. Two days afterward, his dad died.

Following his father's funeral, our sessions shifted from mere strategic interactions to more meaningful conversations about Darren's experiences with his father and his family growing up. The wall that he had built around himself to cover up his resentments, we discovered, eventually became a prison that locked him away from the full experience of being alive.

What Darren began to realize was that he no longer needed this wall to protect himself. He started to open his heart and allow himself to feel some of the pain that for years he had avoided. By having the courage to face the pain he had been running from, he was able to rediscover some of his passions, reconnect with his children, and refocus his life. He became a better leader. He learned to care.

## More humanness

*Guideposts* contributor JoAnn C. Jones relates an experience in which her university professor taught her about the importance of the human touch:

"During my second month of nursing school, our professor gave us a pop quiz. I was a conscientious student and had breezed through the questions, until I read the last one: What is the first name of the woman who cleans the school?"

"Surely this was some kind of joke. I had seen the cleaning woman several times. She was tall, dark-haired and in her fifties, but how would I know her name? I handed in my paper, leaving the last question blank. Before the class ended, one student asked if the last question would count toward our quiz grade. 'Absolutely,' replied the professor. 'In our careers you will meet many people. All are significant. They deserve your attention and care, even if all you do is smile, say hello, and find out their name.'"

"I've never forgotten that lesson. I also learned that the cleaning woman's name was Dorothy."

What JoAnn had missed—and what I have learned by observing leaders in organizations for more than thirty years—is that making the time to learn a person's name, having a connection, giving some recognition, paying attention—in other words caring—makes all the difference in nursing, in leadership, and in life. A life without caring is like a person disconnected from their soul. Their skeleton, nerves, and blood are all able to operate, their body consumes and excretes, but there is no essential life force.

Caring brings meaning and fulfillment to a life. Caring transforms the "bank teller," the "restaurant server," the "janitor," or the "cab driver" from an object into a human being: someone with a name and a story, with needs and wants, with challenges and triumphs, emotions and dreams, goals and aspirations, and a desire to belong and to feel good about their contribution.

Even if the caring we express goes unnoticed, if the seeds we plant fall on unfertile ground, and if no one cares about our caring, deciding to be caring just makes us better people. When we make an effort to care, at the end of the day, we feel better about ourselves. The act of caring—independent of how others respond to our efforts—can in itself bring satisfaction.

Or as Bob Galvin, son and nephew of Motorola founders Paul and Joseph Galvin, said, "Dad once looked down an assembly line of women employees and thought, these are all like my own mom—they have kids, homes to take care of, people who need them."

Leigh Boyle, Executive Director and founder of The Lipstick Project, recently spoke at a Public Salon, a monthly event held in Vancouver and organized by Vancouver's former mayor Sam Sullivan. The Lipstick Project was born out of the journal of Lieutenant Colonel Mervin Willett Gonin, who was in charge of decommissioning the

World War II concentration camp Bergen-Belsen and liberating the camp's survivors. A passage in Gonin's journal involved a wooden case filled with red lipstick that had mysteriously and oddly been donated to their relief effort. The colonel told his men to leave the box in the corner of the yard. And there it stayed for a couple of weeks.

One day, the colonel, on his round of the camp, noticed several "inmates" dressed in their drab striped uniforms but wearing red lipstick. Someone had broken open the crate and handed out the product. Thus, thousands of survivors went from feeling inhuman to human, by wearing a touch of bright color.

The Lipstick Project expounds on the lesson that scared, frail people still want to be recognized as fully human and a part of society. The organization achieves this by going into hospices and care homes, and offering free hairdos, facials, manicures, and pedicures, as well as light massage to the residents. What Leigh Boyle noted in her talk was that people who are sick and vulnerable miss "the touch" of other people. Too often, their loved ones appear afraid to touch or hug them, so they don't. This further isolates and distresses the ones who most need attention and human contact. The Lipstick Project bridges that gap.

In response to this story, my friend Ian West, an executive with an organization that provides care and communities that enrich the lives of seniors, said this, "Most of us take a trip to the hair salon for granted. We see grooming not as a luxury, but as our right. Getting to wear lipstick and having someone fuss over us may seem like a small thing, but these services make a huge difference to how the residents feel about themselves. It's about rising above being a victim of circumstances, and participating fully in the world. This isn't paying 'lip service' to what caring is. The Lipstick Project is bigger than that. It's about the meaningfulness of a human touch."

## Doing the right thing

I recently spoke with an oil executive who, years ago, was in charge of developing a culture of safety in his organization. A large premise of the training was to teach employees to have the courage to say something, to speak up and tell someone when they witnessed a behavior at work that wasn't safe.

This executive, Dale, told me that around the same time, he spotted his neighbor outside on his property performing welding in an unsafe manner, without eye protection. At first, Dale felt disinclined to speak up. The man's actions were none of his business, after all. But then he struggled with himself, knowing he couldn't stand by and watch a possible accident happen, not after what he'd been trying to build around his fellow employees. He could just picture his neighbor's angry response to his "meddling," but he also couldn't live with himself if he didn't do something.

Dale went inside and got his own safety goggles, walked over to the neighbor, and—with misgivings about how this would go over—said, "I'm giving you these because I care."

The neighbor actually welcomed the goggles.

"Gee, thanks," the neighbor replied. "I get careless when I'm in hurry."

Years later, the same neighbor admitted that he always thinks twice about safety when he engages in an action that involves risk—all because of that one caring act.

For a list of strategies to put caring into action, visit Appendix B.

~⁓~

Years ago, I was asked by a client to submit a proposal on culture change. While I felt confident to do most of the work, there was one aspect of the project that I had to subcontract to another consultant. I mistakenly turned the entire proposal over to him, instead of just the portion that would be relevant to his area of the project. As a result, the consultant was able to learn that the client had a healthy budget and deep pockets, and he proposed a project that would have made us both a significant amount of money.

I knew it was unethical to send this kind of proposal to the client. It simply wasn't the right thing to do. We would have been selling them a program they could have paid for, but didn't need. My reputation was at stake, but more importantly, my character was on the line.

I had long made a commitment to only ask clients to pay for services that would bring them value.

So I cancelled the proposal and found another consultant with an ethical foundation and more personal integrity. Doing what is right means learning to accurately gauge the world around us. It means looking inward, being authentic, and being honest with ourselves.

Caring enough to do the right thing takes courage. But the choices we make affect not only our own lives, but the lives of those who rely on us.

# Important Relationships

A man told me once that all the bad people
Were needed. Maybe not all, but your fingernails
You need; they are really claws, and we know
Claws. The sharks—what about them?
They make other fish swim faster. And the hard-faced
Men in black coats who chase you for hours
In dreams?—That's the only way to get you
To the shore.

Robert Bly

## Connecting

Our new hired hand arrived early. When I saw an old man riding a rusted bicycle up our gravel road in the pouring rain and into the yard of our family farm, I wondered, "Who is this slightly scary, weird-looking guy, whistling and smiling, dressed in worn-out coveralls, a flannel shirt, a torn jacket, and rubber boots?"

I was a young teenager and was expected to work with this new hired hand—whose name was Norris—for the summer. I didn't want much to do with Norris at first. I just hung around for a few days and quietly worked alongside him.

He didn't seem to mind that I wasn't talkative. He simply went on about his business. At the time, I thought it was a little odd that no matter what the weather was like, or if we were fencing or building a structure or hauling bales of hay, Norris always showed up on time and was happy. Except for a short lunch break, he never stopped working and never complained. From the moment he arrived until the moment he got back on his rusted-out, single-gear two-wheeler at the end of the day and peddled off, he was always smiling. Always whistling. Always working. Never grumpy. Always the same steady mood.

Eventually, I began to feel sort of relaxed around Norris, but he really got my attention when we started working with our horses. We had a mean two-year-old colt that I'd tried riding before, and been bucked off so many times I'd given up going anywhere near him. One day, I walked up to the corral and in astonishment watched as, after just five minutes with this wild little stallion, Norris had him circling calmly on the end of a lead rope. I climbed up onto the first rung of fence and watched in silence while Norris worked with this formerly willful animal. Whatever the horse did, Norris did. He carefully copied each of the horse's actions. All the fear that this spirited horse had shown earlier in the day seemed to dissolve. The next thing I knew, Norris was on the colt's back and galloping calmly around the corral.

I was captivated. As Norris led the stallion back to the pasture, clearly having established a trusted relationship with the horse, I caught up to him and asked, "Will you teach me how you break horses?"

He stopped and after a moment of quiet, he smiled at me. His response was firm. "You don't *break* horses, son. You *bond* them."

He turned and walked away so abruptly, I had to run to catch up with him. As I hurried alongside, he added, "We can start by building a round paddock. You don't build connection and trust in a square corral."

I didn't get a commitment from Norris that day. What I got was inspired. I somehow knew he would work with me if I earned the privilege to be his student.

Before Norris arrived, I had saved up enough money to buy my first horse. Mom and Dad paid the other half, and so, for fifty dollars, I purchased a retired packhorse. Caesar was a towering seventeen hands tall—over five and a half feet—from the ground to the top of his six-inch protruding backbone. The old gelding was about as tame as a dead dog, and a perfect horse to learn to ride on.

The problem was getting on him in the first place. I didn't have enough money for a saddle, so I had to learn to climb onto him by stepping onto a bucket, grabbing his backbone with both hands, and swinging my right leg over his rump. Norris later taught me to climb onto Caesar without using the bucket to stand on by grabbing hold of his backbone, lifting myself up, and swinging my whole body up alongside the horse. At first, Norris gave me a "leg-up" for this maneuver. I'd step up onto his solidly bended knee until I was able to hoist myself around this huge hulking animal whose back stood almost as tall as I did.

From the beginning, Norris encouraged me to ride bareback. "No need to rely on a saddle," he told me. "Learn first to connect with your horse through your whole body, especially with your inner legs."

Months later, when I started to ride the wild little colt, Norris would sit right behind me, wrap his legs around my legs, grab my hand that held the reins in his hand, and teach me how to connect and communicate with the colt using only my legs. Up against me, Norris's body odor smelled so bad I got nauseous, but I didn't care.

While building the new round corral together that summer, Norris shook his head as he watched me pound in a nail. Quietly he reached his arm around my body, took my hand with the hammer in his hand, and taught me how to pound a nail with accuracy and the least amount of effort. "You have to drive a nail with your whole arm," he told me, "not your wrist. You'll wear yourself out doing that."

He also taught me how to shake someone's hand with firmness and conviction. "Your handshake feels like a fish. If you are going to make something of yourself, you better learn how to shake a hand," he once said to me. He taught me how to bring confidence and solidity to a handshake—and learning that handshake gave me confidence.

Through a combination of Norris's humble competence and my readiness to learn, by conveying that he was with me and not against me, Norris earned my trust, just as he'd earned the trust of the colt. He made me feel safe when I was around him because of his acceptance and honesty, and these, combined with the example of how he lived his life, taught me that happiness comes from our decisions, not from our possessions. He taught me, by way of his inspiring, unconventional presence and love for all of life, to appreciate a good day's work, to connect with animals, and to put pride and passion into whatever I did.

Over the next three years, Norris and I worked together every summer to build barns and fences, and to care for the horses at our place. That old bachelor, more than fifty years my senior, became a friend and a mentor, a man who had a lasting impact on my life. He became my hero. To this day, if I stop to think about him, he still inspires me.

Norris had no title or degree behind his name, only a grade seven education. He had no status and few possessions, except for a dirt-floored log cabin, his rusty bicycle, and a half dozen horses. What he did have was a continual smile on his face and a love for everything he did and every living entity he touched. More than forty years later, if I close my eyes, I can still smell his weird Norris smell and hear his old Scottish drawl speaking one of his favorite sayings, "Happiness is not a destination; it's a method of travel."

Years after I left home, and after my parents sold the homestead, I got a note in my mailbox from one of my former neighbors telling me that Norris had died. The old dirt shack he lived in caught fire and burned to the ground. He passed away in the middle of the night, alone.

I often find myself wondering if Norris had any idea what impact he'd had on my life, and how that impact he'd had on me had filtered outward to make a difference in the world. Teachers and mentors are like that. They come into our lives at important junctures, sometimes intentionally with a request, and sometimes unexpectedly—like a passerby who stops to help us when we're stranded in our broken-down vehicle—while others pick us up and carry us into a new life.

# Teachers and mentors

On the window ledge above my desk are the photos of numerous people who have been teachers and mentors in my life: my parents, my wife and life partner Val, my daughters Mellissa, Hayley, and Chandra, my grandchildren Ethan and Holland, my brother Hal and sister Kate, alongside the many other teachers and mentors who have influenced and made me the person I am today. It was Zig Ziglar who inspired me to create a "Wall of Influence" of the twenty-five most influential people in my life. I've been working on creating this wall over the past several months and as I reflect on these people, I am filled with gratitude and humility.

I've been blessed to have been raised to reach out for help when I need it. Sometimes the help would arrive when I didn't even realize, often until years later, just how important it was. My bookshelf is full of the writings of teachers who have planted their seeds and inspired me with their good thoughts and wisdom. Some of the coaches and mentors whom I sought out deliberately have guided me through the thresholds of adversity into a new, wide world that I could not have reached on my own.

Like mountain guides that escort us into unfamiliar territory, teachers and mentors and coaches come in many forms. Experience tells me, after being so impacted by so many people, that the universe is conspiring to help me. The people who have come into my life and have made such a difference are evidence of this.

We've all known teachers who have taught us how *not* to be. We've known people who insist we be someone they aren't or wished that they could be. But only those rare and precious influencers in our lives help us be more of who we are meant to be ourselves. They hold us and help us hold others, they help us put ourselves back together when we've fallen apart, they provide perspective and wisdom when we have lost our way, and they walk with us as we venture into new and unfamiliar terrain. The ultimate test of a guide is their ability to help us find our own truth, and be more of who we are meant to be.

It's good to be grateful for the caring guides in your life, the people who matter, who continue to inspire and guide you. It's important to reach out for help when it's needed. Then give back what you have so generously been given.

## Caring coaches

A good, wise friend told me one day about a difficult period in his youth when he was struggling to excel at bantam hockey. Pat spoke of two very different coaches he encountered during that time: one caring and one not. "This was 1976," he began.

"I'd made the second level bantam team in the joint communities of Bowness and Montgomery. I was on the third line and felt I was holding my own. We all knew two players had to be cut. One—a defenseman—everyone knew was going. The second cut, the coach's son told some of us in confidence, would be a toss-up between two other players, also both defenseman. I said in the dressing room at one point, 'I'm probably going to get cut,' and a few players said words to the effect that I was out of my mind to say so."

"And then the news broke that the first level bantam team had received a player or two from the northwest based AA team, and they'd had to let one or two players go, and so these players got sent down to our team. One was a defenseman, and one a forward. I knew something was up in the next game when I didn't play the first period, and saw only spot duty the following two periods. My father wasn't happy about it, but what could we do?"

"An evening or two later, I received a call from the coach. He explained to me, in a very caring tone, what the situation was with the team, the number of players we had, and where they each slotted in. 'Pat, I have to let you go,' he told me. He also said I'd be getting plenty of ice-time where I was headed, and that this was the best for me as a player. He really took his time to lay out the whole scenario for me."

"I was thirteen at the time, and already felt like a monster in public and private. So this was devastating news. As was my habit, I held it all inside, told my family I'd been cut and that I was glad. A flat-out lie. It hurt like hell not to be on that team, to be apart from some of my best friends and teammates, to be relegated to the bottom team in the bantam division. One of my friends said, 'It was like you got sent down to the minors!'"

"Inside, I was also grateful and felt respect for that coach for handling it the way he did. He explained it to me in a truly caring way. He kept me on the phone long enough to be sure he felt I understood exactly what the situation was; he was in no hurry, and was truly concerned about how I took it. Even though I didn't end up playing for him that year, he always had my respect."

"Fast forward to the beginning of next season. Word is I'm going to make the first team this time. I'm still in bantam, but it's my second season now. So I practice and play games like crazy with the first team, but we are still early enough in the season that all levels of teams practice together, even though the squads split and use opposite ends of the ice. Again, we learn a couple of players are to go down to the other side. We're gathered in a circle between drills. Actually, we're about to scrimmage with the lower team. Betraying no hint of what is really going down, the coach names a player in our circle, maybe one more, and tells the guys to 'go down there,' meaning to join the lower squad. Most of us imagine they're just evening up the numbers between the two sides."

"And then, almost as an afterthought, he says, 'Pat, you go down there too.'"

"So I go, not thinking anything of it. I can't be cut; they're just trying something out, I reason. But the same friend who said to me last year it was like I got sent to the minors, says something while we're skating some circles. 'The coach's son said you guys are all cut.' And indeed, that was the case."

"This second coach chose to handle things a little differently than the coach the year before. I couldn't actually respect him for it; he didn't tell me I didn't make his team, or why. He didn't tell us anything. A lot of other players were baffled too. And because he never said anything, I wondered what his real motivations were; all kinds of conspiracy theories formed in my mind. Was I too close to his daughter in my grade? Did I not take enough shit from his son? In the end, I was resentful of this coach for many years. I'm not anymore. But it is striking how those two men, coaching teams of similar boys, chose to go about the task in different ways."

## Lessons in fearlessness

For Amanda Timm, having good, caring coaches has made all the difference. Amanda is an all-around athlete and para-alpine skier. She has always loved the mountains, but she went through a difficult time in 2011 after she was injured in a ski accident that left her without the use of her legs. In the weeks and months that followed while she grappled with her new life, she felt uncertain about ever returning to the ski racing that she so loved.

Early on, Amanda was encouraged to try sit-skiing. A sit-ski is a bucket seat attached to a downhill ski that the skier controls using outriggers—adapted poles with small skis on their tips. Despite the similarities, it isn't the same animal as downhill skiing. Sit-skiing has a notoriously steep learning curve. Amanda had to throw out everything she knew about skiing before the accident.

Her initial efforts were discouraging. "It's like balancing on one ski, which I thought would be really easy at first, but it's not. I'd fall. I'd pick myself up and say, 'Tomorrow, I will be a better skier. Tomorrow, I can ski with my friends.' It just took a really long time for tomorrow to come." It was a struggle just to work her way onto the bottom rung of the sport. But with the help of her coaches at the Rocky Mountain Adaptive Program in Banff, along with Amanda's buoyant, never-say-no spirit, she gave it everything she had. She persevered. To conquer the sport, she had to radically change how she saw her body.

There was a point when Amanda asked herself, what was the worst thing that could happen? The worst thing had already happened. So suddenly she found she could take bigger risks. Amanda now seeks out the hardest, steepest runs on the ski hill. She's the first female to sit-ski down Delirium Dive, Sunshine Village's expert-only terrain. She's worked the terrain park and tried aerial jumps.

For Chelsea Archer, a ski instructor, adaptive program coach, and Amanda's friend, watching sit-skiers learn and conquer their fears is inspiring. It's a true balancing act, urging athletes to push beyond their limitations, to try harder, to pick themselves up, and do one more run even when they are frustrated.

"It's amazing being a part of what sit-skiers do," Chelsea says. "There can be a tendency to not push anyone to take risks, but no one can learn without testing the boundaries and leaving their comfort zone. I have seen and felt the frustration after a skier has a difficult run, where it would be easy to call it a day. Instead, I encourage them to see what more they can do and look at how far they have come. Everyone has their challenges. It isn't always easy, but it's important not to lose sight of what you are capable of."

Amanda trains vigorously to maintain her paralyzed leg muscles with a special stationary bicycle that electrically stimulates her leg nerves so she can pedal it, remaining hopeful that one day, when someone finds a cure, her body will be ready. She credits her family and her coaches for getting her through the tough early years. "My entire thing is proving people wrong. When people say, 'You can't do that,' I'm like, 'Oh, yeah? Watch me.'"

Since her success with sit-skiing, Amanda has tried water-skiing, downhill mountain biking, rowing, sailing, rock climbing, and what she calls "aggressive tobogganing." Her fearlessness is a gift. It has allowed her, on her first attempt at downhill mountain biking, to tackle a route that normally only advanced able-bodied bikers would consider riding.

As Chelsea says, "Amanda has ALWAYS taken crazy risks. She always has looked for the craziest lines and pushes herself as though she has nothing to lose. Her injury has only given her more opportunity to push the boundaries in relatively young sports." Amanda recently competed in her first big alpine ski event, on the same team she'd been on before her injury, alongside many of her former team mates, but this time on a sit-ski. "I think she might be the first sit-skier to compete along with able-bodied skiers. She just doesn't stop being awesome!" Chelsea adds.

Sometimes the only way to go on is to face our fears and be firm with ourselves. A good, caring coach sees what's possible and doesn't let those fears get in the way. As Amanda says, "I believe in thinking the best is going to happen."

## Caring enough to have boundaries

Recently, a couple came to see me seeking advice for dealing with their adult son. "We would like some help with a twenty-nine-year-old who is still living at home," they began.

"He doesn't have a job. He sits in front of his tablet all day. He's not motivated to do anything. He's not doing anything to find work. We can't even get him motivated to get a driver's license. We have to drive him everywhere. He wouldn't come in with us today because he said *we* were the ones with the problem, not him ..."

"I know it's frustrating for you, but what if he's right?" I responded.

"What do you mean?" the mother asked.

"He doesn't have any problems because you have taken them on yourself. You're paying his bills, providing him free room and board, giving him complimentary chauffeur service, and all the free entertainment he wants."

"But he's not capable of doing these things for himself," they retorted.

"And why do you think that might be?"

While it may be obvious from the outside what is going on in a family, when we actually live in the system, we can be too close to see the problem. It took an hour of conversation, and many questions asked, before these two mature adults could see their part in the young man's situation and his lack of accountability. It was hard for them to hear it. They eventually came to understand that by not setting clear boundaries, they actually weren't caring for their son.

Over the ensuing weeks and months, the couple slowly weaned their son from his over-dependence on them. The twenty-nine-year-old "boy" was furious when he got evicted from his parents' home for not paying rent and had to find his own way. My first visit with him finally happened when he was facing unemployment and his parents wouldn't bail him out. He came to see me to complain about his horrible parents.

He didn't get much sympathy from me, but over time we developed some trust as I helped him get a job and get his life together.

There's nothing like a good, honest dose of reality to create the potential impetus for change.

The parents, in turn, had to find a new life for themselves. It was not an easy or smooth journey. They were horribly afraid that they had abandoned their son, and that he would end up either on the street or in the morgue. But they realized that this was *their son's* journey and not their own, and they were no longer responsible for the choices he was making.

Some time later, when they began to see their son again, with no burden of carrying him anymore, they discovered that real caring had emerged in their relationship. They were free to fully love him with no demands or criticism or blame or expectations.

## Saving others from their unhappiness?

Years ago, I counseled a thirteen-year-old who was sent to me by the courts for therapy. The young girl had been living on the streets as a prostitute for the previous two years. We were helping her make the transition into a group home and, eventually, into a foster home. She was raised by a mother who did not have respect for herself. As such, she was incapable of caring for others and did not set clear boundaries. From the age of eight, her daughter had no curfew and no limits, and often stayed out all night long. With no clear boundaries, the young girl felt entitled to do as she pleased, but she did not feel cared for.

I appreciate Brené Brown's definition of entitlement: "I deserve this just because I want it." Empowerment, on the other hand, comes when those we care for are given clear consequences for the choices they make, and are supported, not rescued. Empowerment says, "I deserve this because I've earned it." Rather than attempting to save others from their own unhappiness, empowerment comes from caring for others through the challenges of life, and guiding them to find the resources they have within themselves to deal with what life hands them.

One of the greatest obstacles to caring—in organizations as well as in families—is a fear of setting boundaries and holding people accountable. Resentment, frustration, blame, and criticism are often the results of a lack of clear boundaries and an effective accountability process. Understanding the connection between firm boundaries, accountability, and caring has paradoxically made me a more caring person.

Asking tough questions about our own motivations and accountabilities can be complicated. It takes effort. As leaders and parents, we can't avoid the uncomfortable, hard parts of the job. We can't avoid setting boundaries and being accountable, just because they're unpleasant.

Pleasing and caring are not the same thing. Pleasing is caring without boundaries. Pleasing arises from anxiety, insecurity and fear. It takes a strong heart to look a child in the eye and speak honestly, when we know what we say could trigger some anger or hate toward us.

That's the tough part of caring.

# Choices and Accountability

It is wrong and immoral to seek to escape the consequences of one's acts.

Mahatma Gandhi

## Earning people's trust

The CEO of a financial services firm contacted me some time ago to coach his vice president of sales.

"What's the problem?" I asked.

"Don is just not getting the results from his sales team that we need. I wanted him to grow into his role. He was one of our top senior salespeople, but I don't know if he's got what it takes to lead a team. I'd like you to help me assess this and, if he is willing and capable, help him develop his leadership skills."

In my initial assessment interview, the executive was noticeably frustrated with his sales team. He unashamedly blamed them for their lack of effort and weak results.

"It's the millennial generation," Don ranted. "They just don't have the work ethic needed to get the job done. In my day, we worked seventy hours a week. It was about the numbers, and we made sure we got the numbers. Today, these young kids just don't have the commitment. They only want to work thirty-five hours a week, and they still expect the big commissions."

He went on to quote some of the "lame excuses" his team members had for their failure to achieve his targets.

After listening to Don for several minutes, and trying to understand and empathize with his irritation and annoyance with virtually every member of his sales team, I interrupted him. "Before you go further, I have a question for you. I want you to think very carefully about your answer to this question."

"Fine. I will," he responded.

I waited a moment to let the frenetic energy in the room settle.

"Don, do you care?"

"What do you mean? Of course I care. I care about sales results. I've put a lot of years into this company, and my reputation is in jeopardy. The lack of production on this team is evidence that they aren't stepping up and getting the job done. What are we paying them salaries for anyway? I think we should go back to the old days when people worked on straight commission. We've made things too easy for them. They just don't have the drive that's needed for the job. There has to be more accountability here."

I sat quietly while Don ranted on for a few more minutes.

When he ran out of steam, he sat gathering his thoughts, seeming to be building an even stronger case to explain why his team wasn't producing.

"You didn't answer my question, Don."

"What do you mean?"

"Do you care about the salespeople on your team?"

"What do you mean?" he repeated. His frustration, which was obvious before, heightened even more.

"Do you care about what matters to each member of your team? Do you care about their families and their kids and the relationships in their lives? Do you care about what working here is like for them? Do you care about why they come to work? Do you care about how they feel about you as their boss? Do you care about them as human beings with values, feelings, and needs? Do you care?"

There was a long pause … a very long pause … at this stage of our discussion. Don finally shrugged.

"Not really," he said quietly. "When you put it that way, I don't really care."

"Thank you for your honesty. You don't seem to be enjoying this job much," I said.

"No, I'm not enjoying it. It's stressful. It's not a lot of fun working here."

"Have you ever had a boss who didn't care about you?"

There was another long pause.

"Have you ever been pushed by someone, without a foundation of trust, encouragement, and support?" I continued.

"My father was an alcoholic. He would get into uncontrollable rages and take a belt to me. I never knew when the other shoe would drop."

"How did you deal with all that?"

"The only way to get my dad off my rear end was to excel at everything I did. I drove myself hard, mostly in sports. And I could never please him. He didn't know how to show any other emotion than anger. So I got out of the house and got him off my back."

Don, in fact, went on to be an all-star junior hockey player. After being drafted by the NHL, his hockey career was cut short by an injury. He then got a job where he continued to push himself. He was the top salesperson in every company he worked for. Once he made it to the top, he'd move on. Always building, always driven, he could never face the prospect of losses or failure.

"Who do you care about?" I asked him.

"I care about my two sons. But they left home and I never see them now."

"What was it like between you when they were little?"

"I never saw them much. I was out of town a lot ... working."

"And their mother?"

"We split up when the kids were teenagers. I guess there was no reason for us to be together at that point. We've been divorced now for many years."

"Did you care about her?"

"I loved my wife, and of course my kids, but I was working most of the time."

"So ... what does all this have to do with you being the VP of sales on a team that isn't producing?" I asked.

Another long, reflective pause.

"With all the effort in my life to get away from my father, I think I've actually turned into him." Tears had welled up in his eyes.

"You said earlier that you didn't care about your team. But is that actually true? Did you, as a kid, survive the beatings from your father by shutting yourself off from caring? Caring doesn't come from the head. It has to come from the heart. Caring is not the same as being driven. You haven't been very caring to yourself all these years. You've been as hard on yourself as you've been on anyone else. Maybe it's time to stop and learn how to open your caring heart—both to yourself and to the people around you."

"I've actually been thinking of taking some time off to start looking after my health and get rid of some of this stress," Don said.

"Stress isn't so much about hard work as it is about heartache," I began. "You might want to do yourself and your organization a favor and step away, at least temporarily, from a leadership position. Reconnect with yourself, and then decide if a management role is right for you. Because, frankly, leadership is about earning people's trust. And trust starts with caring about people. If people don't see that you honestly care, you don't have any hope of getting them on board with you. You can't fake caring. It's there or it isn't. And if it isn't, then for the good of yourself and others, it's best not to put yourself in a position of leadership."

He listened carefully. I could see that the caring was there, but it was buried deep behind a fortress of self-protection and obsessive ambition.

"What do I do now?" he asked. "If the answer is to learn how to be more caring, where do I start?"

"It's not really about learning to be 'more caring' as much as it is about opening yourself up to the caring that is in you. It's always been there. You cared about your parents. You cared about your wife, or you wouldn't have married her. You cared about your sons. And I suspect you probably care more about your employees than you give yourself credit for. But you have no idea how to show them caring in a way that reaches them. How could you? Who in your life cared about you in a way that made you know they cared?"

At this, Don began sharing memories of his grandfather. "We wrestled together. I would spend the summers on his farm. He taught me to ride a horse. He let me help him fix his old John Deere tractor. We spend hours each day working together, just me and him. When he died, I had no one else to turn to ..."

Over the coming months, Don began opening up his caring heart. He contacted his two grown sons to arrange to take his young grandchildren camping. He took time off work, rented a motorhome, bought some fishing equipment, and took them to a favorite place where he'd spent time with his grandfather. What was most difficult was choosing to let go of his leadership role. He had to let go of not trying to plan and control everything. Just hanging out with the kids had to be good enough. And it was. At first, the boys spent more time on their electronic devices than they did doing anything else, but they gradually became more drawn to the hours they spent with their grandfather.

Learning to be with his three grandkids was awkward, but Don clumsily succumbed to the learning process. He learned, over time, that he didn't have to "do" anything. Just his presence in their lives was a force of good. As he developed a relationship with his grandchildren, the door to his sons began to open. His family started to see him in a different light as he spent time with both his grandchildren and his sons.

By learning to be with his family, he was also spending more time outdoors—a love that he had neglected for years. He started to exercise, eat better, and get himself back in shape. Even though he has a tendency to drive himself with new exercise regimens, Don is learning to relax more and bring some balance into his life. He is working less. He's found new ways to bring caring acts into his daily life, such as offering a kind word to a stranger, being less demanding of a restaurant server, and offering support to the people around him.

When Don started feeling better about himself, he began taking an interest in his staff and co-workers. He listened more—to their concerns, needs, and goals. He opened up and shared things about himself with those he worked with. He was becoming more patient. As he learned to relax, the fortress he'd built between himself and the people around him started coming down, as their trust began to take root. His business results started to come around too.

In the words of John Maxwell, "You have to get to their hearts before you ask them for a hand."

Learning to care is in you. It just has to be opened up. Does caring hurt? Sometimes. But when you care, you find that you would rather have the hurt of caring than the emptiness that comes from being separated by not caring. Connecting to your innate "caring capacity" can change your life.

## Caring and accountability go together

Not so long ago, I worked with a company to assist them in building a culturally aligned business. Following my presentation on accountability, a member of the executive team approached me about the difficulty he'd had trying to build an accountable culture—a place where people knew what to expect from each other and could be counted on to keep their promises.

"I have a manager who cares about his team, but he gets frustrated and criticizes them a lot for not producing the results he knows they are capable of," he explained.

I met with Travis and found the executive's observation was accurate. The manager's frustration level was high.

"I'm not happy with my response to my team. I'm way more irritated and critical than I like to be, and I'm carrying it home."

"What is your process for holding employees accountable?" I asked Travis.

"They know what has to be done and what's expected of them. They just aren't stepping up to the plate and meeting their deadlines." His tone of voice was tense and impatient, and I noticed he was vague in his reply.

"After you clarify your precise expectations for them, do you actually get an agreement that they will meet these expectations within your expected time frame? And do you have a conversation about what support they need, from you and others, to achieve the things they are accountable for?"

Travis's response was hesitant. "I think so?"

"And do you negotiate with them the consequences of delivering on their promises as well as the negative consequences of not coming through with what they have promised?"

There was a long pause in our conversation. Uncomfortable and defensive, Travis said, "Why should I have to talk about consequences? They know the procedures. They know what's expected of them."

"How do you know that you have done everything you can to give them the support they need? And, assuming you have met their support requirements, what would happen if you told them that the next time they didn't meet a deadline, a warning would go on their performance review—and if they continued to not meet their deadlines, their job would be at risk?"

"That would be way too much work. I'd have to get human resources involved and start documenting everything."

"Holding people accountable is work. It's hard work," I told him.

As former US Secretary of State Colin Powell once said, "Everyone on a team knows who is and is not performing, and they are looking to you as the leader to see what you are going to do about it." It's way easier to criticize and blame. But getting frustrated is far less effective than getting honest and doing something, and it's also not caring—to your team, the organization, and to you as a leader.

~

When we fail to set clear boundaries for ourselves, we can feel used and wronged—and in the process end up criticizing, attacking, and blaming the people we "care" about. I know a mother of two adult children who has gone into debt bailing out her thirty-year-old "children" from the financial messes they continuously get themselves into, all in the name of caring. What she doesn't realize is that, without firm boundaries, this isn't caring. It's enabling. And she wonders why she is now angry, bitter, and financially unstable. She can't grasp how she trained her children to constantly take advantage of her.

"When we fail to set boundaries and hold a person accountable," says Brené Brown, "we feel used and mistreated. This is why we sometimes attack who they are, which is far more hurtful than addressing a behavior or a choice."

Saying we care about people while condemning them, either directly or indirectly, and remaining unhappy about them, is far more hurtful than addressing their behaviors directly. For our own sake, and for the sakes of those we care about, it's important to understand the danger of living without boundaries. Caring without boundaries and accountability is not caring at all. Caring is more than just a thing we say. It isn't just a statement or affirmation. It means action. Without action, we probably won't get the outcomes we desire. Worst of all, when we're angry and we criticize others, the message that we care about them will invariably be lost.

## Making better choices

I owe much of the heart and soul of my business to my long-time assistant and sales manager, Laurie Hutchinson. Laurie and I started working together back in the early nineties when she had her own Speaker's Bureau, *Listen International*. The first time she heard me give a talk, I thought I would have wowed her. Instead, she took me to lunch and gave me ten pages of suggestions on how I could improve my presentation. Thus began a lifelong friendship. I could always count on Laurie to be honest, forthright, and wise.

A while after our first meeting, I worked with Laurie when I contracted exclusively with the speaker's bureau she then represented. Teamed up with Laurie, my speaking business was launched to a new level. Laurie came to work with me full-time in 2004, and was with me until her retirement. At that time, she lived in Edmonton, but when she wanted to be closer to her aging parents, son, and grandson on the West Coast, she moved to Nanaimo, British Columbia and managed my business from Vancouver Island. I can easily say that with her passion and commitment, it was Laurie who helped us through many rocky times.

It's been a tough year for Laurie. She lost both her parents, happily married for more than seventy years, when they died peacefully within two days of each other. Fortunately for Laurie, a few years ago, after many losses in her personal life, she found the love of her life. I know that this next leg in her life's journey will be filled with joy as she travels it together with Jack.

I owe much of my success and business growth to Laurie. Without her, I would not be where I am today. Her caring presence with clients, her passion and belief in me and my work, her skillful attention to detail, and her ability to create value for each client will all be missed.

Many years ago, when the government department that Laurie was working for laid off sixteen employees, they were all offered jobs in another department. Laurie was the only laid-off person who did not accept an alternate government position. She did not want the job that was offered to her. She decided to leave government work and open her own business. Her husband had left her eight months before and she had three teenagers to support. Her co-workers hassled her about the decision, telling her she was crazy. They simply could not understand why she would leave the security of a public service position.

Laurie, who has since run her own business and was my sales manager for more than twenty years, has never looked back. In the years I have known Laurie, I've admired her courage of character to follow the dictates of her heart and the spirit of her convictions.

Her decision all those years ago has spawned a legacy. Laurie said to me one day, "That act of courage to save my soul has taught my children to follow unusual careers, to open businesses, and follow their dreams."

For her colleagues at the time it seemed crazy, but for Laurie it was the only choice that fit. Choosing the right path and finding the best solution for ourselves can be tough, a matter of balancing different needs. We can tune out those who don't see the full picture of us—or we can try to enlighten them.

## Pressing the reset button

When a client called me for help with a situation she was facing with her team and her boss, it became clear to me within the first few minutes that I had encountered this situation before. In fact, it seemed like an easy solution. After a few moments of listening, I proceeded to give Giselle what I thought was sound advice. "After all, this is my field of expertise," I told myself. "I have a great deal of experience and knowledge in this area."

After giving her some recommendations, a silence fell on the other end.

"Do any of my suggestions speak to you?" I asked.

After another lengthy pause, Giselle began explaining, in a respectful and polite way, the situation from a completely different direction.

I realized that I had lost a connection somewhere in the conversation. I might as well have hung up for all the good I was doing her. The help I had offered was not helpful. While my intentions were worthy, in my over-exuberance to be supportive, in my self-assurance at having quickly guessed the "right" solution for her, and in my need to "fix" things, my caring was not caring.

After listening closely while she enlightened me, I apologized and asked Giselle to keep helping me understand the situation in a new way. I needed to regroup and come at the whole thing with a new approach.

We all have our cognitive biases. We often identify the root of a problem from our own familiar perspective and offer a quick, easy solution without properly listening or thinking the problem through. Maybe the problem and the solution speak to a pattern we've seen before. As humans, we tend to seek out patterns routinely and automatically. Patterns are wonderful tools. They help us understand the world with greater ease and efficiency.

But when Giselle asked for my advice and I immediately gave her my own familiar solution, I wasn't seeing the world from her perspective. I wasn't tuned in to her or to her reality. I wasn't giving her situation the care and attention it deserved. Avoiding this kind of mistake sometimes requires stepping back and, in a sense, reprogramming ourselves to find a solution that is attuned to the problem presented.

Caring can be like that. It's like pressing the reset button and starting again.

# An Authentic Life

The purpose of life is not to be happy. It is to be useful, to be honorable, to be compassionate, to have it make some difference that you have lived and lived well.

Ralph Waldo Emerson

## That "caring kid"

Some of my earliest memories of caring are my attempts to mediate in the midst of my parents' fights. They both brought a great deal of personal pain into their relationship and, at a very early age, I believed it was my job to stop my parents from killing each other. Even as a young child, I cared, but this caring was really my attempt at surviving the tension and trauma. Alone and scared, caring in this light became a mask to cover up the fear and insecurity I felt.

This kind of caring, while a sincere and unconscious intent to heal the pain in our family, actually became my escape from reality. It may have looked great to the outside world, as I developed a role that identified me as that "caring kid" at school and in my church, but caring eventually became an obsession. I was driven to care. I *had* to care because caring is what I used to prove myself. My caring capacity eventually led me to a career as a family therapist, and then as an organizational consultant and an educator. While I was a good therapist in that early role, what I didn't realize at the time was that my efforts to care were an attempt to fill a hole inside of me—a hole that could never be filled. Caring, rather than a natural expression, was driven by a ceaseless determination to make myself whole. I was using caring to heal myself, and before long it exhausted me. Because caring defined me, I worked far too hard at it, and it eventually consumed me.

As a young family therapist, in private practice with little support, I went for months when I would sometimes see over forty families a week. My clients would often call with a crisis in the middle of the night. When I wasn't helping, I would feel tense, worried, and vulnerable. Unable to separate my identity from my work of helping, I didn't know how to say no or have clear boundaries in the work of caring. Bolstering my sense of self-worth became my reward as a helper.

Like an alcoholic who has to hit their bottom, my "chronic caring" or "help-aholism" led me through the dark journey of burnout, depression, and eventual collapse. My life, which was devoted to helping and caring for others, ironically became empty and alone. I grew so depressed and exhausted trying to prove myself by taking care of others that I eventually ended up lying for days on the couch, depressed, exhausted, and completely unable to work, much less to care. My wife at the time grew increasingly exasperated with the months of unavailability and distance in our relationship, and we eventually divorced.

What makes an addiction to caring difficult to diagnose is that it is normally a very legitimate way to spend your day. At some point, however, I had to admit to myself that my life was unmanageable. I started to be honest about what the work of caring and helping was doing to me and about what I was running from. I began reaching out to others. I allowed myself to be cared for as I sought help from a good therapist (who was at first difficult to trust; after all, I thought I was the only good therapist in town!). Eventually I was led to a program of recovery as I sought mentors to guide me out of the darkness. As I began getting a sense of myself away from my need to care in order to define myself, I uncovered my gifts as I gave myself permission to care for myself. Caring started coming from overflow rather than emptiness.

I stumbled upon many writers and teachers during this time of recuperation, guides who introduced me to the concept of authenticity and the notion that exhaustion, depression, and burnout were not "pathologies to be *fixed*" but actual indicators of being off course and drifting away from my authentic self.

"Burnout," in the words of Rabbi Ira Eisenstein, "is not about hard work, but about heartache." So the question of how to deal with this soul pain I had became not what to do *about* it, but what to do *with* it.

Caring is more than a simple impulse to respond to the suffering around us. Caring that comes from a need to please, to feel secure, or to define our worth, ends up leaving us empty, depleting us of life energy. Conversely, when caring comes from a voice within rather than an impulse without, a voice that invites us to honor the nature of our true self, it nourishes both the soul and the world. An authentic call to care is a call that heals *and* sustains.

Over a hundred years ago, the German poet Rainer Maria Rilke wrote a poem that sheds clues on connecting with the true, essential self.

> This clumsy living that moves lumbering
> as if in ropes ...
> reminds us of the awkward way the swan walks.
>
> And to die, which is the letting go
> of the ground we stand on and cling to every day,
> is like the swan when he nervously lets himself down
> into the water, which receives him gaily
> and which flows joyfully under
> and after him, wave after wave,
>
> While the swan, unmoving and marvelously calm,
> is pleased to be carried, each moment more fully grown,
> more like a king, further and further on.

The swan doesn't cure its awkwardness on land by moving faster, working harder, criticizing itself, or being evaluated in a performance review. It frees itself from the stress of its environment simply by moving toward the element where it belongs. Simple contact with water breathes life into its tired body.

Touching and connecting with the essential waters of one's own life—and discovering the authentic self—can change everything. As simple as this sounds, lowering oneself into the water from the familiar ground we find ourselves on can be difficult, especially when we think we might drown.

The authentic journey, this seeking to return to the life-giving waters of my essential self, is for me a lifelong voyage. Yet when I care from that place, and I am comfortable with myself, caring feels a whole lot more enjoyable.

## The authentic journey

The kind of caring I am coming to know—caring that is aligned with my authentic self, that transforms and sustains me as a caring person— can be blocked when my caregiver's inward, essential self goes unacknowledged. In the work of caring, it's important to somehow find a way to give birth to our own essence. Rather than a destiny to be achieved and admired, it's a journey to be embraced.

When we listen primarily for what we "should" be doing with our lives, we may find ourselves hounded by external expectations that distance us from who we are authentically. When we care from a place of obligation, because we "should" care, or in order to feel secure or less fearful or somehow more worthwhile, it can eventually violate our soul and diminish our energy. The telling signs are: guilt, resentment, and exhaustion. Instead of being life-giving, which is how caring could and can be, caring that comes from an inauthentic place becomes life-taking.

By listening more deeply and getting past the noisy demands of the world, beyond the loud cravings of emotion, I've discovered and been guided by a deeper voice within me. Unlike the strained and even violent concept of caring as an "ought" and a "should," I am coming to a more generous, gentle, and human image of caring as "the place where your deepest desires meet the world's deepest need." Caring, to be sustaining, is more than being guided by a simple, impulsive emotion that directs us away from the discomfort of *not* caring.

Sometimes we care by "not caring." When an addiction has settled in our home, sometimes stepping back, building a clear boundary, and letting go are the best ways to care, even when at the time it feels completely uncaring. If there are no consequences and no boundaries in our relationships, if we fail to acknowledge our own deeper voice, that really isn't caring.

At the back of the book, in Appendix C, I explore more fully the stages of the authentic journey.

## Live honorably

The training program for U.S. Olympic coaches at the Josephson Institute Center for Sports Ethics contains this illustration of virtue:

"'In the 1936 Berlin Summer Olympics,' Hitler said, 'Americans ought to be ashamed of themselves for letting their medals be worn by Negroes. I myself would never shake hands with one of them.'"

"Jesse Owens, the great American track and field star, had already embarrassed the German dictator by winning gold medals in the sprint and relay. But in his first two attempts at the long jump Owens stepped over the foul line. He recalls being scared stiff that he would foul on his third attempt and not make it to the finals. His fiercest rival in the event was Luz Long, the German athlete. Despite the risk of infuriating Hitler and the chance that Owens would beat him, Long took a towel and laid it a foot before the foul line and advised Owens to use the towel to assure that he would qualify. Owens did, and he ultimately defeated Long to win the gold medal."

"Long's extraordinary display of sportsmanship, courage, and character went well beyond duty, but demonstrated the highest standards of ethical virtue in sports. As an aftermath, Luz Long was sent to the Russian front where he was killed. And when his daughter was married years later, Jesse Owens walked her down the aisle."

Deep inside each person lies a conscience, a "still small voice," an "inner guide," a "moral compass." Unless a person is a psychopath and has been so brainwashed and damaged as a child that they have no conscience, everyone develops, somewhere in their upbringing and at some point in their life, a sense of knowing what is right and wrong. Character is about living an honest, authentic, and honorable life in accordance with our conscience. Character is doing what's right and not necessarily what's easy, popular, or comfortable, or what will give us financial gain.

When people came to say goodbye to hockey legend Gordie Howe at Joe Louis Arena following his death in 2016, the line for the public visitation stretched well around the rink. The waiting time was more than ninety minutes. There's little doubt that Gordie Howe was admired as one of the best athletes in the world during his era, and is still considered one of the best hockey players ever. I think he was *loved*, though, because of his humility, his politeness, and his respect for people. It was his character that made him special. As great as Gordie Howe was, and as legendary his stature, in the words of journalist Bob Duff, "it never infected him with the disease of self-importance … Howe was a first-ballot hall of famer in hockey, humility, and humanity." For Howe, the hullaballoo was never about "Gordie," but about the fans. In his travels he always made the time for photographs and autographs whenever he was recognized. It seemed that his character inspired people as much as his capability. "There is no real excellence in all this world that can be separated from right living," writes David Starr Jordan.

I once counseled a father who was charged with child abuse for repeatedly striking his children with belts and a bamboo stick. When asked about his purpose for doing such a thing, his response was that he wanted to "teach them a lesson about honesty, obedience, and respect." Too frequently character is something others feel must be beaten into us rather than cared into us.

I certainly learned about character from years of attending Sunday school classes and listening to sermons from the podium. But character can't be "taught" like mathematics. It was instilled by years of living with caring parents and being around adults who exemplified honor and integrity. Whether it was observing my parents' honesty at the border crossings as they declared everything they brought into the country, or going out of their way to hire adults on our farm with mental disabilities, or watching my father stand in front of politicians to fight for the rights of minorities in our community, character was instilled in me through daily exemplary actions, love, and observation.

Through the lens of caring, we come to see character as inspiring others through the power of example: character as a matter of choice. The decision and commitment to live with character is caring. It means caring enough *about* the world to bring goodness *to* the world. Being a good and decent person inspires others to be good and decent. If you attend an Alcoholics Anonymous meeting where men and women become honest with themselves and commit to living sober, respectable lives and recover their integrity, you'll find a room full of caring people committed to their own recovery to heal the wreckage of their important relationships. Character is an expression of caring, because character is what makes the world a decent and civil place to live.

Care enough to seek to be a person of strong character. It's not the fierceness of the storm that determines whether we break or not, but rather the strength of the roots that lie below the surface.

In my leadership development workshops, I often use this exercise. Think of three people you admire. They could be people who have made a positive difference in the world, Nelson Mandela or Mahatma Gandhi, or people who have made a personal contribution to your own life, say your grandmother or a schoolteacher. For me, three people I deeply admire are my wife Val, my parents Joyce and Harlie Irvine, and Viktor Frankl, the Austrian neurologist and psychiatrist.

There's a second part to this exercise. Think of the character traits that make each of your chosen people admirable to you. In my case, I admire Val for her unconditional capacity to love. I would not be the person I am today without Val's loving presence, acceptance, and support. I admire my mother for her wisdom and my father for his compassion, and I admire Viktor Frankl for his courage, resilience, and perseverance. From his harrowing survival of the holocaust, he emerged with a philosophy of living that is centered on the pursuit of purpose and finding meaning amidst deep anguish.

Finally, I ask workshop participants to compare these fine, admirable traits with the typical success markers in our culture, the kind of character traits featured, say, in *People* magazine. After using this exercise with literally thousands of people, I have yet to observe anyone choose their admired people for the character qualities most frequently popularized in magazines and online, such as fame, beauty, power, youth, or wealth. It's fascinating that, culturally, we gravitate unconsciously to those things that ultimately mean so little to us.

I learned from my parents that there is a difference between success defined by the world's standards, and *real* success, success built to last, success defined by the strength of our character.

For a Character Inventory to assess and strengthen your own character, visit Appendix D at the back of the book.

## Reaching in

There's a story about a troubled mother in India, during the time when Mahatma Gandhi was in office, who had a young daughter who was addicted to sugar. One day, the mother approached Gandhi and explained the problem to him and asked if he would talk to the young girl. Gandhi replied, "Bring your daughter to me in three weeks' time and I will speak to her." After three weeks, the mother brought her daughter to Gandhi. He took the young girl aside and spoke to her about the harmful effects of eating sweets excessively and urged her to abandon her bad habit. The mother thanked Gandhi for this advice and then asked him, "But why didn't you speak to her three weeks ago?" Gandhi replied, "Because three weeks ago, I was still addicted to sweets."

Character means that the way you change the world is to change yourself. Before you reach out in an effort to change the environment around you, care enough to look inward to see what needs changing within you. Character is an attitude and an approach to life that is built on the foundation of personal responsibility. Whether that means having a positive impact on climate change, or making a difference in your workplace, or improving your marriage, the day you decide that blaming others is a waste of time will be the day you change your life forever.

If it is to be, let it begin with me.

## Reaching out

Clara Hughes, a six-time Canadian Olympic medalist in cycling and speed skating, exemplifies reaching out. There is far more to Clara than athletic achievements and earning medals. Real success for her means having a voice and using her athletic achievements as an opportunity to reach out and help others.

Since winning her Olympic medals, Clara has donated thousands of dollars and hours of her time to help give youth at risk a better direction in life. She became the national spokesperson for Bell Canada's Mental Health initiative and the "Let's Talk" campaign. In sharing her past struggles with depression, Clara is helping to break down the stigma associated with mental illness. Although she has pursued her dreams in a big way through the world of sport, her ultimate goal is to motivate youth and inspire hope in others through her actions. By setting an example of sportsmanship and creating a supportive environment on every team she has been a part of, Clara has supported and aided the growth and development of many young athletes.

Character amplifies your impact on the world. It gives you freedom. Character is having a strong enough sense of yourself, so you are able to live life on your terms rather than on the whims of approval or definitions of others. Character gives you inner peace and the self-respect to look yourself in the eyes when you see yourself in the mirror. It means you are authentically the same person in public as you are in private.

I'm not ascribing to a life devoid of self-doubt or mistakes. However, with strong character there's no pretense or hidden agendas. You are who you are. Character is, perhaps, the ultimate expression of caring: to others, to the world, and, perhaps most importantly, to yourself.

William Makepeace Thackeray captured the essence of character in these lines:

Sow a thought and you reap an act;
Sow an act and you reap a habit;
Sow a habit and you reap a character;
Sow a character and you reap a destiny.

It takes time to build character. You don't discover or develop it overnight. Great acts of character come from years of small habits, diligence, and persistent living each day. The payoff is profound: self-respect, freedom, peace of mind, and the courage, clarity, and capacity to build a better world around you through the power of your example.

# A Radical Notion

Creative leaders find ways of stepping into the shoes of other
people and asking, "How would I feel and what would I want if
I were this person?"

Gay Hendricks and Kate Ludeman, *The Corporate Mystic*

## Paying attention

"How long to the airport?" I asked the taxi driver as we pulled away
from the hotel. I'd been waiting for his cab for a quarter of an hour
and was impatient to get going.

"Forty-five minutes," responded the driver with a smile. "I'll get
you there as quick as I can."

Silence filled the cab as I sat back and took a deep breath. It had
been a long day, and I would be glad to be home. If things lined up,
I might even catch an earlier flight. A few minutes into the drive, my
cell phone rang. It was a coaching client I enjoyed working with. This
was a good time to touch base, I decided.

Her call was brief. She caught me up on her recent progress with
managing anxiety in her role as leader of a large division. She'd been
paying closer attention to where the anxiety registered in her body.
She was taking a few minutes between meetings to breathe and get
centered, and to focus on releasing the tension in her shoulders and
her upper back. Overall, her call was upbeat. It was good to learn of
her progress. She'd found she was earning the trust of her team as she
became less stressed.

After we hung up, I closed my eyes.

"I used to have anxiety too!"

I realized the driver was trying to get my attention.

"So sorry for intruding, but I couldn't help overhearing your last conversation. I have been working very hard myself on my anxiety. I used to be so stressed. I used to drive like a maniac and get so uptight when a customer was in a hurry. I couldn't sleep at night. The pressure was getting to me."

He was obviously excited to tell me this, and I couldn't help but let him continue. His enthusiasm was contagious.

"So what did you do to learn to be more relaxed?"

"I started to meditate. Each morning now, I pray and get close to God. I take deep breaths during the day. And I am eating less sugar. That helps too. I'm not cured but I am learning. I have a doctor who gave me medicine. I tried it for two weeks, but all it did was make me tired and numb. So instead I made up my mind to be happier. I realized that I have to be happy on the inside. Even if I don't get a customer and I start worrying about my wife and my three children at home and wondering how I am going to feed them, I realized I might as well still be happy, because being unhappy doesn't help them."

"How do you deal with customers who are in a hurry and want you to rush to get them places?"

"Nobody gets me stressed now." He smiled. "I get them there when I get them there. I will shave off a minute or two if I can to help them out, but you know what? You can hurry without being stressed!"

I looked up and realized that we were pulling to the curb at the airport. The cab driver jumped out to help me with my door and my bag. We smiled warmly at each other as I handed him my taxi fare.

"What is your name?" I asked, reaching out my hand.

"Ajit," he smiled, firmly taking my hand with both of his.

"Thank you, Ajit," I said. "It was my good fortune to get a ride from you today. Thank you for gracing me with your presence."

"The pleasure was all mine."

I paused as Ajit pulled away. He was no longer an unnamed, soon-to-be-forgotten cab driver. He was Ajit, husband and father of three, committed to a family he was determined to feed and care for, a man who was learning to be less anxious, and who knew how to make a difference in the life of a customer in the backseat of his Prius.

As the vehicle drove out of sight, I wondered why I'd been so impatient waiting for his cab for a mere fifteen minutes.

## The making and sharing generation

I'm biased about millennials, those born between the early nineteen eighties and the turn of the century. I'm biased because these brilliant young people represent my three daughters' generation. Millennials are a curious breed. In some fundamental ways, they face the same things previous generations always have. As young people, they question what to do with their lives, whom to spend time with, and how and where to live in the world. In other ways, though, they face a very different future than I did at their age. Yet, because of some differences in how they see the world, they are starting to have an impact on that future.

Millennials make up a cohort of young people who are less inclined to own a vehicle and are learning to drive at a later age than their parents. They are also less inclined to purchase a home. This is due, partly, to overinflated real estate markets, but also to the fact that kids are taking longer to permanently move out of the nest. The fact is, for all intents and purposes, millennials seem to be taking longer to grow up. Interestingly, this has put them in a position to change the way we use our resources.

Being of an older generation, it's hard seeing the effects that humans have made on the planet—the bad effects, I mean. Species extinction, polluted oceans and rivers, smog-filled cities, extreme weather, the list goes on. The truth is, we're starting to see the effects of our misuse and abuse of resources more and more, so this questioning of how we use what we have is timely. It's a fact of life that millennials can't assume ownership of things like houses and cars the way their parents did. So it's a practical thing, but it's also a philosophical question. Why buy a car when you can share one? Why purchase a house when you can carve out a rental suite in your parents' or grandparents' home? Why buy tools when there's something called a tool library close by? Are millennials really the generation that refuses to grow up? Or are they a generation that thinks more creatively, and more caringly? Maybe sharing speaks to being able to get along, to being more social-minded. Why wouldn't we want to live together as generations, as opposed to existing as isolated nuclear islands?

This generation also embraces online media, webinars, and emojis—along with craft fairs, cyclepaloozas, role play meetups, and social activism. There's something particularly caring and heartfelt about this generation, despite reports of the opposite. In a 2013 Time magazine issue, famously devoted to "The Me Me Me Generation," journalist Joel Stein called millennials "lazy, entitled, self-obsessed narcissists." Maybe there's some truth in this statement, but I could say the same thing about my own generation of baby boomers. Stein adds that millennials are stunted, unable to leave the nest, and they don't make very good rebels. They appear ready to consult their parents on nearly every decision, big or small.

This is all speaking broadly, of course. But I believe this upcoming generation has something profound to offer, and they're already making an impact. Two millennial brothers, Marc and Craig Kielburger, whose organization comprises non-profit and social enterprises, specialize in getting people to embrace the concept of "We" instead of "Me," to think beyond ourselves, and to help others. They achieve this mission with mostly millennial staff. I have personally witnessed hundreds of their generation who are committed to giving back, my own daughters and the friends they associate among them.

Some of the innovations I'm seeing driven by this generation include the craft and maker movements, the urban gardening movement, and the sharing economy. Millennials face some pretty intractable global problems that they've inherited from us. Yet from what I can see, they are ready to tackle these issues head on. In general, their parents believe in them, so they tend to believe in themselves.

Perhaps their relative disinterest in rebelling leaves them more time and energy to actually make a difference in the world.

For my part, I don't see them as lazy. I see young people who aren't afraid to take risks or to explore creative solutions, who aren't afraid to show they care.

## Caring solutions for a changing world

People respond to leaders who take the time to listen, to encourage and welcome, who visibly care. But what happens when a leader also purposely seeks out the least skilled people, those who are mostly marginalized, and who draws out their knowledge and talents, and develops and supports these people to perform skilled work in their communities?

In 1972, Barefoot College founder Sanjit "Bunker" Roy had a radical idea. What if he were to teach technical skills to the lowest of the low, the untouchable classes, the poor and illiterate, the grandmothers and widows? What if the school's training tapped into the local traditional knowledge base, along with modern technologies? What if the teachers were allowed to be learners, and the learners to be teachers?

Alongside various other useful trades and skill sets, Barefoot College has been training mostly illiterate grandmothers from three different continents to be solar engineers. In six months, students learn to install and connect solar panels to the rooftops of local homes. The technology provides a relatively simple solution with far-reaching benefits to the homeowners. It allows them to power LED lighting inside. For the first time in their lives, the residents can perform useful work in the evenings or early mornings, such as studying, learning to read, doing needlework, or weaving.

The "barefoot" approach values simple solutions. It values community control and ownership of businesses and projects. There is no overarching organization to manage or oversee each solar project. Everything is owned and run by the workers.

The key to Bunker Roy's approach comes from noticing and observing what people in rural communities needed the most. He spent years doing that "noticing." With a degree from a prestigious

New Delhi university, which he soon learned meant relatively little on a practical level, and with nothing more than an innate curiosity and a desire to do something meaningful with his life, Bunker proceeded to spend half a decade digging wells in rural communities. That was only the beginning.

There, he was exposed to "the most extraordinary skills and knowledge and wisdom that very poor people have. It does not come from books. It does not come from a university ... You don't read about it—you have to feel it. I felt that this extraordinary knowledge and skill and wisdom needed to be brought into mainstream thinking. That was when I started the Barefoot College ... in a very small village called Tilonia."

Since its humble beginnings, the college has trained almost seven thousand "unassuming housewives, mothers and grandmothers, midwives, farmers, daily wage laborers, and small shopkeepers." Bunker says middle-aged grandmothers are his best students. They are invested in their communities. They won't take their training certificate and leave their village for a job in the city. And they tend to "need the employment opportunity and income the most."

The Barefoot College is a model that works because Bunker Roy was humble and honest enough to care. He cared enough to recognize that even top universities may not have all the answers, that large institutions may not have all the answers. As John Maynard Keynes wrote, "The difficulty lies not in new ideas, but in escaping from the old ones." Roy noticed what people needed the most, and realized that homegrown knowledge could offer as much value as a university degree.

Most importantly, he saw the potential in several thousand illiterate grandmothers and convinced them that they could be solar engineers. The changes they've brought to their communities have been transformative. As one recipient of a solar array in Kashmir said, "This is the first time I see my husband's face in the winter."

## It's in everyone to nurture

"Our offices and direct level managers, 60 to 70 people, get together quarterly to review results, discuss plans, examine ideas, and directions," writes Max De Pree, former CEO of Herman Miller, the world renowned office furniture company. "Shortly before one of these meetings, I had received a wonderful letter from the mother of one of our handicapped employees. It was a touching letter of gratitude for the efforts of many people at Herman Miller to make life meaningful and rich for a person who is seriously disadvantaged. Because we have a strong, albeit a quiet, effort going on in the company to empower the disadvantaged and to recognize the authenticity of everyone in the group, it seemed to be a good idea to read this letter to the officers and directors."

"I almost got through this letter but could not finish. There I stood in front of this group of people—some of them pretty hard-driving—tongue-tied and embarrassed, unable to continue. At that point, one of our senior vice presidents, Joe Schwartz—urbane, elegant, mature—strode up the center aisle, put his arm around my shoulder, kissed me on the cheek, and adjourned the meeting. That is the kind of weeping we need more of."

Being a nurturing guy is sometimes tough in our culture, not as tough as it once was, say, fifty years ago or so, but macho expectations are still deep-rooted. We feel the pressure to take action, to be the boss, to smile awkwardly when we're stuck holding the baby, and at all costs to never, never cry.

From a young age, boys are encouraged to be daredevil adventurers, not caring nurturers. They are taught, "don't be a girly man." Playing with dolls? Playing house? Anything that smacks of caregiving or "mothering" is likely to get a guy bullied. It's unfortunate, because there are a lot of nurturing males out there. It's a tragedy when boys allow their caring side to be bullied or peer-pressured out of them.

The macho narrative is a myth. It's a fiction that's been foisted on us by an artificial testosterone culture. Caring and nurturing are qualities in every one of us as human beings, observable across the breadth of every animal species.

Studies have shown that when men in the workplace were assertive about their ideas, they were praised and often promoted. But when women were assertive "in exactly the same way," they were often deemed "too aggressive" and "difficult to work with." Men get rewarded for being trailblazers. They are rewarded for their hard argumentative natures and for bossing others around.

"Unconscious bias against women—and indeed against everything coded as 'feminine'—is pervasive in our society," says Nancy Fraser, Professor of Philosophy and Politics at The New School. "I could give lots of examples, but one of my favorites is a riddle. It concerns an emergency room surgeon who is set to operate on a boy who has been critically injured in a car accident in which his father was instantly killed. The surgeon takes one look at the boy's face and says, 'I can't operate; he is my son.' The riddle is, how can this be?"

"You'd be amazed how long it takes most people, women and feminists included, to figure out that the surgeon is a woman—many are more likely to say that it's a gay man. And of course, there are lots of more consequential examples, such as the way that sexist bias influences judgments about the qualifications of job applicants."

What does it take to change the narrative? Fraser says that a key approach is to challenge the current distinction between two separate kinds of labor. Men have long been associated with "productive" labor and remunerated by wages, while women often take on society's "caring" activities, much of which remains unpaid. This division between production and reproduction is a defining structure of our society, Fraser says, and "a deep source of the gender asymmetries hard-wired into it."

A recent Dove advertising campaign celebrates men's everyday acts of kindness. "The strongest men are those who care," says the slogan. In the advertisements, men are still described as "strong" and "heroes" but not for the usual macho reasons. Dads are shown caring for children, feeding and consoling them, kissing them, helping a son dress, combing a daughter's tangled hair, helping another child with toilet training. The campaign "points to a larger shift that is slowly taking hold in advertising: depicting men more frequently as considerate husbands, caring fathers, and active members of their households," writes Susan Krashinksy. These ads, in other words, depict men as they really are.

The world changes at a slow creep, and then suddenly there's a shift. The angry male boss or domineering father is becoming a thing of the past. It's not just in girls and women to be caring and nurturing: it's in everyone.

# The Joy in Caring

We must tell ourselves
Who we want to be
And then act accordingly.

Epictetus

## Summer camp

Our daughters Hayley and Chandra have been involved in an unusual summer camp program since 2007. CISV International is a global organization dedicated to building inter-cultural friendship, cooperation, and understanding among young people around the world. Founded in 1950, and formerly Children's International Summer Villages, today CISV is a federation of more than 70 member associations with over 200 chapters. For over six decades, it has given countless young people the experience of their lives and the opportunity to build lasting friendships through its international education experiences.

Starting at age eleven, my daughters have attended programs around the world, in Austria, Brazil, Costa Rica, Denmark, Ecuador, and Norway. They have attended youth leadership development programs in Toronto, Ottawa, and Victoria, and count themselves lucky to have close friends in over thirty countries. CISV has afforded them life-changing experiences and a place to belong. And over the years they've learned a lot about themselves and others, and about how they can contribute to the world. This extraordinary program has taken Hayley and Chandra from early adolescence into adulthood. During this time, Val and I have watched our beautiful daughters grow into remarkable young women.

## The joy in caring

Chandra met Joanna in a seminar camp, a program for seventeen to eighteen-year-olds in São Paulo, Brazil. Unlike her peers at camp, who all had extensive experience with CISV, this was Joanna's first experience with the organization. Scared and shy, she was out of her comfort zone with the twenty young people who'd arrived from all over the world. After five days in camp, Joanna was done. She wanted to go home. The leaders called everyone together and helped Joanna announce her plans to the rest of the camp members. "CISV is just not for me," she told everyone. She would be heading to the airport to fly home as soon as she had packed.

Her camp mates were deeply affected by "losing one of their own." Although Joanna was shy and withdrawn, the group had quickly grown loyal to her—as they had with each person—and felt reluctant to let her go. Even those who hadn't managed to get to know Joanna were hurt and shaken. Everyone was stunned. Tears were flowing in the group.

While Joanna was in her room packing, the rest of the camp participants had a chance to talk about her decision. They were all in shock. It is just so rare for anyone to leave a CISV camp early, and they wondered if there was anything they might have done to prevent this. Together, they decided to individually write letters to Joanna, expressing caring messages she could take away with her on the airplane.

When she returned from packing, Joanna was given hugs and presented with everyone's letters. Brian, a participant from the US, approached Joanna. "Before you go there is something very special I would like to give you. I have a bracelet that was given to me in a suicide prevention program at my school last year. The bracelet reads, 'I am irreplaceable.'"

Brian's eyes were moist. There was a long pause as he regained his composure. "Once you feel you are truly irreplaceable, Joanna, you are to hand this bracelet off to someone else, someone who needs to know *they* are irreplaceable. All of us here in this seminar camp know that *you* are irreplaceable. So now we want you to find this out yourself."

By now, everyone was in tears except Joanna. A protective barrier kept her closed off, because she did not yet know how to let caring permeate it. Joanna graciously accepted the bracelet and envelope containing all the hand-written notes from the other participants. She thanked Brian and the young people standing around her, then she averted her eyes as she walked away to the car that would take her to the airport.

The joy of caring comes as much, if not more, from the person who cares as it does from the person receiving the caring. Sometimes people aren't ready to be cared for. While some simply aren't grateful, others don't know how to receive or show their gratitude. Maybe the seeds of caring have yet to take root and grow. Nonetheless, it's important to keep on caring, because you never know who will need it and who is ready to receive it. You may never know whose life is changed through your caring. You might not know if you are saving someone's life.

Most importantly, even if it isn't accepted yet, you keep caring because it brings you joy. "Find a place inside where there is joy, and the joy will burn out the pain," wrote Joseph Campbell.

CISV joins youths together in the spirit of caring. This remarkable organization is where a true understanding of others begins for many of these kids, and where the seeds of caring are planted. Camp participants learn lessons that are carried over, not only to personal choices they will make for themselves, but in every facet of their lives: with family and friends, their communities, and their careers. By seeing how others live, by appreciating their commonalities amidst radical differences, these youths can imagine making their mark in the wider world.

## The undervalued virtue of human goodness

The heartlessness of others led Eugene Bostick to take in abandoned animals and become a train conductor for rescued stray dogs.

"We live on a dead-end street, where my brother and I have a horse barn," said the eighty-year-old Fort Worth, Texas native. "People sometimes come by and dump dogs out here, leaving them to starve. So we started feeding them, letting them in, taking them to the vet to get them spayed and neutered. We made a place for them to live."

Bostick keeps them safe and cared for, and he's found an adorable way to keep them happy, too. The rescued dogs have plenty of room to run and play on the Bostick farm, but the retiree thought it would be nice to be able to take them on little trips to other places as well. "I'm a pretty good welder, so I took these plastic barrels with holes cut in them, and put wheels under them and tied them together."

Twice a week, Bostick sits in his tractor, hitches the barrels behind him, and pulls his custom dog train around town or through the forest near their home. Often he stops by a local creek so the dogs can drink and play in the water. It's something these formerly unloved dogs have come to relish in their happy new lives. "Whenever they hear me hooking the tractor up to the train, man, they get so excited. They all come running and jump in on their own. They're ready to go."

For Bostick, it's all about bringing a small amount of joy to a handful of dogs that have been run through the mill and discarded. I can just imagine his cheerful canine passengers.

⁓

A sequoia can live two thousand years. A domestic cat does very well if it makes it to twenty. A mayfly: born at sunrise, gone by nightfall. Each life is complete in itself. The quality of an individual life has nothing to do with how long it lasts, and everything to do with how it is lived.

Years ago, when I took a course from Margaret Wheatley, author of *Leadership and the New Science*, Meg spoke of the values that guided her organization. The first was, "we rely on human goodness." When people come to work they want a chance to help others, to learn, to be acknowledged, and to find meaning in what they do. In short, when they come to work, they want to live well.

"It's difficult to understand the sum of a person's life," penned screenwriter Justin Zackham for the film *The Bucket List*. "Some people would tell you it's measured by the ones left behind. Some believe it can be measured in faith, some say by love … Me? I believe that you measure yourself by the people who measure themselves by you."

## The undervalued virtue of play

When Troy Scott landed in alcohol rehab at a men's shelter, he had already lost his apartment, his girlfriend, and custody of their four-year-old daughter. Then he started playing street soccer at a local school gym. He was out of shape and hadn't exercised in years, but he kept going every Monday night.

Troy Scott is now one of over five hundred homeless Canadians who play "street soccer" weekly across the country. Recently, he joined a team that represented Canada at the Homeless World Cup.

Street Soccer Canada gives marginalized citizens a place to belong. It offers them a challenge to better themselves and the experience of being truly alive. The initiative began when housing advocate Paul Gregory put together a team for the Homeless World Cup in 2004. Since then, Street Soccer Canada has become a thriving network of over twenty soccer programs in a dozen cities across the country. Each year they send a Canadian contingency to compete against more than seventy countries around the world. Last year, Troy Scott headed to Amsterdam.

For more than a decade now, hundreds of underprivileged individuals living in shelters or on the street have been given a chance to be part of a team. One of the side benefits for participants is the health boost they receive. Their diet gets better, they are stronger and fitter, and being active helps reduce their drug use. Plus, it gives them something positive to focus on. Marc and Craig Kielberger, founders of Free the Children, and advocates for social change, talk about street soccer as "a sport that interrupts lives of grinding poverty, self-doubt, and social exclusion with exercise, confidence, and camaraderie."

Sometimes, all it takes is one small step to get the ball rolling—in this case through physical exercise and new friendships. Street Soccer Canada is helping individuals go from living in poverty and having no social standing, and from being ignored on the street, to pulling on a Team Canada jersey and representing their country. And when they score, they get something few homeless people do—a chance to cheer and celebrate.

In Appendix E, I offer more guidance on getting the ball of human goodness rolling in your own life.

## Giving away the lottery

"Happiness is not a goal; it is a by-product," Eleanor Roosevelt once said.

In early 2015, Randall Rush won the lottery. When he was asked how he felt about winning fifty million dollars, he said, "I think I started hyperventilating. I was screaming, and the girl at the till was screaming."

The forty-eight-year-old Lamont, Alberta man had played the same numbers at the same store where he bought his cat food for his cat, Conway Kitty, every week for the past six years. "I can pay off that parking ticket in Moncton, New Brunswick now," the heavy equipment operator said with a laugh. "It's on the front of my fridge and it's been like, ugh, next paycheck, next paycheck. Now I've got no excuse."

In the middle of the press conference and in the midst of all the excitement, Randall Rush stopped and a serious look overcame him. "It literally is a ton of money and it's a huge responsibility. You can't take this with you; this is a tremendous amount of money. I'm going to set up a trust fund and the interest that spins off this trust fund will go to feed hungry kids and homeless children around the world."

"A lot of people have nothing and I have so much. I want the money to do a lot of good even after I am gone." In this short inter-view, Randall Rush poignantly illustrated the difference between the emotion of *happiness* and the deep and sustaining experience of *joy*: the calmness and contentment that comes from within, from knowing that you are right with the world.

Happiness is winning the lottery. Joy is giving it away. Happiness is exciting. Joy is gratifying. Happiness is about pleasure. Joy is about peace. Happiness is an agreeable emotional response to a situation—happiness is fleeting and transitory. Joy is deeper; it's more sustained.

Happiness is certainly an emotion worth experiencing. It's fun to laugh until your belly hurts. These kinds of experiences can even stay with you for a long time. But joy is different. Unlike the excitement we get from buying a new wardrobe item or purchasing a new car, or the happiness we get from a boost in pay, joy is the inner sense of wellbeing that comes from having *earned* that pay raise. Even if we don't get a raise, we can still feel the joy of putting our heart into our work. Happiness is being told that we are appreciated. Joy is knowing that we are dedicated to our customers, clients, and fellow employees. Happiness is about birthdays and holidays and romantic encounters. Joy is how a grandfather feels the day his grandchild is born. Happiness passes quickly, while joy lingers. Joy is who we are authentically, at our core.

It could be that the secret to a joyful life is to forget about happiness as a goal. Does it matter if we're happy from minute to minute? When we care with joy, it has a lasting effect; it grounds us. In the long run, we create a wellspring inside ourselves, something to tap into. That's what joy is.

## Hal's legacy

Caring teaches us the undervalued virtue of human goodness. This is Hal's legacy, his life's greatest lesson. Caring has made him a good person, and being a good person has enabled him to care. Being a good person has made him better at everything he has done.

These past months, being with my brother—as horrible as it has been for everyone involved, especially Hal—has made us all better for it. We have all grown through the grief and shadows. Through caring, we've learned that the only thing we can ever take with us to the other side is what we have given away on this side. Caring teaches us that there is no line between the giver and the receiver, and that both benefit. It breathes life into our efforts to make the world a better place to live in. Caring truly is everything.

It's a precious gift to recognize the value of simple human goodness in each act of caring. Caring is not some special skill reserved for the arena of extraordinary individuals. It is not confined to some kind of compartment in your life. It's not a destination, or a place to get to. Caring is a method of travel, and a rickety imperfect one at that! You simply heed the call of this natural caring impulse within you, and follow, in your own human and imperfect way, where it leads to.

You can resurrect the ordinary through caring. Your caring actions are what change history. Whatever caring you are called to, may you realize more fully how important your actions are. Know that you have much more to offer than you may realize.

# What Home Means

Would that I could gather your houses into my hand, and like a sower scatter them in forest and meadow.

Would the valleys were your streets, and the green paths your alleys, that you might seek one another through vineyards, and come with the fragrance of the earth in your garments.

Kahlil Gibran, "On Houses"

## Fathers

"The best way to find yourself is to lose yourself in the service of others," Mahatma Gandhi said.

A few years ago, my sister-in-law's family lost all their possessions in a horrible house fire. Among the many personal effects lost in the blaze were the war medals and badges of my late father-in-law Malcolm McMillan, who served with the Bomber Command in the RCAF in World War II. Those medals were graciously replaced this past year by Veterans Affairs Canada and recently arrived at Val's mother's home. Our family examined this package of beautiful medals and badges, and took some time to honor Mac who, like so many others, served his country valiantly.

Intrigued and inspired by the sacrifices of those who served in the Royal Canadian Air Force, I spent some time researching what it might have been like to serve in Bomber Command.

The men who served in it faced some of the most difficult odds of anyone fighting in the war. One tour of duty consisted of thirty combat raids and the risks were so high that almost half of all aircrew never made it to the end of their tour. Despite its heavy losses, Bomber Command was able to maintain a steady stream of aircraft that flew over enemy targets in occupied Europe, from Norway to France.

Life as a bomber aircrew member was arduous. Usually seven men flew in a Lancaster bomber. These men worked together under intense pressure on their night forays. Take-offs were stressful as the roaring aircraft, loaded with tons of bombs and thousands of gallons of highly flammable aviation gasoline, raced down the runway. At high altitudes, in sub-zero temperatures, oxygen masks often froze. Enemy fighters used powerful searchlights and flak batteries against the bombers, turning the skies into a hail of shrapnel. Evading the enemy defenses sometimes caused a Lancaster to go into a spin, and the pilot would have to fight for control of the heavy aircraft.

Although Mac talked little of his experience overseas—few who served in Bomber Command ever did—he told his kids of a time when his plane was hit and when he stood in the open doorway of the Lancaster, waiting for his pilot to command him to parachute into the unknown. By good fortune the command never came, and the wounded aircraft landed safely back in England.

Of every one hundred airmen who joined Bomber Command, forty-five would be killed, six would be seriously wounded, eight became Prisoners of War, and only forty-one escaped unscathed— at least physically. Among those killed in the war was Ted Harling, my mother's first husband, a pilot with the RCAF. His death left my mother a widow and single parent of a three-year-old daughter, my sister Kate.

When I talk with Kate about her father, most of what she retains of him are emotional, visceral memories from her three-year-old self—and our mother's memories of him, which are more about our mother than about Kate or her father.

"Perhaps, what my sense of him is really about," she tried to explain to me recently, "are the losses that come from war, losses that shaped our life forever. There was a space, an empty shape left when my father was gone. My mother and I, each in our own way, have tried to fill that empty space, which was unfillable."

In her own words, here are Kate's memories of her father:

"I lost my father on November 4, 1945, when I was three. His plane crashed on Tuetoburger Wald in Halle Westfalen, Germany as he was flying a full load of penicillin and other medical supplies to Warsaw, Poland on a post-war mercy mission. Edward Pattern Harling joined the Royal Canadian Air Force on September 10, 1939, when Canada joined Britain in declaring war on Germany. He flew Transport Squadron throughout the war, and his last tour of duty was as a volunteer on a humanitarian mission, flying penicillin to Poland. His plane crashed, and my father and his four crew mates were all killed."

"What I do know and remember of this man, my father, whose genes I carry, is that I have visceral memories of being close to him … the smell of him, the sound of his voice, the laughter in his eyes as he looked at me, the strength in his arms as he lifted me up. He was a God to me, a bigger than life being, and then he would be gone on his next tour of duty. I remember the sadness in my mother's eyes when he left, the tension in her body while he was away. She would go from me to some other place inside of herself where I could not follow. Upon his return, my mother would release that tension and come alive again, and my world would feel whole once more. When my father didn't come home after his plane crashed, there was a space in our lives that would never be filled. In some ways, this empty space that's filled with old memories of my father is what connected my mother and me."

"My father was a war hero who sacrificed his life going to the aid of others. Obviously, he was a man who cared for his country, his crew, his family, and the people he wanted to help. Am I proud of him? Absolutely! And yet his death changed my life forever, in ways I can never know. I lost a caring father, my mother lost a caring husband. He was no longer with us and we had to go on without him."

Not every father makes that kind of sacrifice or endures the unimaginable hardships of those who've served in the military. My own father was not allowed to join the forces because he failed his eye exam. His service during the war was with youth who lived on the streets in downtown Calgary.

In each father's life a sacrifice is made. Many sacrifice time with their family in pursuit of their career or in a contribution to their communities. Many sacrifice some aspect of their career aspirations for the sake of their family.

Regardless of whether your father was a role model who inspired you, a friend who encouraged and loved you unconditionally, or a man who taught you how *not* to live your life, if you look deep enough, you might grasp that even if your father didn't give you everything you wanted, he probably gave you everything that you needed. No matter what, he helped shape the kind of person you are today. Perhaps it is time to send your father the only message worth giving a parent: thank you.

## Dianne

When a climber's partner unexpectedly plunges off a rocky cliff and into a raging river, the response is to take immediate action and jump into territory neither have navigated before.

When Hal lay in his hotel room experiencing his first fateful seizure, it was Dianne, his devoted life partner, who held him in her arms as she reached for the phone to call for an ambulance. Through the chaos that ensued in taking Hal from the hotel to the emergency room, Dianne never left his side. As he lay in the hospital bed waiting for a diagnosis, Dianne was there holding his hand. In the midst of all the confusion, she worked desperately to reach each of their children to share the awful news.

A dedicated wife and mother, Dianne organized and arranged for family members to visit, and she advocated for her husband during arduous medical explanations. She arranged to have Hal transported back home where he could get the care he needed—close to the friends, family, and community who continue to care so deeply for both Hal and Dianne.

Such is the life of an individual whose partner is dealt the hand of a plunge into terminal illness. You hear the call to care and you can't help but respond with an open, courageous, committed heart.

The trajectory isn't easy. Once the endless medical procedures, assessments, diagnoses, and visits from physician specialists are over, and the initial shock begins to wear off, you are suddenly faced with the realities of living with a spouse who now has an inoperable brain tumor. And while you may come to grips with the cancer, you still have to handle the ordinary everyday stuff of life—meals, dishes, laundry, bills, shopping, home repairs, and so on.

At the same time, you may be forced to take on roles you would never have dreamed of and have little facility with.

- Pharmacist: sorting out and managing a myriad of medications whose names and purposes are baffling.
- Financial manager: accessing on-line accounts you don't know the password to, and making decisions in a new and often confusing medium.
- Researcher and student: learning anatomy and all there is to know about brain cancer and brain functioning.
- Nurse: undertaking patient procedures heretofore unfamiliar.
- Patient advocate: learning how the health care system operates and the best way to navigate it.
- Gatekeeper: managing the flood of well-wishers and visitors.
- Chauffeur: driving a wheelchair-bound partner to and from all of the medical appointments and other necessary outings.
- Employer: hiring caregivers and managing all the employment and government forms.
- Booking agent: locating suitable accommodation while getting treatments at the out-of-town cancer center.

There are too few hours in a day to do it all, and too much to learn in such a short time, that it's hard to keep your own head above the raging river you are both now trying to navigate. With all the extra work and attention this entails, you may have to let go of certain things, including regular self-care. So now, stretch this grueling ride out over weeks and months, and sometimes years, as the illness wears away your last glimmer of hope. All the while, you're required to be the consummate optimist and a stable, strong partner through every turn.

Dianne has risen to this task—with unimaginable courage, caring, and commitment. Every step along the way, through Hal's adventure with an astrocytoma, Dianne has been responsible for making all of the arrangements required, a responsibility she has shouldered with grace and a sincere, genuine devotion. She's tackled every task with determination and researched every aspect of my brother's treatment—following up with calls about MRI results and medical trials and drug experimentation. She had to find immediate answers to questions such as:

When does too much Dexamethasone cause excessive nausea, mood swings, thinning skin, vision problems, and weakness? Will too little of the drug cause more seizures?

How much of the side effects are the results of the drugs, and how much are the results of the tumor?

What do you do when the seizures come?

When do you call the ambulance?

When she learned of a new drug that was believed to help slow brain tumor growth but was not approved for use in our province, Dianne proceeded to contact the drug manufacturer and arrange to make it accessible to Hal—a mammoth undertaking in itself that required enormous tenacity and energy.

Hal and Dianne's kids come as much as they are able whenever they possibly can, and my sister Kate has repeatedly travelled from San Francisco to help out. An amazing community of friends has pitched in so very much, but Dianne has done most of the heavy lifting.

A life raft appeared when an incredible, caring person arrived in Hal and Dianne's world. This most amazing caregiver, Val Sarsons, has become Dianne's indispensable "strong right arm" and because of her presence, Hal has been able to live as safely and comfortably as possible while in palliative care in their home.

Hal and Dianne had planned to spend their semi-retirement years in a beautiful mountain community in southern British Columbia. They had purchased a townhouse, and Hal had plans to practice family medicine in the community part-time. The astrocytoma had different plans. Its arrival meant that their lives have taken an altogether other route, one that is tied to the proximity of treatment and care in their own home town and province.

Dianne's children will tell you that their mother delivers a "Herculean effort of devotion and care." I don't know how she does it. But she finds a way. It's what we do because it's who we are. Such is the world of a loving partner transformed into the unmapped life of a caregiver.

## Grandparenting

Mellissa, my oldest daughter, gave birth to our first grandson Ethan in 2006. The day I first held Ethan and gazed into his eyes, the love that consumed me was incomprehensible. The impenetrable magic I experienced in that moment will forever exist between Ethan and me, as it will with all my grandchildren. That moment was the start of a lifelong special bond between a grandson and his grandfather.

We're never wholly prepared for the feelings that a first grandchild's birth inspires. Even though I was there for Mellissa's ultrasound and I saw the image of Ethan as a twenty-week-old fetus, I was still astonished by the rush of joy his arrival brought. Grandparenting indeed takes parenting to someplace even grander.

Ethan lives twelve hundred kilometers away. With the miracle of technology, we Skype and talk regularly, and although we see one another far too infrequently, there is an enduring, special bond between us. "The new child has just come from the Other World, and the grandparents are going to be there soon, so they have a lot in common," is how the poet Robert Bly puts it.

Or maybe it's simply that there is something about caring as a grandparent that invites a little more ease with the love. Many grandparents will tell you, "If I knew it was going to be this enjoyable, I would have become a grandparent first!"

Grandparents bring a different perspective to caring than a parent, something more lighthearted and yet more mindful, because it comes without the added stress of parental responsibility. There is a difference between being responsible *to* your children and being responsible *for* your children.

Grandparenting has taught me that parents are not responsible for the choices their children make. I did not know this when I was a parent of young children. Through parenting teens and young adults, and now grandparenting, I have come to understand in a whole new way the truth of these words by the twentieth-century Lebanese-American artist and poet Kahlil Gibran.

Your children are not your children ...
They come through you but not from you,
And though they are with you yet they belong not to you.
You may give them your love but not your thoughts,
For they have their own thoughts.
You may house their bodies but not their souls,
For their souls dwell in the house of tomorrow,
which you cannot visit, not even in your dreams.
You may strive to be like them,
but seek not to make them like you.

The message I want to convey to my own children about parenting is this: learn from your children as much as you give to them. There is no need to carry your children, for they have their own unique journey. We walk beside our children, but they must journey up their own mountain. While at times we will carry them over the difficult places, and occasionally carry their packs, be careful not to carry their pain. Always remember, our children will need to eventually walk on their own. Let go a little bit and enjoy the experience more. While it's important to be a conscientious parent, don't take it all quite so seriously. Kids grow up quickly! You don't want to miss being with them by being a worried, fearful, overprotective parent.

A grandparent once taught me that the best way to determine if you are being a good parent is to ask yourself how much you *enjoy* parenting. "If you want to be a better parent," she said, "don't 'try' to be a better parent. Just find a way to enjoy yourself when you are with your kids, and you will naturally be a better parent."

I remember seeking my parents' advice about bedtimes when our children were young. "Your kids may not need a bedtime," my father said to me once. "But *you* need them to have a bedtime. It's for your sanity as much as it is for theirs. Set one that works for you and it will work for them. The best limits for yourself will be the best for your children."

Grandparenting is about mentoring and passing on wisdom and our perspective by showing our grandchildren how we live our lives. It's about those times we hold them in on our laps and tell them stories, or we listen to *their* stories while their parents are busy trying to make ends meet and pay the bills.

Our grandkids have things to teach us, practical things like how to make better use of that tablet we have sitting in our kitchen. In turn, we can help them learn how to relate face to face before the Internet, computers, and smart phones invade their lives, and help prepare them for those future times when things become more complex, confusing, and demanding for them. We can share our love of fishing or knitting, of climbing or playing music. We can support and encourage some interest they themselves may have. The important thing is to allow them to feel the warm presence of an adult role model who is willing and eager to take the time.

Being with adults who love us unconditionally, who provide a wise and stable presence, and who go at a slower and more natural pace in the world, this is what grandparenting is ultimately about.

## Companions furred, feathered, and otherwise

My earliest memory of having a dog in the house was as a toddler, by way of a sweet and lovely mutt named Snuggles. I don't remember much about her, only that I have fond recollections of her being around. I recall my mother sobbing inconsolably when she died. Snuggles had been my mother's constant companion in those post WWII years, after her husband died and she'd been left as a single parent.

I got my first, very own dog two months before my sixth birthday. The three-month-old Dachshund puppy arrived in my Christmas stocking. I also got pet birds at a time when my brother had a cat. Cats and birds don't get along too well in general, due to the feline's natural instincts, and his cat killed all my birds. That incident didn't earn me much fondness for cats—until our daughters came along and managed to turn my heart around. Since then, cats have joined our household and we've all adapted to living side by side. Our home has also provided shelter to a host of critters that seem to come with having children: hamsters, frogs, fish, and even a short-lived gecko. While these companion animals never wiggled their way into my heart, I learned to tolerate them because they each meant something to the girls.

I grew up downwind from a pig farm. I liked the smell of pigs and couldn't figure out why everyone else thought that was weird. As a boy, I walked up the road one day and asked our pig farmer neighbor Art Wiebe for a job so I could earn enough money to buy my first horse. He agreed and I worked for him through my teenage years. He had sheep too, and I learned to care for them as well. Art Wiebe ended up being a teacher and mentor for me in many ways. He taught me to care for animals, how to take pride in my work, and how to live an honest life.

After a year working with Art, I'd saved enough to buy my retired packhorse Caesar. I learned to ride him with some help from my sister, but especially with help from our hired man Norris who tutored me to ride Caesar bareback and grip my inner thighs to his withers.

Once I'd developed enough confidence with riding, the next horse I saved up for and bought was a grey Appaloosa gelding named Tex. I don't think I knew it at the time, but Tex helped me through most of my adolescent torment. After a rough day at school, or in the middle of a fight with my parents, I would go off and spend time with Tex. Some days, I would ride for hours through the woods and around the lake just beyond our home farm.

Everyone needs to carve out some form of sanctuary—adolescents especially so—and riding Tex was certainly mine at the time. Companions in our lives, whatever form they take, can help us through our tough times. There were moments when I would stop mid-ride, lean forward, and gently wrap both arms around his neck. I could lie on Tex like this for minutes at a time, taking in his earthy, sweaty scent. His spirit and solid presence gave me strength.

## Kano, a companion in the truest sense

When Val and I were first married, we bought a Norwegian Elkhound from a breeder in our neighborhood and we had the privilege of having him spend his life with us. Kano had many gifts over the years, but his greatest was a capacity to love. A companion in the truest sense, Kano became the center of our family life. We lived on the edge of a ravine, and, after work, Val and I would walk him each evening in the river valley, sometimes for hours. With Kano at our side, we would talk about our day, reflect on important issues in our lives, and enjoy the simple pleasure of being together in nature.

Kano was the first pet our youngest girls were exposed to and, fortunately, he had a loving disposition. This exposure instilled a deep affection and compassion for animals in our daughters, which has carried through into their adult lives. Admittedly, during those early childrearing years, it was more often my children who jumped up on my lap, so there was little room for a dog. In those days, I neglected Kano more than I care to admit, relegating him from a companion to a chore.

Still, through all those busy years when Kano seemed to get the short end of the stick for our attention, he was a giver and a receiver of love, and a beautiful constant presence. His later years coincided with the death of my mother, and a transformative time for me both in business and in life.

I have noticed that, during both times immediately following the deaths of my parents, I had a sense of being guided by an unexplainable force from beyond. The year my mother died, Kano took on an important role in my life. Beginning with the loss of my mother, that year evolved into a time of grief and reflection, a time of turning corners and embarking on new terrain. Animals can be a great source of strength during those times, when we find it important to step away from the outer world and go inside. "Until one has loved an animal, a part of one's soul remains unawakened," writes Anatole France. Simply being with my canine companion, and being away from the demands of others, was an important awakening and help to me.

This was also the last year of Kano's life, so while I sought contemplation and quiet time, his slowing down—and mine—became a big part of our journey together. I introduced the habit of observing scheduled Sabbaths, away from the demands of the world and unplugged from the emerging around-the-clock technology that was beginning to creep into every aspect of my life. I carved out time to simply be with my kids and with my dog. During the weekdays, I would take extra time after lunch to walk him along his favorite river trail that he and I loved so much. He was a great sounding board for my grief, and for my reflections on a new direction.

Kano, during that time, was my connection to the divine. To sit with a dog by a river on a splendid afternoon, I've come to believe, is to know peace. "A person can learn a lot from a dog," writes John Grogan, "about living each day with unbridled exuberance and joy, about seizing the moment and following your heart. [Marley] taught me to appreciate the simple things—a walk in the woods, a fresh snowfall, a nap in a shaft of winter sunlight. And as he grew old and achy, he taught me about optimism in the face of adversity. Mostly, he taught me about friendship and selflessness and, above all else, unwavering loyalty."

Having a companion also means caring for a companion. Along our journey with Kano and the many animals we have had in our home, came a friendship with our veterinarian Gerry Smith.

Any pet owner will tell you they expect their veterinarian to be competent. If the doctor is unable to diagnose and treat what is ailing your animal, you won't be coming back. As the humorist-philosopher Will Rogers said, "the veterinarian is the best doctor in the world. He can't ask his patients what's wrong. He just has to know." Yet there's a difference between competence and caring. A veterinarian can be good scientist, a diagnostic expert, a skilled clinician, but caring adds something more.

Gerry Smith has been tending to our dogs and cats for more than twenty years. He is competent *and* caring, and he makes it his art to care. He doesn't just give an exam or a shot or a pill to one of our animals. He takes the time to connect with them as well as with us. From the touch of his hand or in the calm of his voice, he settles the nerves of our anxious cat or fretful dog. He understands that a relaxed patient actually feels better and will respond more quickly to treatment. He also understands that the patient in his examining room is as much the handler as the animal.

Gerry and his team cared for Kano for over ten years—through routine examinations, vaccinations, surgery, and prescription medicine—as part of the healing, caring veterinary journey with our beloved companion. In the last few weeks of his life when Kano started to show his age, his health deteriorated rapidly. There came a point when a decision had to be made. We could give him medicine and be patient for a considerable time, for as long as veterinary science would allow us, but the time had come to ask if his quality of life was just too poor and it was time to put him down.

Our answer came from a desire to care for our canine friend in the best way we could, in other words, by trying to imagine what Kano would want. So we called the clinic and booked his last appointment. When Gerry heard who it was, he called us back and insisted that he come and euthanize our dog at our home.

On the last day of Kano's life, he couldn't walk or stand to feed himself. I carried him into the backyard, a place he'd loved sniffing and rooting and lazing around in, and there we lay together most of the day while everyone took their time saying goodbye. Each of the girls spent time just being with him alone. We cried and took pictures.

Gerry and his then wife Jan, who is also a vet, arrived shortly after supper. They asked what place we would like Kano to be at for the procedure. As a family, we decided they should put him down in his favorite corner on the backyard deck. Gerry and Jan helped us make him as comfortable as possible. A small section of his leg was shaved. This, we knew, was where the needle would be inserted. They gave him the injection. Our family surrounded Kano as he peacefully closed his eyes.

—◆—

We had Kano cremated and held a short memorial for him as a family. We told stories to each other of times we'd spent with our dear companion. Then we went down to the river that he loved so much and scattered his ashes in the water. Another Will Rogers gem goes like this: "If there are no dogs in Heaven, then when I die I want to go where they went."

Animal companions are part of my life, and always have been. I've been there for the birth of foals and puppies and pigs and kittens and sheep, and I've been at their sides many a time when they've passed on. I've cleaned up their messes and I've held them close to me. Since Kano's death, we've had many more pets, more wonderful dogs, and, yes, even cats.

Our companions—furred, feathered, scaly, warty, and otherwise—show us that life, like caring, isn't wrapped up in a tidy box. Life is full of messes to clean. It's imperfect. It's painful. It can, at times, be difficult to endure. Most of all, it's wonderful, or mostly so. That's the blessing of it. In whatever form our companions take, whether domesticated pets or the wild friends we encounter in nature, they help us realize we are not alone, that we share this earth with others, that we are part of something so much bigger.

# The Gift of Adversity

Sometimes it's the very people who no one imagines anything of who do the things no one can imagine.

Joan Clarke, *The Imitation Game*

## The gift of being different

Sydney is a music major attending her first year of college. In high school, she played trumpet in several ensembles and was a member of the marching band. Over the past several months, she's experienced some transformative changes. It's been a time of transition and reversals, yet paradoxically a time of coming back to herself. For the first time in her life, Sydney is free to express her true nature, to live and be the person she is.

On a crisp day in November, I spoke with Sydney and her mother Amy about the transitions they've both experienced in recent months, and the evolution of their mother-daughter relationship.

David:   I have great respect for Amy's caring, and with Sydney's courage. Sydney, how do you feel today?

Sydney:   I feel nervous that maybe I can't answer all your questions.

David:   I feel nervous too, that maybe I'll ask the wrong questions. Can we make a pact that there are no wrong questions and no wrong answers?

Sydney:   Sure. That sounds good.

David:    Okay. Where should we start? Let's begin with Amy and
          Sydney's relationship. Amy, what was Sydney like grow-
          ing up?

Amy:      She was always quiet. As a mother, I was always protective
          of her, maybe overprotective. When Sydney approached
          adolescence, she started keeping to herself more and
          more. Because I was busy, I didn't take much notice of
          this. I remarried during that time. In any case, I didn't
          find her quietness was unusual. When she started band,
          I saw her come out more. It made a big difference for her.
          I want to say that band grounded Sydney in a way she
          hadn't been before.

Sydney:   I'd say our relationship was always strong. I trusted Mom,
          it was just a given.

Amy:      While she was growing up, Sydney and I didn't show our
          affection a whole lot. We didn't talk much either. We are
          not really affectionate people in my family. That's just
          who we are. But her coming out has changed that. We've
          become more loving to each other. We have long conver-
          sations about all sorts of things. We share so much and
          we're very close now.

David:    Sydney, tell me about the band and being forced to cut
          your hair.

Sydney:   My high school marching band has 300 members, and
          there is a strict uniformity. Before I joined, I really ad-
          mired the band director. I admired how clean and refined
          the band was under his direction. He was strict and he
          had strict rules. I respected many of these rules, like when
          you're representing the band, don't talk badly of oth-
          ers, you never know if another band member's parent is
          nearby. Or don't leave your trash around. Be respectful.
          These are good rules. But the band director took the
          rules too far. He put up walls and un-crossable lines.

The cost of uniformity felt too high, and there were no other options. The cost of uniformity meant that all the boys had to have short hair, and all the girls had to wear one earring per ear. These are just two examples. The band director wanted you to give up yourself, be nothing but a part of the group, nothing but a perfect band member. Some of the rules felt absolutely pointless; it was all about his strict ideas and nothing about the band members. I absolutely hated these rules.

Having long hair has been a huge part of my identity. My whole life, I always felt I was female. I just always knew. When I discovered in my junior year that I would have to cut my hair for band, it was hard. I cried.

Amy: By senior year, I finally asked myself the question, is this necessary? I had a long talk with the band director, but there was no way I could convince him. Allowing Sydney to keep her long hair just wasn't an option. It's easy to say it's just hair, that it will grow back, but it became a decision. It became a deciding moment. I felt torn between two things that Sydney valued very much. I wanted her to know I supported her keeping her hair long, because I knew what that meant to her. Since there was no way to keep it, I wanted her out of marching band. But I knew this wasn't much of an option either. So she had to choose.

David: Sydney, when did you feel different? Did you feel separate from yourself?

Sydney: Not really. I've always known I was different. I always felt that I wanted to be a girl. An important point in my life came when I met someone, a girl who would become my girlfriend. She knew about being transgender, and what that meant. She knew way more than I did at the time. She had read a lot about it. I was still presenting as Caleb when we met. I was still presenting as a male. Suddenly I was able to open up to someone. I was able to share so much with her, about how it felt to be me, to the point that she finally asked me the question, do you think you might be transgender? She had to describe what that meant. But when she told me, I said, yes, that fits who I am. I didn't even know there was a word for it. Where we live in Oklahoma it's so conservative. It was funny. I'd been exploring for a long time. I'd been around a lot of different people, I was on the football team for a year. I did wrestling. I've always gotten along with all sorts of people. That's me. In general, I get along really well with others. But somehow I just couldn't find the right place for me. In band I had sort of carved out a place for myself, and I was happy with my bandmates—but marching band wasn't exactly the right place for me either.

David:    How did you first come out then?

Sydney:   When I first found out from my girlfriend what it meant to be transgender, I could see that it fit me and that was who I was. But for a while I really couldn't see how I would ever be able to share that with anyone else. I didn't know how to live as a transgender person, certainly not in my band or my school or my town. So I couldn't envision a point when coming out might actually happen, when I could actually be that person I knew I was, freely. I thought, if I could move to a place where no one knows me, maybe then. But as long as I stay here, I won't be able to tell people who I am.

In secret, my girlfriend brought me girls' clothes to try on, and she let my try her makeup. She helped me practice being a girl with her. One time in English class, I picked a female role to read. I wore a woman's peasant costume. It was so freeing. In addition to that, I got great marks for doing it, and for being so bold with my performance! This was a bit like coming out, in a way. After that I thought, okay, I can do this. Take one single step further. Tell one friend. So I told one friend, then I told a few more, and they all accepted me, just like that. I chose a new name. I picked Sydney because I didn't know anyone called that.

I still hadn't told my mom though, even though my coming out had been going on for a few months. Finally one day, I knew it had to happen. So I sent Mom a text. "I have something to tell you when you come home." That's what the text said. She called back immediately and said, "What is it? What's going on? Tell me now."

So right there and then, we had this epic phone call, and I could tell right away she understood. She really did. It was a big deal for me. Telling her was the biggest step I took during this whole process. I didn't know what to expect from Mom when I started telling her, even though it made perfect sense when she was so accepting and understanding. I guess I knew this was a big moment, that now things would actually begin to happen. Once I told her, she could get me on this big huge path to being who I am. Even though I knew it would happen eventually, and I knew that no matter whatever else took place in my life, this being who I am *had* to happen. This was the next step I was taking! It was a really defining moment for me.

David:    What was that conversation like for you, Amy?

Amy:      Sydney asked me, do you know what transgender means? That was her first question. And from there she kept talking. Sydney just started telling me what that meant. She explained everything she knew about being transgender. She told me she knew she was a girl.

David:     What was it like telling other people about Sydney? How did your family react?

Amy:       I was worried about telling my mother. She's been vocally against same-sex marriage for a long time, and I'd been hearing all about those views leading up to the Supreme Court decision last summer. So I knew Sydney's coming out wouldn't exactly align with her. My family is very conservative, and I was afraid they wouldn't think being transgender was *real*. When I told my mother about Sydney, it surprised me how good she was about it. My whole family was supportive. My mother said, "I don't really understand it, but I guess I'll just have to work on that."

Sydney:    I decided a long time ago that people don't get to make me feel a certain way. Nobody gets to do that. I won't let people hurt me. I won't be scared of anyone. It would be sad losing the people I care about, but I could always get past that. It would suck a whole lot, but if I had to, if a person hurt me, I would break whatever emotional attachment I had with them.

David:     I'm really blown away by your strength, Sydney. Your courage is amazing.

Amy:       It's true. Sydney came out to me this past March during her senior year. We've been through so much since then. We spent a lot of time during the summer working through everything, getting ready for Sydney to start college this fall.

Sydney:    We had a lot to talk about. I knew it was going to be a long process, and I knew I wanted to start right away. The first two things we did were to find a therapist and to get the process going to legally change my name. Changing your name takes a long time. And I had to find a doctor so I could begin hormone treatments.

Finding a therapist was the really important step. After several sessions, I was able to get a letter so I could get into the girls' dorms at college, and start the treatments, and so on. The stage I'm in still feels temporary. I'm still seeing my girlfriend. We've been together for three years! She's in her last year of high school back home. My girlfriend's parents are super strict Oklahoma people, so that's another hard part. She has to refer to me with her parents as "he" and she still calls me Caleb around them. It's hard, I know, but I have to trust her. This falsehood is what I have to put up to be with her. When she graduates next year, we'll be able to move in together and that will be that. Her parents won't have any say in it.

David:     So what's your message in all this?

Amy:       We're all human. And we're all different, everyone in our own way.

Sydney:    Every single person should be themselves. We shouldn't be who others want us to be. Nobody gets to say who and how we should be or how we should live. My message is, live life as your own person.

David:     Amy, how does it feel to have your daughter surpass you in some of her wisdom?

Amy:       (Laughing.) It makes me feel like a really good mom. I'm inspired by her strength. For me personally, I've had a chance to really grow as a person. We don't always get the opportunity to grow this much at this level.

David:     How do you feel about Sydney being in college?

Amy:       I don't want her to get hurt. It's hard sometimes. I want to protect her from anyone who tries to hurt her.

David:     Sydney, how has college been so far?

Sydney:   I wasn't expecting my whole family to be so support-ive, or for the college staff to be so accommodating. The college staff are so incredibly helpful. And I'm surrounded by classmates who support me. One day, a substitute teacher called me "he" and my whole class corrected him to call me "she." It was amazing to feel so supported. The teacher just said, "Okay. She, I guess." With other teachers, though, I've been impressed by their subtle understanding of me and what I'm going through now.

David:   How does it feel to be you after all these transitions?

Sydney:   It's incredible how much better it feels! The hormone replacements and getting to wear feminine clothes and having breasts. This all feels so much more me. There are subtle expectations to present as a specific gender, one or the other, and I've finally been released from these expectations that didn't fit me. Presenting as a male, I felt like so much less, like I wasn't that, like part of me was being nullified.

David:   It's freeing to be who you are.

Sydney:   Yes. Freeing is a really good word for how it feels.

Amy:   I was always criticized for being overprotective with Sydney, but maybe it was good that I was overprotective with her early on! Maybe that allowed her to be herself.

David:   Is there anything else you'd like to add?

Sydney:   I didn't get to tell my version of the haircut story. Be-fore, when I was told I had to cut my hair, I always refused. I just said no, I am not going to. That's where I was when the band director told me I had to cut my hair, and this time I wasn't given a choice. I thought, it doesn't matter what he wants, there's no way I'm cut-ting it. It isn't his choice to make. It doesn't matter what he says. What changed my decision was when I talked to my step-dad. He said cutting your hair is just something you do. He knew what he was talking about. In the army, he'd had to shave his head. It's just what everyone did. So I decided, okay, I have to do this. And so I stopped any emotional response. I got my hair cut off and I just cut myself off from caring about it, even though my long hair felt like the one thing that truly identified me and set me apart. It had been my defining feature for so long. But I decided, no, my hair isn't me. I will cut it, and it will grow it back. Happily, it did grow back and now it's long again.

David: So was there a huge dividing point in your life where you went from male to female, from Caleb to Sydney? Do you feel the same or different since you came out?

Sydney: I feel the same. I feel exactly the same as I've always felt. It's the outside world and outside things that have changed. Other people's perception of me has changed. I haven't.

As we wound up our conversation, I thought about Sydney's courage and wisdom, and how proud Amy is of her daughter. These words by Shakti Gawain sum it up: "We will discover the nature of our unique genius when we stop trying to conform to other people's models and expectations, and allow our natural channel to open."

## The beauty of a hard road

After a summer of working long hours in a camp for people with disabilities, our daughter put every free cent into saving for her first car. There's nothing quite like the pride of sacrifice and ownership. One winter morning, during her third year of university, on her way to the school where she was student teaching, a driver went through a yield sign and broadsided her. Hayley was okay, but her pride and joy was totaled. She was in tears when she told me what it was like to see the tow truck take away her "little baby." The only thing salvageable was the Ford hood ornament that now sits on her desk in her basement suite.

Parents know that it hurts to see our kids hurt. It took painstaking effort to not reach into my pocket and buy her another car in an attempt to rescue her from her unhappiness.

Philip Simmons, in his inspirational memoir *Learning to Fall*, relates a childhood memory about adversity, when he took it upon himself to perform his "first road improvement project at age seven." He spent most of an afternoon removing pebbles from the dirt road near his family's house and tossing them into a nearby field—certain that he was "acting for the general welfare" of the family by making the road absent of any rough obstacles.

"But then my father came out and told me to stop. We needed those stones in the road, he told me. This made no sense: wasn't it better to make the road smooth? No, he explained, the stones made the road hard. We needed a hard road more than a smooth one."

Adversity, if we can somehow face it honestly, has the capacity to transform us. My mother used to say that adversity was necessary to plumb the depths of our own resources and find out what we are made of. People with strong character, who can find a way to step back from adversity and befriend it caringly and courageously, will see growth opportunities in their difficulties. It's through coming to grips with adversity that we realize our potential as well as our destiny.

My mother knew this from her own suffering—the loss of two siblings as a child, having an absent father who worked three jobs to support his family during the depression, giving birth to a stillborn child, the death of two husbands—to name but a few of the difficult journeys she made in the course of her lifetime. There is value in pain. It can teach us to love and to be a stronger human being.

Caring can't always occur without pain. My mother would tell me that when adversity hit, it was worth seeing what I might learn and love about myself and the world around me. When we bring curiosity into adversity, we may find that a new level of caring capacity emerges from the wreckage.

Within suffering and adversity our purpose often awaits us. The great Celtic poet and scholar John O'Donohue teaches, "You were sent to a shape of destiny in which you would be able to express the special gift you bring to the world ..."

"Sometimes this gift may involve suffering and pain that can neither be accounted for nor explained ... Each one of us has something to do here that can be done by no one else. If someone else could fulfill your destiny, then they would be in your place, and you would not be here. It is in the depths of your life that you will discover the invisible necessity that has brought you here. When you begin to decipher this, your gift and your giftedness come alive. When you are in rhythm with your nature, nothing destructive can touch you. Providence is at one with you ... To be spiritual is to be in rhythm."

If you don't live in a chaotic world that confronts you daily with inequality and injustice, then practice embracing adversity. You might fall on your face, and it could feel terrible for a while. Maybe, like hard pebbles underfoot, facing adversity will always be rough going. With practice, facing adversity can get easier—and if not easier, than somehow worth the pain. Sometimes a hard road can be beautiful.

At times it's caring to step in. At times it's more caring to step back. That's the nature of caring—taking the time to go through the rigorous process of asking the questions of how, when, where, and why to care.

# Our Shadows

If we gain the ability to look in to ourselves with honesty, compassion, and with unclouded vision, we can identify the ways we need to take care of ourselves. We can see the areas of the self formerly hidden in the dark.

Gabor Maté

## When we fail to acknowledge our shadows

I was settling into my seat on the Airbus A320, waiting for the usual flight preparations. About a dozen passengers had boarded when the yelling started. Every other word was an F-word. This aggressive, abusive, shouting originated from the guy in the seat behind me. When I turned around to see what was going on, I saw he was on his cell phone. I had no idea what the context was, or what had triggered such a rage of temper. I saw only his swollen, flushed face absolutely full of fury.

The next thing I heard was his cell phone being thrown onto the floor under my seat. There was a distinct sound of plastic breaking. I could only imagine the condition of his phone after that kind of treatment.

I sat quietly for a few moments getting myself grounded in the aftermath of the emotional turmoil behind me, and as the next group of passengers began settling in to find their seats. Curious, I turned to observe the man again. He was still shaking and raging from the trauma he had just put himself through.

Minutes later a tall, attractive blonde woman stood next to me. Having just entered the aircraft and made her way down the aisle, she now placed her small, red carry-on bag in the overhead compartment above the seat of the man with the temper. Within moments, the two had struck up a wholly polite conversation. And over the next four hours, the man actually charmed her into accepting a date with him. Watching them cheerfully disembark, I wondered how long it would be before the woman would be introduced to the man's rage.

When sunlight hits a body, the body turns bright but casts a shadow. Each of us has a darker part of our nature that lives behind what we see. We don't know as much about ourselves as we think. We act as if "what you see is what you get," but that's only part of the truth: what you don't see is what you get too. The only thing worse than being around an obnoxious person is being around an obnoxious person who doesn't *know* they are obnoxious.

All my life I have carried around too much unacknowledged anger, irritability, and impatience. People close to me never knew when I would impulsively explode or be indiscriminately critical, and they'd constantly feel they were walking on eggshells. Oblivious to their feedback, I was blind to my anger and how it concealed the other shadowy aspects of myself: my anxiety, fear, and insecurity. "This is just the way I am," I would rationalize.

It's an act of caring to have the courage to take an honest look at the entire spectrum of ourselves, to take a truthful appraisal of the impact of our actions on others, and to have the willingness to make necessary changes.

## The long bag we drag behind us

As preschoolers, we have a divine personality that radiates energy out of every pore of our body and our psyche. We are artists and singers and actors and lovers and builders and healers. Then one day, we notice that our parents don't like all this emotion and activity and disruption. After all, they are tired and they need their children to be orderly and well-behaved. They say things like, "Can't you be still?" or "It isn't nice to be so angry," or "Can't you be quiet?"

Later on, maybe we go to school and church, and the adults there understandably try to keep order and tidiness in their classrooms and their choirs, and we are told by people in authority what our art and music and self-expression are supposed to look and sound like, and we are told how we need to behave. And what do we do, when our innate and unique personality doesn't fit the mold of a tidy classroom? We put these beautiful parts of ourselves into what Robert Bly would describe as a "the long bag we drag behind us, heavy with the parts of ourselves our parents or community didn't approve of." The shadow is that repressed side of ourselves that we hide from the world and, often, from ourselves.

Our parents and teachers weren't evil by having us do this. They just needed a little peace in the house and in the classroom. It's also important to realize that no one put these aspects into our bag. You can't blame anyone in your life for what you have been carrying around, buried in the bag over your shoulder. We put these parts of ourselves out of sight because we thought we had to keep them hidden in order to survive.

Yet within this bag lies tremendous untapped possibilities. We simply don't know as much about ourselves as we think. Whatever is hidden from us may be good, bad, threatening, liberating, creative, or dreadful. We just don't know until we take a look at them. We won't know until we approach each one and draw it into the light, and get to know it. What we do know is that if we don't somehow get these things out of the bag, they become a burden to us and to those whom we are close to. They unknowingly hold us back from our freedom. Whatever is hidden has the power to be either destructive or blind us to our potential. That power is increased when it remains unacknowledged.

As a youngster, Bob Chartier loved to sing. He sang at church. He sang at school. But he was told by family members, teachers, and others that he couldn't carry a tune. What happened, Bob will tell you, is that it became a self-fulfilling prophecy. Because important adults in his life told him he couldn't sing, he became what he would describe as a "horrible singer." And what do "horrible singers" do? They stop singing. Exactly what Bob did.

It took almost fifty years, when he was in his early sixties, for Bob to sign up to attend a music camp. He wasn't a serious musician. He loved music and enjoyed hanging out with musicians, and he played a bit of bass. That all changed at camp. "They have a band scramble," says Bob. "You put five strangers together and they form a band and you have twenty minutes to come up with a song and perform it in front of a hundred and twenty people. I'm playing the upright bass by this time. I'm just hiding behind my bass and this woman Sandy says, 'You know, Bob, you're going to sing the third verse.'"

Bob responded, "I don't sing ... but I thought, these are friends and no one is going to die here. The third verse came along. I took a big deep breath and out came a voice that nobody had ever heard before, including me. It's a really emotional thing at age sixty-one to find your voice."

Ever since then, Bob has become a fixture in his music community. He has become an arts producer and has been instrumental in kick-starting an entire music community in Calgary. Bob has also become an accomplished songwriter. He's written over a hundred songs, and runs the songwriter sessions at the Gravity café.

"Music is my life," Bob will tell you today.

My own family upbringing was filled with enormous love, wisdom, and support. But the hidden side was the rage in my parents' relationship, my parents' anxieties, and my father's struggle with mental illness. Of course, these aspects were not necessarily "hidden" to our family like they were to the world, but we didn't have permission to talk about and acknowledge them openly with each other. So it all went underground, into our respective bags. I didn't think it was safe to say no, to get angry, or to open my heart fully to the experience of life. My courage and creativity went into my bag. I was the "good kid." I was loved by teachers. I had an abundance of friends. I was popular. To the world, and even to myself, I was so caring. But I had no idea of how anxious and depressed and full of anger I was. And buried amidst all this was a concealed artist. I believed that it was not safe to be exuberant and stand up for myself, to express my voice and allow my creative energies to come out without being continually edited. I did a lot of complying with the rules and, in disconnecting from the wild side of my nature, I spent my early life pleasing other people. I've been spending most of my adult life learning how to bring into the open what I put in that bag so many years ago.

My brother had his own bag that he filled. I don't know what was in there, but I know that what he showed to the world was a magnificently brilliant science and mathematics student. What I saw was his anger. When we were teenagers we got into such a fight one day that he pummeled my head into a brick wall. Hal learned to care through his work. You knew he cared, but it was difficult for us to get to his heart. It wasn't until he became a doctor that his heart opened.

## Light and shadow

Where there is light, there is a shadow. Whatever brings us joy will also produce darkness. In the process of deciding whether to buy a new house a few years ago, I brought over a good friend to have a look around and to help us with our decision making. After he had a good tour of the place, one of the first things he asked was, "What is it that you *don't* like about the house?"

I had a strong emotional reaction to the question. I believed my friend wasn't seeing all the beauty I was seeing. Whenever I have a strong emotional reaction, I've come to know I am touching on the dark side. "Well, I know it's an older house and it needs some fixing up. But it will be minimal," I rationalized, a common response in avoiding the shadow.

The truth was, I was so in love with the house that I was blinded from reality by passion. I was so convinced that this was the house I was "meant to have" that I avoided a thorough inspection. My friend was wise, and the decision to not pay attention to the shadow cost us a lot of money in unexpected renovation expenditures. In hindsight, we still would have bought the place, but we would have had the courage to actually see what was wrong with it, to pay for an extensive inspection, and be tougher in the negotiating process. Staying in denial about the shadow can cost you.

# The shadows in organizations

My understanding of the shadow has deepened since working as an organizational development consultant. Every organization contains both the visible system and the shadow system, and all employees are part of both.

The visible system consists of formal hierarchy, recognized lines of authority, rules, and communication patterns. The shadow organization isn't as obvious. It consists of hallway and coffee conversations, the grapevine, the rumor mill, and those informal unspoken rules for getting things done.

While the visible system is often focused on procedures, policies, job descriptions, and routines, the shadow system has few rules or constraints. In an organization, it's important to listen to the shadow. To have a lasting impact as a leader, it means you make time to go into the cafeteria or meet people in the hallways, or you go to the areas where people take their breaks.

You can talk about the small things in people's lives, or you can talk about what matters most. Either way, you have to take the time to listen to the hidden network. If you try to battle against the shadow by attempting to "overcome resistance," or if you pretend it is not there, the shadow will go underground and sabotage any opportunity for trust and growth.

The shadow in the organization is also found in the enormous gifts that people bring to their jobs. "How often," I ask participants in my leadership development programs, "have you been in an organization where you found that there is far more talent, brainpower, wisdom, and resourcefulness than the job required or even allowed? What happens to your soul when your special gifts cannot seem to find their place in what you are doing?" Indeed, we bring more to work than our bodies and what is visible in a resume.

In the midst of the demands for results, time pressures, and immense and conflicting priorities, the employee's unique abilities can get buried under all the strain and be hidden in the organizational bag. As a leader, taking time to get to know yourself and your employees, assessing strengths, listening to the dreams, passions, and desires that people bring to work, and doing the best you can to evaluate their fit, can be a way of bringing what is hidden within you to what you do. Herein lies the key to real engagement.

Every culture, like every life, has a shadow. What makes a culture dysfunctional is the lack of awareness or lack of courage to bring it to the surface and shine a light on it.

When National Hockey League player Theo Fleury announced publicly that he'd been sexually abused by his former junior hockey coach, it helped release Theo from the trauma. Over the years, that trauma had driven him to drugs, alcohol, and promiscuity. He'd managed to hold the secret inside himself throughout his otherwise impressive sixteen-year NHL career, but it was steadily destroying him.

Through a concerted desire to heal himself, Theo is now helping to heal others. By speaking out and becoming an advocate for young players and sexual abuse victims, he has brought healing and recovery to thousands of hurt and struggling individuals who have experienced similar traumas in their lives. Searching our shadows is not only good for the soul. It's good for the world. It's the work of caring.

## The importance of facing our shadows

My reason for writing a chapter in a caring book on facing the shadowy aspects of ourselves is that if you are hurting others or yourself by being habitually critical, impatient, angry, or abusive, then it is more fully caring to stop and acknowledge what is going on, and to have the courage to take responsibility and do something about it. It's caring to resist the natural tendency to say to ourselves "this is just the way I am." But shadow work doesn't just have to do with bringing the darker sides of our nature into the light. It also has to do with finding our voice at a music camp. Or taking up ballroom dancing. Or traveling to India. Or doing something that is important in our lives that we may have been told for years "isn't good for us," or that "we aren't good at it," or "nice girls don't do such things."

In Appendix F, you will find some strategies for honoring and bringing your shadow into the light and thus into recovery and healing.

# Allowing for Hope

Impermanence is life's only promise to us,
And she keeps it with ruthless impeccability.
To a child she seems cruel, but she is only wild,
And her compassion exquisitely precise:
Brilliantly penetrating, luminous with truth,
She strips away the unreal to show us the real.

This is the true ride—let's give ourselves to it!
Let's stop making deals for a safe passage:
There isn't one anyway, and the cost is too high.
We are not children anymore.
The true human adult gives everything for what cannot be lost.

Jennifer Welwood

## Sharing cousins

"Go ahead, Tim." We stood in line waiting to place our order at the coffee shop. The sharp fall morning air reminded us both that these warm September days were coming to an end. Tim and I hadn't seen each other in months and I looked forward to getting caught up.

"How was your summer? Did you and Karen get away?"

After our few minutes of niceties, there was suddenly this long pause.

"I've had the most fascinating summer of my life," Tim said. There was an inner peace about him I had never seen before. "I'll get you caught up when we sit down."

We got our tea and pulled our chairs up at the last empty table. "So what happened?" I asked.

"I donated one of my kidneys to my cousin," he answered. "I've spent the past two months recovering from the surgery. It's been slow, but I should be ready to get back to hockey in a month or so. The only thing that's changed in my life is I can't take ibuprofen. I guess it's too hard on a kidney when you only have one left."

His calm manner impressed me. "That's pretty major surgery. How did you decide to go through with the procedure? You don't just wake up and decide to give up a kidney."

"Well actually, that's sort of how it happened."

I was inspired by Tim's generosity, and his matter-of-fact account of what he'd given to his cousin, truly the gift of life. "Could I sit down with you both some time? I'd like to hear more about this incredible thing you've done."

## Crushed hopes

A few weeks later, we were gathered in Tim's living room where Tim offered us tea and banana bread. "One of my favorite ways to eat bananas," Julie said, laughing. Bananas, a source of potassium, had been recommended to manage her potassium levels.

Tim and I sat across from each other while Julie settled by a window, her slight dancer's body engulfed inside the overlarge, stuffed armchair. A tattoo circled Julie's wrist. The ink had the appearance of barbed wire, but on closer inspection the circle turned out to be writing. The words are Gaelic and are drawn from Julie's Scottish heritage. The inscription is her personal mantra.

Julie was first diagnosed with kidney disease at eighteen, she told us, during a hectic time in her life. She was in the throes of adolescence and high school diploma exams and ballet school, and was coping with the symptoms of lupus disease, a condition with which she'd been fairly recently diagnosed. It was then that the Jenga blocks came crashing down. Julie noticed something was seriously wrong. Her legs grew painful and bloated, and she began throwing up everything she ate, while at the same time gaining fifteen pounds—in fluid as it turned out.

Over the next few months and years, she would learn to cope with the disease in, as Julie put it, a "totally driven" way. She didn't let herself think too hard about her condition. She pushed her emotional needs out the window in an effort to be strong, and, like the dancer she was, refused to reveal any weakness. She'd been highly successful with the approach, and now was the head of a program at the ballet school where she taught.

But the disease and the dialysis treatments were taking their toll. Before Tim came along with his offer to help, Julie was close to hitting rock bottom. She was nearing forty, she wasn't bouncing back so easily, and she'd been on dialysis full-time for a decade. Doctors and other healthcare workers had told her the odds were low that a third kidney transplant would succeed—assuming she even got one. Kidneys, when they come available, tend to go to younger recipients, and Julie was no longer one of the young ones. There was also the problem of locating a donor who matched her blood profile. And having lupus disease meant she was more prone to rejecting foreign bodies like a new kidney.

"Would a fourth kidney ever be a possibility?" I asked her. "If this one doesn't work out?"

"Getting this one was a long shot. So a fourth? It just doesn't happen," Julie said. "The message I've had from healthcare workers since my second transplant was always this: don't set your expectations too high. So they pretty much crushed my hopes. I expected to be on dialysis forever."

I asked Julie to tell me what it was like when she discovered she had the disease, back when she was a teenager. The first indication that something was wrong, she said, came when she was taking medications for pain and bloating, symptoms she thought were caused by lupus disease. She'd been carrying on with her usual heavy load, going to school, taking ballet, stoically enduring the pain. Finally, an unstoppable nose bleed brought her to the hospital. Blood tests would later show that her hemoglobin was crashing and her blood had no more platelets. Doctors had to cauterize her nose to stop the bleeding, a terribly painful procedure. Finally, after more rounds of misdiagnoses, Julie learned she had kidney disease.

She was in ICU for two weeks. The day before she was admitted, she was still taking dance classes and yet, Julie would find out later, her doctors at the time were preparing her family for her possible death.

Soon after her admission, they started her on dialysis—a treatment that performs the normal job of a kidney by filtering out toxins from the blood, but all at once instead of little by little. The procedure was an ordeal every time. It took three to four hours, was invasive and draining, and basically wiped an entire day off Julie's calendar. Afterward, she would be weak and exhausted, often plagued with migraines and a terrible malaise.

In her early months with the disease, Julie's dad Brian prepared to donate one of his kidneys for her first transplant. The surgery was successful, but her dad's kidney had been damaged upon removal, and Julie's body struggled for a year and a half until the donated organ failed. She then returned to dialysis—three times a week—and waited for another suitable kidney to appear. It came a couple of years later when she was twenty-two, from an anonymous, deceased donor. The second transplant was more successful, and for nine years it worked well enough to keep her off dialysis—until the second kidney also failed, and Julie was back to her regular treatments at the renal clinic.

Initially, Julie didn't know the seriousness of her condition since she wasn't given much information. She just wanted to get out of the hospital and back to her old life, the way things had been before. "When you don't know how serious things are," Julie said, "you just go along for the ride." Eventually, she learned the truth, and the ordeal of coping with kidney disease hit her like a ton of bricks. From then on, she just buckled down. Julie became driven and did whatever it took to cope.

## It's what family does

Flash forward to early 2015. By now, Julie was juggling regular dialysis treatments with her growing administrative duties at the ballet school and continuing to teach classes. Life was getting harder. She could feel her spirits spiraling downward when she got the life-changing call from Tim.

"Sometimes cousins can be matches," he told us.

Tim had been to visit his aunt, Julie's mom, three months earlier when the topic of donors came up, and it was then the truth finally dawned on him. He felt so dumb. How could he have not known he could be a match? Immediately, Tim called the living donor program. He didn't hesitate. He had three kids who were mostly grown, his health was good, and his was business stable, but more importantly, Tim knew he had no choice but to donate his kidney to Julie if he possibly could. His and Julie's families had spent a lot of time growing up together and, despite their age differences, all the cousins had been close. As Tim tells it, the donation was no big deal. "It's just what family does."

Without telling Julie, Tim initiated testing to see if he might be a match, a rigorous process that would take seven months. Partway in, when a match seemed likely and being a donor was a real possibility, Tim called Julie to tell her what he'd been up to. At this point, he offered her his kidney.

At first, Julie's answer was an unequivocal no. She refused him outright. She didn't want to see him put his health at risk. Tim had three kids, he was responsible for a family, plus he was her cousin, for heaven's sake. That's the paradox of kidney donations. Often, it's the closest family members who make the best donor matches. And transplant surgery is a serious procedure—which means putting two family members at risk at the same time.

Tim would not take no for an answer. He told Julie he was continuing with the tests. Seeing he was adamant, she reluctantly agreed. They had a few more hurdles yet, and she didn't think he would be a match anyway—so for that reason she relinquished control and put her fate into someone else's hands.

For Julie, it meant opening herself up, one infinitesimal crack, to hope.

One aspect of Tim's testing was determining if his kidney could be a match, a compatibility test, in other words. There were additional tests to assess his overall health. He had to visit a social worker who tested his mental state and cleared him of any possibly he was trying to sell his kidney to Julie. Tim had EKGs and CAT scans done, and he spent an entire day in the hospital one time, beginning with a visit to the lab where they drew fourteen vials of his blood. For the final critical test, called a cross match, Tim and Julie visited the blood lab together. The lab technician mingled their samples in a petri dish and waited to see if their blood cells would fight each other.

Tim heard the results first. The test result was negative. No fighting. They were a match.

When he called Julie to tell her the news, she was in a class, teaching. The message he left on her voicemail at work was cryptic, Julie said. She couldn't decide what it meant. After she'd listened a second time, she sat and stared at the wall. She was so terrified of having her hopes dashed, she choked and couldn't call him back. Eventually, her colleague and close friend Maria came in and asked her what was wrong.

"Call him." Maria picked up the phone and dialed, and handed the receiver to Julie. This time Tim's voicemail picked up. He didn't answer because he was driving. Julie left a shaky message and hung up. "We're going for dinner," Maria told her.

They were at the restaurant when Tim called back. "Looks like game time," he told her. "We're a match."

Julie could hardly believe it. She kept saying, "You don't have to do this for me."

They were admitted to the hospital the night before their surgeries, on the same ward. Tim would go into the operating room at seven the next day to have his kidney removed, hopefully by the least invasive method, and Julie would go in about an hour later in the adjacent operating room to receive his kidney.

In the morning, Julie waited with her mom. Eight, nine, ten o'clock. By ten-thirty, Julie was frantic, and when a nurse finally came by for a routine check, Julie asked her what was going on with Tim.

"They've booked you in the same operating room. When he's done, you'll move into his room."

Julie struggled to calm herself, but she was terrified that things weren't going well for her cousin. They were taking far too long. Later, after it was all over, she would learn that Tim's doctors had hoped to remove his kidney with laparoscopic surgery, but because his stomach muscles were in the way—scar tissue, Tim says—the surgeon had to open him up and access the organ via a larger opening.

She recalled briefly waking up in the operating room, and then nothing until she was back on the ward. Tim recalled coming to in the operating room and feeling nothing, until a huge wave of abdominal pain hit him, accompanied by an immediate desire to pull in his knees to his chest. Tim stayed recovering in the hospital for a week, on morphine and IV fluids, unable to eat for six days while his abdominal cavity slowly deflated, its swelling due to the surgical procedure. He and Julie were on the same ward together, recovering, essentially forging an indestructible cousin bond. They left the same day.

Sharing a set of kidneys, their bond has grown even stronger than it was when they were growing up together, sharing holiday time as kids. In the tradition of organ donations, they have named their kidneys together. Tim's is Casey and Julie's is Finnegan, partly to honor Tim's Irish heritage, but mostly after two puppets from the children's television program, Mr. Dress Up, that they had both watched as kids.

## Giving up a part of one's self

Since the operation, Julie's life has been transformed. In Tim's living room, she spoke about her cousin fondly, with humor, honesty, and respect. At one point, she broke down, telling him, "I don't think you know how much this means to me. I keep a lot inside." Julie has always been tough and resilient, and she's always been private and protective about her disease. She didn't want anyone to view her as being sick. Tough like a dancer, she tended to compartmentalize her life. Dialysis, when she was on it, stayed where it belonged, at the clinic. The rest of the time, she was the head of a program at the ballet school, and a teacher. Few people know about her disease, and if they do, she mostly avoids talking with them about it. That's how she's always preferred things to be.

At one point in our conversation, Julie turned to Tim and asked him if his feet smelled. "My feet never smelled before you gave me Finnegan."

"Of course my feet don't smell," Tim said defensively. Then he chuckled. "There are stories about donated kidneys causing changes in the recipient's body, even eliciting old memories from the donor sometimes." He addressed Julie again. "If your mind wanders over to Hawaii 1987, don't go there."

This was the kind of thing that only close family could say to each other. It was clear that Julie had opened up. She'd hated when her father donated his kidney that first time. She was relieved when her mother and sister underwent testing and were both unsuitable matches. She didn't want to put her loved ones in jeopardy. The risks were too high. But things had changed. She had shared this huge experience with Tim, and had let the light in by sharing her burdens. Julie was still tough and independent, but now there was this bond that wouldn't ever go away, even if Finnegan couldn't go the distance.

Throughout our conversation, Tim's sense of wonder and curiosity was palpable. He was so calm about the whole thing, and he didn't seem to recognize how brave he was. He embodied caring for his cousin, one hundred percent.

"But Tim," I said, "wouldn't you call what you did altruistic? This takes a lot of courage. It must have been life-changing."

"Nothing at all has changed in my life," Tim responded abruptly. "The experience didn't change me. Rather, my perspective on life allowed this experience to happen. I was just lucky that this came at a time when I could do it so readily. This wasn't a sacrifice. I have my uncle Brian, Julie's father, as a role model. He was Julie's first kidney donor more than twenty years ago and he's still out there playing hockey, at sixty-nine years of age. Why anyone *wouldn't* do this is beyond me."

I nodded, full of admiration for Tim. Not everyone would give up a part of themselves in such a huge and permanent way. "But you gave up one of your kidneys. You underwent a serious operation."

"It's not altruism. It's just family," Tim told me.

This surgery is probably Julie's last chance. If Finnegan doesn't work, then she'll have to go back on dialysis for the rest of her life. But she is grateful for even the few dialysis-free months she has gained so far. No matter what, she has to take drugs continuously to prevent organ rejection, drugs that have bad side-effects. And because of her lupus disease, she suspects even the most perfect, ideal kidney match will slowly, over time, be rejected.

"None of that matters. I got a new life," Julie said. "I'm allowing for hope."

She won't let the disease define her. Instead she just deals with it. She focuses on the words around her wrist. Light. Health. Strength.

# PART III

# Cultivating Caring

I slept and dreamt that life was Joy.
I awoke and realized that life was Duty.
And then I went to work—and lo and behold I discovered that
Duty can be Joy.

Rabindranath Tagore, Indian Spiritual Leader

# Gratitude

It's not joy that makes us grateful. It's gratitude that makes us joyful.

Brother David Steindl-Rast

## Transforming impatience into love

I'm sitting having lunch with my good friend Dr. Peter Nieman, a person who inspires me every time we get together. Peter is the author of *Moving Forward: The Power of Consistent Choices in Everyday Life*. We have our usual lunch place, a hotel restaurant in northwest Calgary that's generally pretty quiet. But today is a family holiday, and it's full of families and kids running around like wild monsters. I think Peter can sense my irritation as I attempt to create a meaningful conversation amidst the chaos.

Peter has many qualities, but two in particular stand out. First, he brings gratitude with him wherever he goes. Peter is one of those people who inspires me and reminds me of all the good things that happen in my day-to-day life. Peter is also a pediatrician. He adores kids.

Detecting my irritability with these chaotic children, he announces unreservedly, "Isn't it wonderful that we have children around us that are enthused about life and spending time with their families! I mean, what's the alternative? Having them all drugged up to the point of being comatose? And isn't it amazing that we have been given the gift of a mind that has the capacity to process noise, so we can actually experience the miracle of sound?"

Peter stops me right in the middle of my irritated, judgmental, self-centered, non-caring tracks, and I smile. In one short statement of gratitude, Peter shifts my whole reality of the moment. Gratitude, with one small decision, has the power to transform annoyance into harmony, impatience into love, and indifference into caring. Gratitude bypasses right and wrong. It stops criticism, rage, and anger. Gratitude dissolves fear and heals a troubled heart.

Gratitude is one of the sweetest expressions of caring.

## A guy without legs

"Life is difficult," Scott Peck maintains in *The Road Less Traveled*. "It is a great truth because once we truly see this truth, we transcend it. Once we truly know that life is difficult ... then life is no longer difficult. Because once it is accepted, the fact that life is difficult no longer matters."

I'd arrived late for the first speech at the conference and was headed for a seat along the side of the crowded ballroom. I was the wrap-up speaker, so I knew I had plenty of time to sit through presentations during the day to get a good sense of the audience. Sitting off to the side of the assembled seats was a man with crutches at his side. I pulled up my chair next to him without speaking to him, not wanting to disturb any of the nearby audience members. I'd been hoping to make a connection with someone in the audience, but it wasn't until now that I realized that I was sitting beside a guy without legs. Now here was a conversation opener.

As I glanced over, he gave me a welcoming nod and a smile. I reached out and shook his hand. He had a warm, inviting presence. He was calm and relaxed. Inner peace seemed to surround him. I was certainly more drawn to this man's contented manner than to the CEO's opening remarks. We didn't look at each other after our initial greeting, but I enjoyed sitting next to him for the remainder of the opening address.

After the speech was over there was a break, and I turned and introduced myself to the man sitting beside me.

"I'm Paul Franklin," he replied, smiling.

"What happened to your legs?" I asked.

"Afghanistan."

"How can you be so happy and contented?"

"Gratitude. Every day is a new day, because in reality I should be dead."

As with most of us, there are a handful of important years that have defined Paul Franklin's life. He explained that 1999 was the year he found his life's work with the Canadian Forces. A year later, he welcomed his son Simon into the world. He completed his first marathon in 2005.

According to Paul, the best year of his life, however, was 2006—the year a suicide bomb ripped through his vehicle in Afghanistan, killing Canadian diplomat Glyn Berry, and seriously injuring two fellow soldiers. Paul nearly died that year. He lost both of his legs, and he fought anger, hatred, unbearable pain, and fear, but he now maintains that this horrific tragedy eventually led him to his life's purpose: to improve the lives of Canadian military and civilian amputees. Now, so many years later, Paul makes a point of spending time with his son and with friends, while ensuring his family is well cared for.

Paul Franklin reminds me of the saying, "I used to complain about having no shoes, until I met a man who had no feet." He also reminds me that to care enough about one's life and the people who care about us, to care enough to work through the anger and the injustice and the hurt, is to care enough to choose service and contribution over narcissistic self-pity.

This honorable veteran is an inspiration and a great illustration of what it means to be caring. You can read Paul's story in its entirety in the book *The Long Walk Home*.

## Being alive is a privilege

I once asked my mother Joyce, when she was in the final stages of her life, how she felt about dying. "I am so grateful to have had seventy-eight years of life! I have been blessed beyond belief to have this one precious experience. How can I possibly be upset about dying? What a privilege it was just to have been alive!"

"No matter what happens to you, remember to spend a little time each day in sincere gratitude. Don't ever fail to recognize the good things that happen in your life every day that the sun rises."

In *The Hiding Place*, Corrie Ten Boom tells of her involvement in the Dutch resistance during World War II, and how she managed to survive Hitler's concentration camps and afterward travel the world as a public speaker. "Every experience God gives us, every person He puts in our lives, is the perfect preparation for the future only He can see."

The practice of gratitude carried her through the years of torture and the death of her family members. At one point, she even practiced gratitude for the fleas, for they were a part of "all circumstances." She was a courageous woman who brought to life that precious perspective of seeking the gift in everything.

## Gratitude in exchange for anger and grief

An attitude of gratitude inspires. It was just after Christmas, and Lee was heading out with friends for her first ski of the season. En route, a large buck recklessly threw itself into the side of the car, causing her shoulder to slam against the door. Combined with significant whiplash, the impact yielded what doctors suspected was a spinal tear in Lee's upper back. The trauma resulted in the dura (the sack that surrounds the spinal cord and contains cerebral spinal fluid) to spring a leak.

For months afterward, she was unable to tolerate any exertion or upright position. She couldn't sit or stand. Being in any other position than horizontal caused her excruciating head and neck pain, due to low intracranial pressure that caused her brain to sag into her spine when she was upright. This put a squeeze on her brain stem and cerebellum. Erratically and spontaneously, her condition would stimulate a sympathetic, autonomic—otherwise known as "fight or flight"—response.

Her life became, in Lee's words, "a crazy race to do even small tasks, such as making lunch, before the pain would take me down. My head pain would escalate until I had to be horizontal again. At first, I would push to do more, but the more I pushed, the harder the pain took me out. I struggled with my inability to take on any activity, be it yoga, going out with friends, or unloading the dishwasher. I spent much of my time lying on the couch contemplating the ceiling, urging my body to maintain equilibrium."

Pain is a big motivator for change. Being conscious of the importance of adversity in her own human development, Lee eventually, after much anger, grief, fear, and depression, began to move the experience of pain into gratitude. She stopped fighting a battle she realized she would never win, and started watching and listening to the entire situation with a form of acceptance and appreciation.

"I made the decision that I would go for the ride, and let it play out with as much patience as I could. I found peace in the stillness amidst even the most excruciating pain. Time seemed to stand still. My everyday fears and stresses of managing the demands of the fast lane of life faded away and I became more present than I ever had been."

During the ten months of convalescing, mostly on her couch in a horizontal position, Lee faced many lessons. She learned to be grateful for and accept her anger, fears, and grief. She told me how this whole wounding and recovery experience was guiding her to discover and deepen her own healing gifts. During the journey she was led to explore biodynamic craniosacral therapy, a system of healing that had helped her so much, and for which she decided to take the two-year course to learn the art.

Lee is now learning to help others support their bodies to process old physical and psychological traumas. As she expressed to me recently, "I did not know the power of real caring before this experience of having my spine spring a leak. By learning to genuinely care for myself, I acquired new skills and strength to care for others in new ways. That's something I'm tremendously grateful for. This challenging experience has been one of my best teachers."

There's an old joke about a man who is sitting in a bar one night, drinking his problems away, and feeling sorry for himself.

"Why are you so miserable," the bartender asks him.

"My uncle died three months ago," the drunk replies.

"That's awful, but don't you think it's about time to get on with your life?"

"But you don't understand. He left me half a million dollars in his will."

"What are you so unhappy about?" asks the bartender.

"Well, my father died two months ago."

"I'm sorry. That is horrible. But drinking isn't going to help you get over it." replies the bartender.

"Yes, but he left me a million dollars in his will."

"What on earth do you have to be depressed about?"

"Nobody died this month."

So many of our problems reside not in the world but in our own minds. The joke also illustrates the high price of living without gratitude. This poor guy, like so many of us today, did not know what *enough* feels like.

## The fuel for healing

Several years ago, I co-facilitated a bereavement group for parents dealing with the death of a child. In our group was a woman whose daughter and husband were killed by a drunk driver fifteen years earlier. She knew a pain that I have never known.

What touched me during the months I worked with Emily was her amazing capacity, in spite of her inconceivable grief, to bring gratitude to her life every single day. She was grateful to be alive. She spoke of the marvelous fall colors in the trees that I had failed to notice. She spoke of the wet pavement. "Always make gratitude greater than your abundance, because you are always more abundant than you perceive yourself to be. Gratitude is the fuel required for healing," she told me.

This grateful heart that Emily radiated was genuine. Years of rage, tears, and torment merged into a grateful heart that was authentically hers. Out of her appreciation and gratitude for the blessings that she saw in her life came freedom. While grieving and healing are much larger than mere appreciation, gratitude is important fuel to take with you on the journey.

## Every disaster a potential blessing

There's a monument in Enterprise, Alabama that stands as a paradoxical tribute. It honors one of the worst agricultural scourges of the last century, the boll weevil. The plaque on the monument reads: "In profound appreciation of the Boll Weevil and what it has done as the herald of prosperity."

The explanation for this tribute is simple. Over a hundred years ago, the cotton fields in the region were devastated by boll weevils, and farmers there were forced to turn to peanut crops in order to survive. The next year, peanuts provided the area and its people with the greatest prosperity it had ever known.

An old Sufi story tells of a man whose son captured a strong, beautiful, wild horse. All his neighbors told the man how fortunate he was. The man patiently replied, *"Well ... maybe."* One day the horse threw the son, breaking the son's leg. All the neighbors told the man how cursed he was that his son had found the horse in the first place. Again, the man answered, *"Well ... maybe."* Soon after the son's leg was broken, soldiers came to the village and took away all the able-bodied young men, but the son was spared. When the man's neighbors told him how fortunate his son was to have a broken leg, the man would only reply, *"Well ... maybe."* At last, the people were no longer confused.

Every blessing is a potential disaster, and every disaster a potential blessing. We can never fully predict the fortunes, or misfortunes, that chaos and change may bring to our lives. Like the person who gets laid off and eventually discovers that this is the best thing that ever happened to them, there is always something more going on than we can know. Gratitude helps us step back and realize that there is a larger context in which our narrative is unfolding. Seeing our life as a greater story can fill us with renewed purpose and passion. Gratitude softens a heart that has become miserly and spoiled, and it nourishes the soil for caring to grow and flourish. When we see that everyone we meet and everything that happens to us brings lessons that are important, we become grateful for everyone and everything.

# A Caring Universe

I will love the light for it shows me the way, yet I will endure the darkness for it shows me the stars.

Og Mandino

## The power beyond

After Albert Einstein saw the needle of a compass at the age of four, he always understood that there was "something behind things, something deeply hidden."

My own experience of connecting with a power beyond my being was planted early in my life, growing up in a rural community in western Canada. Everywhere, I saw things growing. I witnessed the conception and birth of foals, lambs, and litters of puppies. I observed cultivated fields turn green in a matter of weeks. I saw tiny seeds I'd placed in the garden turn into plants. I remember as a child being filled with a sense of mystery, excitement, and awe. To this day I marvel at how a cut on my hand can heal without any effort on my part. With little more than that to conceptualize it, I experience a life force, an existence of something greater than myself. Connecting with this power has been a great source of strength and support in my life, as it has guided me and helped me in finding ways to help others.

While I was raised in a church that had well-defined, explicit, clear beliefs and teachings that sought to erase the mystery and provide clarity on the purpose of life, I have come to accept that uncertainty is an inescapable corollary of being alive. An abundance of mystery is not just part of the human experience; it is necessary on my faith journey. I don't lament this realization, and I have no expectation that this be true for anyone else. For me, accepting the essential mystery of existence is just preferable to the opposite: capitulating to an inflexible doctrine with its illusion of certainty.

My faith is emerging from a traditional way of thinking into what theologians would describe as moving away from a *transcendent* God and embracing the idea of an *immanent* one. Thus, I am growing away from a concept of a distant, invisible, and otherworldly God— to an experience of godliness that is present and working within me and within every aspect of my life, and within every other person.

My mother had a profound impact on my experience of spirituality and faith. Shortly before her death, she wrote of her love for the mystery, wonder, and miracle of life. "Every day is truly a miracle!" Joyce said.

"The word mystery means something secret, as if we see it with closed eyes. When we close our eyes, we draw on a deeper kind of sight. We see at a deeper level. We see something we have not seen before. We learn to trust that a new creative expression will come to us from within. It flows out of inner vision. As we go down into the darkness of the soul, we discover a darkness that offers unlimited possibility. We discover a faith in our own 'being' that is unnamed, undefined, unmanifest."

Joyce once shared an experience of discovering a cave on a journey she'd taken to Ireland some years before. "As I descended into its darkness, the sacred walked with me. A stillness, a holiness consumed the experience. Faint lights guided our path, but at one point, as we gathered in a circle, our guides extinguished the lights. We were in complete darkness."

"Only faith held me there in those few moments. I had never been in such dark, dark darkness. I surrendered to my faith and settled into the obscurity. I let my surrender have full range. And I was held. New energy and an overwhelming feeling of awe embraced me!

I experienced the untold beauty of darkness. I felt I was in the womb of the earth and I stepped into unlimited possibilities of new creations. It was one of the defining creative moments of my lifetime."

## A rescuing hug

At times, caring happens as a reflex. It isn't something we think about or "try" to do. It's an instinctive response of an open heart. Someone slips, our arm goes out. A pregnant woman struggles to stand in a crowded subway and we gladly give up our seat. The car in front of us is in an accident and we stop to help. A colleague at work is down and we let them know we care by taking a few moments in our busy day to simply listen. Babies will often begin to cry when they hear another baby cry nearby. This underscores the infant's innate ability to recognize emotional cues, to experience empathic contagion in their environment, even if the child is not able to fully comprehend the emotion. It all seems natural and appropriate. We live, and caring is a part of who we are.

Expressing our innate generosity, caring naturally for one another, we sometimes glimpse an essential quality of our being. We may be sitting alone, lost in self-pity, feeling sorry for ourselves, when the phone rings with a call from a friend who is *really* depressed. Instinctively, we come out of ourselves and are there for another. It doesn't matter so much what is said, but when a little comfort is shared, we put the phone down and feel a little more at home with ourselves. We're reminded of who we really are and what we can offer one another.

Caring is everywhere if we open our eyes to be a part of it. Caring seems to come not so much *from* us as *through* us. In 1995, a photo appeared in *Life* magazine with the caption "The Rescuing Hug" and featured premature identical twins, Kyrie and Brielle Jackson. Kyrie had wrapped her tiny arm around her sister Brielle, whose breathing and heart function were weak and failing.

This caring moment heralded a change in how hospitals manage premature twin and triplet care. The usual protocol was to place all babies, even twins and triplets, inside their own separate incubator. It was the twins' nurse Gayle Kasparian who used her caring instincts and brought the two sisters together—a desperate move, she admits, that went against hospital rules.

"When I put Brielle in with her sister, it was amazing. She immediately calmed down. Her heart rate stabilized and her color changed." Over twenty years later, the Jackson sisters are grown up and attending college. They remain close and still share a bedroom, albeit not an incubator. As their dad Paul says, "They're each other's best friend."

Caring fosters caring. Learning to be caring is really simply awakening what's inside and around us.

## The unexplainable life force

"I was in about forty feet of water, alone. I knew I should not have gone alone, but I was very competent and just took a chance. There was not much current, and the water was so warm and clear and enticing. But when I got a cramp, I realized at once how foolish I was. I was not very alarmed, but was completely doubled up with a stomach cramp. I tried to remove my weight belt, but I was so doubled up I could not get to the catch. I was sinking and began to feel more frightened, unable to move. I could see my watch and knew that there was only a little more time on the tank before I would be finished with breathing!"

Ram Dass and Paul Gorman open their inspirational book *How Can I Help? Stories and Reflections on Service* with this story about natural compassion, a tale that illustrates the universe's inherent caring nature.

"I tried to massage my abdomen. I wasn't wearing a wet suit, but I couldn't straighten out and couldn't get to the cramped muscles with my hands. I thought, 'I can't go like this! I have things to do!' I just couldn't die anonymously this way, with no one to even know what happened to me. I called out in my mind, 'Somebody, something, help me!'"

"I was not prepared for what happened. Suddenly I felt a prodding from behind me under the armpit. I thought, 'Oh no, sharks!' I felt real terror and despair. But my arm was being lifted forcibly.

Around into my field of vision came an eye—the most marvelous eye I could ever imagine. I swear it was smiling. It was the eye of a big dolphin. Looking into that eye, I knew I was safe."

"It moved farther forward, nudging under, and hooked its dorsal fin under my armpit with my arm over its back. I relaxed, hugging it, flooded with relief. I felt that the animal was conveying security to me, that it was healing me as well as lifting me toward the surface. My stomach cramp went away as we ascended, and I relaxed with security, but I felt very strongly that it healed me too. At the surface, it drew me all the way in to shore. It took me into water so shallow that I began to be concerned for it, that it would be beached, and I pushed it back a little deeper, where it waited, watching me, I guess to see if I was all right."

At times, caring comes through us, expressed as the divine life within us, and we are ourselves the vehicle. It's difficult to remain faithless when we become joined with a power greater than ourselves. Caring is not something we do, or even something that is done for us. It's something unexplainable we are a part of.

## The power that grows our fingernails

"The art of medicine consists of amusing the patient while nature cures the disease," wrote Voltaire. My good brother, who practiced medicine for almost four decades, once told me, "In all my years as a doctor, one thing I could never do is cure anyone. I could set a broken bone. I've put in stitches. I can make a diagnosis. I can prescribe antibiotics when the body needs some help. I can care. But what I can't do is cure. Curing is beyond any conscious act. The body will take care of itself if it's able to."

Hal is not a religious person. From the time he was about sixteen, he never went to church—at least not "religiously." If I pushed my brother hard enough on where he stood in any philosophical or theological stance, he'd call himself a humanist. But that is about as far as I would get with him. I'd say what Hal understands is that there is a power beyond oneself, and beyond any human understanding and rational comprehension, that is at play in the work of a physician.

It's the same power that grows our fingernails when we sleep, heals a cut on the back of our hand as we go about our day, grows a plant toward the light, gives birth to new life, and sends a dolphin to save a diver. This power, of course, goes beyond healing. It's about trusting the natural life force that animates all living things to bring the fullest expression of life to the world.

Accessing the power of this unexplainable life force in the work of caring comes through faith. Faith is not the same as hope. Hope waits. Faith, on the other hand, trusts, claiming strength through a decision to let go. Caring, without some kind of faith or access to the universal healing presence, becomes burdensome and exhausting. But when we remember to trust—whether it's conscious or not—caring inevitably brings us joy.

How each person defines or conceptualizes this power beyond ourselves is less important than tapping into it in our own unique way, particularly in the work of caring.

## Spiritual beings

When I pause after a busy day and reflect upon the incomprehensible depth of space above me on a dark starlit night, or stop and feel the magnificence of a simple flower, or begin the day by listening carefully to the silence of early morning just before dawn, something within me reverberates with the recognition of an unseen and indescribable power. When I tap into this power that evolves every living thing toward wholeness, I find caring becomes natural and flows more fluently through me. I see the world, in the words of the late W. Clement Stone, as an "inverse paranoid."

Stone grew up in poverty on the south side of Chicago and, by age six, was out on the streets hawking newspapers to help out his widowed mother. In time, he would become a billionaire, an inspirational author, and a philanthropist—and he would live to be a hundred. As author Jack Canfield writes, "Instead of believing the world was plotting to do him harm, [Stone] actually chose to believe the world was always plotting to do him good. So, instead of seeing every difficult or challenging event as negative, he saw it for what it could be—something that was meant to enrich him, empower him, or advance his causes."

Pierre Teilhard de Chardin, the French philosopher and Jesuit priest, said we are spiritual beings who face a human experience, and not the other way around—human beings experiencing the spiritual. In this light, caring can be a reconnection with the divine as we reach out to help others.

Exhaustion and caring fatigue can be indicators that we have disconnected from this natural flow of life, and are trying too hard and wearing ourselves out, rather than trusting in the power beyond us. No matter how much rest we take in our work of caring, we won't recover from caring fatigue until we can tap into a power that is there to help us. Relaxation, serenity, and ease in the caring process come from a deep sense of the fundamental good of the universe. Rather than trying to *make* caring happen, it's about releasing the constraints to the caring that is already there. Caring is not something you "do." Caring is something you are a part of. When I remember this, caring is far less tiring and far more enjoyable.

## Suffering

"But how," I can hear many of you say, "can I see this compassionate universe when there is so much abuse, pain, illness, and death that surround me?"

In part, having a faith journey means stepping back far enough to be able to place suffering in a wider context. The abused woman who suffers and arises as a stronger person when she musters the courage and strength to get out of that relationship? The many recovering alcoholics who have told me that, without their alcoholism, they would never have become the person they are today? Their journeys into recovery have made them so much stronger and better people. Without problems, how would we possibly learn and grow and evolve?

Having faith—both in the caring process and whatever is beyond— is a decision. It is a decision to believe in an unseen power, to embrace uncertainty, and to reach for caring in the midst of pain.

Besides, without illness, there would be a lot of unemployed health care professionals. Without broken-down cars, how many mechanics would have nowhere to express their unique talents and gifts? How would we learn to care without someone to care about? If we come to believe that the tragedies of the world are caused by an uncaring universe, think for a moment of the alternative. What would the world be like without pain, death, and what we have come to call tragedies? It seems, whether we judge things harshly or like and approve of them, the world seems designed exactly the way it is supposed to be.

Take a moment to fill in the rest of this line. "Because I have suffered I am able to ..."

People tell me when I ask them this question, and after they reflect upon it long enough, "Because I have suffered I am able to empathize and care about others more deeply." Or they say, "Because I have suffered I began a spiritual journey." "Because I have suffered I can appreciate my life with more gratitude." "Because I have suffered—and come through it at the other end—I am able to offer the strength and hope of my experience." The list goes on.

However we define or conceive of it, our faith partnership with the divine can help us relax and *allow* caring to happen, rather than working so hard to *make* it happen. No plant I have had has ever grown better because I demanded that it do so, or because I threatened it. Plants grow only when they have the right conditions and are given the proper care. Finding the right place and the proper nourishment for plants—and people as well—is a matter of continual enquiry and attentiveness. The universe is conspiring to help us. As my mother used to say, "Whenever you set a goal, there is an unseen force, an energy that moves you toward that goal."

## Ubuntu

An anthropologist once proposed a game to the children in an African tribe. He put a basket of fruit near a tree and told the kids that whomever got there first would win the sweet fruits. When he said "go," they all took each other's hands and ran together, then sat in a circle enjoying their treats. When he asked the children why they did it this way, when they could have had all the fruits for themselves if they got there first, they said: "UBUNTU! How can one of us be happy if all the other ones are sad?"

Ubuntu, an ethical value that originated with the Bantu peoples of Africa, has been upheld by African societies for centuries. It is a belief in a universal bond of sharing and respect that connects all of humanity. Ubuntu emphasizes our connectedness to each other in the past, present, and future, what we can be for each other, and how we belong to each other. It is a short version of the Zulu phrase, "Umuntu ngumuntu ngamantu," which roughly translates as: a person is a person because of other persons. I am what I am because of who we all are. My humanity is tied to yours, and we depend on each other for our wellbeing. I am because *we* are.

Ubuntu teaches us that it is only through others that we become fully human. It illustrates this principle of caring for each other's wellbeing in a spirit of mutual support—and that a person cannot be complete unto themselves. If one group within society is denied its full humanity, then no individual in that society can fully realize their own humanity. "We are all human beings and no human being is more human than any other," says humanitarian and retired general Roméo Dallaire.

Atrocities that have scarred the human race in recent history, such as the Holocaust in Europe, the genocide in Rwanda, or the civil war in Syria, remind us that as a global community we still have a long way to go to incorporate the value of Ubuntu. And you don't have to see a world news report to experience the absence of Ubuntu. Even in our own communities we experience inhumanities and cruelty toward other human beings. Caring means wanting to make a difference, realizing that a lack of Ubuntu anywhere in the world is a lack of Ubuntu everywhere in the world. Ubuntu, by its very nature, reminds us of the global community in which we reside. Everything affects everything.

Who cares? How do you make a difference? How can each of us bring Ubuntu into our day-to-day lives? For some, it is to act globally, to join international peace-keeping or military initiatives. For others it is to take action politically and to work to change the international governmental systems. For some, like my niece, Lauryn Oates, caring is about removing barriers to education for women and children in Afghanistan and other developing countries.

## Living Ubuntu everyday

Ubuntu can be brought to everyday living through self-awareness, self-acceptance, self-responsibility, and the courage to bring light into the darkness. We are made to pick ourselves up and bring goodness to the world.

> **Be self-aware.** When the seventy-five member Stanford Graduate School of Business Advisory Council were asked to recommend the most important capability for leaders to develop, their answer was nearly unanimous: self-awareness. Without self-awareness, it's difficult to regulate your emotions or avoid impulsive outbursts when you feel threatened or rejected. Without self-awareness, it is not easy to see that your judgment or hostility toward others stems from fear, self-doubt, insecurity, or shame that you experienced at an earlier time in your life. If you were abused by an adult at five years old and did not have a safe place to heal from it, the pain becomes subconscious and is directed toward others. This is where bullying on the playground and in our corporate offices originates.
>
> Hostility and discrimination toward others is generally about hostility, abuse, shame, or trauma that you've had in your own life. Unless you become aware of it, you not only cannot change it, you likely don't even know when it's happening. Most people who are prejudiced or abusive toward others have no idea what impact their behavior has on others, much less why it is happening and what to do about it.
>
> "Great leaders make it look easy," write researchers Ginka Toegel and Jean-Louis Barsoux. "But in truth, the majority of effective leaders that we have observed … have worked

hard on themselves." We all have blind spots to some degree or another, facets of our personalities that make our actions toward others invisible to us. Some of us are more self-aware than others, but few can see the world as it sees us. It takes honest effort to solicit feedback from people who will be honest with us.

This is where coaching, mentoring, counseling, or a recovery or support group can be extremely beneficial, and even necessary. Self-awareness, an understanding of how your behavior affects yourself and others, starts with being open to hear how the people around you view your actions. Clinging to an outmoded view of reality is destructive. Ubuntu becomes possible with self-awareness: a willing, honest, thorough appraisal of yourself.

**Be okay with yourself.** Without self-acceptance, a basic respect for who you are, it is easy to get caught up in chasing external symbols of success rather than being the person you are meant to be. More than that, a lack of self-respect erodes Ubuntu. How can you possibly respect and be okay with others, if you don't have a fundamental sense that you are okay with yourself?

So many caring people, myself included, will take all that shame and judgment directed toward us as children, and internalize it as hostility toward ourselves. Just as the bully on the school ground who is being abused by his father, or the chauvinist in the boardroom who was shamed by his mother, we can abuse ourselves with thoughts of self-judgment and hatred when we don't meet inhuman standards of perfectionism.

Your ability to care for and respect others, your ability to practice Ubuntu, has a direct correlation with your ability to be compassionate and non-judgmental toward yourself. Self-honesty and courage to trace the origins of prejudice, judgment, and hostility toward others contributes to your wellbeing. Integrity, as defined by Henry Cloud, is the "courage to meet the demands of reality." Integrity is the value you place on yourself that has resulted from your actions. When you are no longer owned by unconscious scripts and outdated beliefs that at one time may have helped you survive, you earn yourself a good dose of self-respect. This kind of self-respect is the ultimate source of Ubuntu.

The late Virginia Satir, recognized by many as the pioneer of family therapy, taught me, in a month-long retreat in the early 1980s, the role that self-acceptance plays in the role of respecting others' humanity as your own—and in so doing, becoming "more fully human." Virginia introduced me to what she called "survival myths." These are what you did to survive, say, as a ten-year-old. For instance, you may have learned to withdraw in the face of your parents' rages, internalizing the anger and not speaking up for fear of further abuse. This was necessary then to survive. Forty years later, it is important to realize that, when faced with an abusive boss, you can rewrite the script and find a different way to respond. You are no longer ten years old, and your boss is not your parent. These survival myths are destructive and limiting when you don't pinpoint and create a renewed perception of reality as you step into the new context of being an adult.

Virginia keenly observed that many people learn to deny certain senses in their childhoods, thus limiting their capacity to appreciate, accept themselves, and respond as adults. Noting the significant role that our senses play in our survival, she devised the following "five freedoms" to help us connect to ourselves and attain greater self-acceptance:

- The freedom to see and hear what is here, instead of what *should* be, was, or will be.
- The freedom to say what we feel and think, instead of what we *should* feel and think.

- The freedom to feel what we feel, instead of what we *ought* to feel.
- The freedom to ask for what we want, instead of always waiting for permission.
- The freedom to take risks on our own behalf, instead of choosing to be only secure and not rock the boat.

These five freedoms, Virginia felt, not only help us accept ourselves, but also our own uniqueness, and enable us to take risks and be vulnerable; in other words, to respect ourselves and, in so doing, become more open and caring toward others.

**Be self-responsible.** Being open to others means being able to step back and change, if necessary. Anwar Sadat, the former president of Egypt, "had been reared, nurtured, and deeply scripted in a hatred for Israel. 'I will never shake the hand of an Israeli as long as they occupy one inch of Arab soil. Never, never, never!' And huge crowds all around the country would chant, 'Never, never, never!' " writes Stephen R. Covey. "[Sadat] marshaled the energy and unified the will of the whole country with that script."

While his script was patriotic and roused unity and strong emotions in the citizens of Egypt, it was also unwise and destructive. "It ignored the perilous, highly interdependent reality of the situation." It also demonstrated a lack of Ubuntu.

When Sadat saw the foolishness of his words, he "re-scripted himself." As a young man, he'd been confined in a solitary cell in Cairo Central Prison, and had there gained a deeper awareness of himself. Learning to meditate, he re-scripted his view of reality and began to question the country's divisiveness he'd been raised to believe in. Years later, when Anwar Sadat became president of Egypt, he was able to confront the new political realities and begin to mend fences with Israel. When he visited the Knesset—the legislative branch of the Israeli government in Jerusalem—he pried open a peace movement between Egypt and Israel, a move that would eventually lead to the Camp David Accord.

Mark Twain once said, "We should be careful to get out of an experience only the wisdom that is in it, and stop there lest we be like the cat that sits down on a hot stove lid. She will never sit down on a hot stove lid again and that is well, but also she will never sit down on a cold one anymore!" Human beings are the only species that have the capacity to step back, observe themselves, and make changes in the courses of their lives. Responses that helped us survive as children, but then become unconscious, destructive adult scripts and patterns, can be changed. The same wall that keeps out our pain also keeps out the sunlight of an enriched life. Allowing our hearts to open, to be touched by human experience, is transformational. Political walls come down as the walls within us come down.

If you change the way you look at things, the things you look at will change. Self-awareness and self-acceptance are only the beginning. Self-responsibility means taking necessary action to stop destructive patterns you inflict on yourself and those around you. It takes strength, honesty, and courage to know when and how to apologize.

**Pick yourself up.** "I was told the story of a pregnant Rwandan mother of six whose village was destroyed by a massacre," wrote my teacher Meg Wheatley. "She was shot first, buried under the bodies of each of her six slain children, and left for dead. She dug herself out, buried her children, bore her new child, and, soon thereafter, chose to adopt five children whose parents had been killed in the same massacre. She expressed her belief that her life had been spared so that she might care for these orphaned children after losing her own ... This young African mother teaches me what it means to have a vocation to be fully human." Sometimes the way we change the world is by picking ourselves up and doing what's in front of us.

Ubuntu is about each of us, one person at a time, consciously and courageously opening our hearts and our humanness to each other—through courage and caring. It starts at home. There is plenty of work to do in our own backyards. Within our own communities, we've all witnessed an absence of Ubuntu: violence, misuse of authority, racism, abuse, bullying. Be part of the cure, rather than part of the disease. Keep progressing into a better life.

— ~ —

"The pupils and disciples of a Hasidic rabbi approached their spiritual leader with a complaint about the prevalence of evil in the world," wrote William B. Silverman, author and former rabbi of Temple Ohabai Sholom in Nashville, Tennessee. "Intent upon driving out the forces of darkness, they requested the rabbi to counsel them."

"The rabbi suggested that they take brooms and attempt to sweep the darkness from a cellar. The bewildered disciples applied themselves to sweeping out the darkness, but to no avail. The rabbi then advised his followers to take sticks and to beat vigorously at the darkness to drive out the evil. When this likewise failed, he counseled them to go down again into the cellar and to protest against the darkness and to shout imprecations to drive out the evil. When this, too, failed, he said: 'My children, let each of you meet the challenge of darkness by lighting a candle.' The disciples descended to the cellar and kindled their lights. They looked, and behold! The darkness had been driven out."

There is a Greek word, politeia, which when translated means "your highest sense of purpose for others." I interpret politeia as the realization that while we may not be capable of curing the world of its suffering and sorrow, what we can do is find a way to bring our own wellbeing to the world. Francis Bernadone, referred to often as St. Francis of Assisi, perhaps the most universally loved of Christian saints, had to face his own demons. From his pain emerged a prayer that expressed what he would wish to become, his own form of politeia:

> Lord, make me an instrument of thy peace. Where there is hatred, let me sow love. Where there is injury, pardon. Where there is doubt, faith. Where there is despair, hope. Where there is darkness, light. Where there is sadness, joy. Lord, grant that I may not so much seek to be consoled as to console, to be understood as to understand, to be loved as to love. For it is in giving that we receive. It is in pardoning that we are pardoned. It is in dying to self that we are born to eternal life.

The remedy for absence is presence. Evil is an absence and, as such, it cannot be healed with an absence. By hating evil, or by hating someone who is engaged in evil, we contribute to the absence of light and not its presence. Hatred begets hatred. What we do to others, others will do to us. That's called karma.

The answer to an inhumane world begins with inner peace and the courage to open our hearts. In spite of the setbacks of war, hate, and greed, the world is sure to get better when we open our hearts. There is a First Nations saying that goes, "What we do not listen to, we do not understand. What we do not understand, we fear. What we fear, we seek to destroy."

# Forgiveness

As I walked out the door toward the gate that would lead to my freedom, I knew that if I didn't leave my bitterness and hatred behind, I'd still be in prison.

Nelson Mandela

## Transforming hate into caring

Jack Kornfield, a Buddhist teacher, recounts the following true story he heard from the director of a rehabilitation program for juvenile offenders, many of whom were gang members who had committed homicide.

"One fourteen-year-old boy in the program had shot and killed an innocent teenager to prove himself to his gang. At the trial, the victim's mother sat impassively silent until the end, when the youth was convicted of the killing. After the verdict was announced, she stood up slowly and stared directly at him and stated, 'I'm going to kill you.' Then the youth was taken away to serve several years in the juvenile facility."

"After the first half-year the mother of the slain child went to visit his killer. He had been living on the streets before the killing, and she was the only visitor [in jail] he'd had. For a time they talked, and when she left she gave him some money for cigarettes. Then she started step by step to visit him more regularly, bringing food and small gifts. Near the end of his three-year sentence, she asked him what he would be doing when he got out. He was confused and very uncertain, so she offered to help set him up with a job at a friend's company. Then she inquired about where he would live, and since he had no family to return to, she offered him temporary use of the spare room in her home."

"For eight months he lived there, ate her food, and worked at the job. Then one evening she called him into the living room to talk. She sat down opposite him and waited. Then she started, 'Do you remember in the courtroom when I said I was going to kill you?' 'I sure do,' he replied. 'I'll never forget that moment.' 'Well, I wanted to,' she went on. 'I did not want the boy who could kill my son for no reason to remain alive on this earth. I wanted him to die. That's why I started to visit you and bring you things. That's why I got you the job and let you live here in my house. That's how I set about changing you. And that old boy, he's gone. So now I want to ask you, since my son is gone, and that killer is gone, if you'll stay here. I've got room, and I'd like to adopt you if you let me.'"

"And she became the mother he never had."

## Cultivating forgiveness

Dale Lang became a hot air balloon pilot in 1974, and for the next ten years, he ran his own full-time balloon business out of Calgary, Alberta. Dale won the first Canadian National Hot Air Balloon Championship in 1979, and the next year, he went on to co-pilot the first balloon to cross over the North Pole.

Over the years, he changed careers, had a family, and moved to Taber, Alberta, an agricultural town about three hours east of Calgary. On April 28, 1999, the family's life was shattered. Dale's seventeen-year-old Jason was shot dead by a fourteen-year-old boy in the hallway of the Taber high school he attended.

How does a person respond to such an unimaginable tragedy such as this? How could a father not become embittered and poisoned with resentment? Instead of becoming cynical and defeated, Dale Lang chose to respond to his son's death by forgiving, and by making it his life's work to ensure that Jason's life and death made a lasting difference to all Canadians.

Forgiveness did not come easily to Dale. Over the years, he's frequently spoken with brutal honesty about his initial anguish, bitterness, and anger. He attributes his deep and sustaining faith and the grace of God in his life for being able to forgive. "Forgiveness," he will tell you, "was the only response that I could give."

Dale's message, both in his book *Jason Has Been Shot!* and in his presentations to high school students, teachers, business leaders, and spiritual communities across the country, is about making forgiveness a priority, stopping the violence of bullying, and treasuring our teenagers.

Jason Lang was in many ways a typical teen, according to his dad. He enjoyed sports and had bought his first car—a 1983 Camaro—three days before he died. The morning of Jason's death, his father Dale had helped him learn how to pilot the five-speed Camaro.

"On the last day of Jason's life, he and I were the best of friends," said Mr. Lang. "I hope you understand how thankful I am that April 28, 1999 was not a day we argued."

Dale Lang's example of forgiveness in the face of unimaginable tragedy inspires love, hope, and healing in everyone he comes in contact with. Being around Dale, like being around anyone with a forgiving heart, makes you a better person. Our family has been personally touched by his amazing example of forgiveness. Our daughter, as a university student, was twice a recipient of a scholarship set up by the Lang family in Jason's name.

Dale's life and his message prove that love is stronger than hate, and forgiveness is stronger than revenge.

While these two stories present us head on with heavy issues, we also realize that forgiveness is more than the big stuff. Sure, if someone murders someone you love, you will wrestle with the issue of forgiveness. But what about when someone offends you, steals your ideas, or takes credit for something when you know you did all the work? What if a business partner burns you? What if someone breaks into your vehicle in broad daylight and steals your briefcase? What if you find out your spouse has been having an affair? And, if you really want to learn how to forgive, what about the guy who cuts in front of you in the line at the grocery store? Life never seems to stop creating opportunities for us to grapple with what it means to forgive.

## Doorways into forgiveness

"Without forgiveness, there is no future," said Archbishop Desmond Tutu. So just what does it mean to forgive? Here are some of my thoughts:

**It takes courage.** "Forgiveness," writes George Vaillant, "is not some bleeding-heart, Sunday school platitude." Forgiveness is having the courage to honestly face the emotions that come from being unjustly injured, and then *letting go* of the right to be resentful. It takes maturity be able to bear an injustice without wanting to get even. Forgiveness does not abdicate the importance of justice; rather it removes revenge from the justice process. Forgiveness transforms vengeance into freedom.

**Anger is different from resentment.** Anger is the initial response to a person who injures us. Resentment—whether directed toward another or ourselves—is the result of not letting go of that anger. When bitten by a poisonous snake, it isn't the bite that kills; it's the poison. Nelson Mandela, who had many reasons to not forgive, yet had the courage to let go, was said to have spoken these words: "Resentment is like drinking poison and hoping it will kill your enemies."

**Give it time.** You can't rush forgiveness. Forgiveness is personal. It must come from within you. Forgiveness is being willing to let go of anger to prevent it from turning into the poison of resentment.

Several years ago, I had a secretary who embezzled several thousand dollars from my company. Filled with shock and anger, I know how difficult it can be to forgive. While she was charged and eventually spent time in jail, I never saw the money again. At the time, I wished the justice system had handed her more punishment. But even if it had, I still wouldn't have had any of my money returned. While forgiveness requires time, with consciousness and courage, along with support and perspective, you can expedite the process.

**Forgiveness is a decision.** Forgiveness is not an event. Forgiveness is a process. At least four important decisions surround the process of forgiving:

- The decision to let go of the right to be resentful toward another who has unjustly injured you. The question that surrounds forgiveness is: "Do you want to be right or do you want to be at peace?"
- The decision to accept the apologies you never get. Let go of the attitude that you are entitled to a life that is fair. Freedom comes from letting go of the notion that you deserve something just because you want it.
- The decision to make an effort to understand the world through the perspective of the person who has hurt you. Empathizing doesn't excuse the perpetrator. It means instead, to care enough to seek to understand the humanity underneath an act of destruction. And even if you are unable to find it in another, empathy opens the door to the humanity in *you.*
- The decision to step forward into a life with self-respect. When you decide to let go, you manifest one of the most evolved skills of homo sapiens: the capacity to envision the future.

**It's about freedom, not erasing grief.** Forgiveness does not eliminate grieving, nor does it eradicate the pain. It opens the door to your freedom.

Some time ago, I counseled a woman who had suffered years of sexual abuse from her father. Anguish, bitterness, and hatred had built up for some time before our first session, and most of these emotions, sadly, were directed at herself. The woman's healing process began when she started to direct her rage toward her perpetrator. She was able to see that her father be brought to justice for his wrongdoing. Even though the legal system did not punish him to the degree that she felt he deserved, she knew that she had done all she could, and that at some point she had to choose to let it go and move forward in her life. She recognized that the resentment and anger she had held onto so tightly was making her sick. It was from this woman I learned that forgiveness won't eliminate grief, take away pain, or bring justice. "What I need," she said confidently to me one day, "is to find freedom. And right now, the bitterness is holding me hostage. It's time to take back my freedom."

Forgiveness, the decision to let go of the resentment both toward herself and her father, didn't bring her childhood back. It didn't end the grief. It didn't take away the past pain. What it did do was bring an end to the bitterness, make room for acceptance, plant a seed of love amidst the anguish, and open a door for a new adulthood. At one point, this courageous woman expressed how the experience had made her a better person. Gratitude became a big part of her healing and forgiveness journey as she began discovering her gifts of compassion, healing presence, and a courage that emerged from her wounds.

"I'm strangely grateful for this whole experience," she said to me, after years of anguish. "It's given me what I needed, even though it wasn't what I wanted. I would never be who I am today were it not for the suffering and healing path I traveled." A decision to forgive and let go was the key that unlocked her prison of hatred. Mark Twain said it this way: "Forgiveness is the fragrance that the violet sheds on the heel that has crushed it."

**The person forgiving is the one freed.** An absence of forgiveness destroys the unforgiving person more than the person they might forgive. Unexpectedly and paradoxically, peace of mind comes more from the one who forgives than the one being forgiven.

Forgiveness is one of the most courageous and precious acts of caring. So ... how do you know if you have forgiven a person? Forgiveness doesn't mean that you are obliged to befriend the person you are forgiving. You don't have to like them or in any way condone what they did. Forgiveness merely means that, if you were to meet this person on the street, you could look them in the eye without any diminishment of respect for yourself or for them.

You have forgiven if you've made a decision to no longer allow the person who has harmed you to take away your freedom by turning you into a bitter person.

# Your Fundamental Purpose

Believe in your heart of hearts that your fundamental purpose, your reason for being, is to enlarge the lives of others. As you enlarge the lives of others, your life will be enlarged. And all the other things we have been taught to concentrate on will take care of themselves.

Pete Thigpen, Former President of Levi Strauss

## Your unique personal contribution

Recently, I led a three-day leadership development program with a long-term client, Marilyn, and her team of managers who run a successful grocery business. The first day, I arrived an hour early to set up, and was eagerly met by Dwayne, the Vice President of Information Technology, who already had the audiovisual equipment all ready for me. In the process of getting organized, we discovered that I didn't have the right adapter for his television screen. Accountable and enthused, Dwayne sped off across town to get what I needed. He was obviously motivated, passionate, service minded, and wholeheartedly engaged.

I asked a long-time executive team member what he felt led to his colleague's passion for his job. Dwayne's story is a fascinating one. It turns out he had worked for fifteen years on the floor, stocking shelves, before he joined the senior executive team. While his work on the floor was up to par, he was unmotivated, unhappy, and pretty miserable to be around. He used up every sick day he had available, he came in not a minute early and went home not a minute after his shift, and he didn't really talk or interact with anyone. He was a classic, disengaged employee. He was, in fact, on the verge of being fired because of his attitude when the new general manager arrived three years ago.

How does an unhappy employee get from the shop floor to the executive suite in three years?

Good leadership is the answer. Marilyn, the new GM, took the first several months of her tenure to wander around, listen to people, and make a personal connection with everyone on the floor. She saw potential in this disengaged employee. Marilyn saw something that perhaps he couldn't even see in himself. She found out that Dwayne was a leader in his home community, and she started to wonder why she couldn't bring that capacity out in his work. She thought he had good ideas and asked him if he would be interested in taking on the role of shop steward. She then worked with the union to make this happen.

Dwayne thrived in his role. And as a result of more conversations, it was soon discovered that he also played in a band, and he had unique computer and technical abilities. Informally, he took on the role of the organizational "techie" and before long was promoted to VP of IT. The more responsibilities Dwayne was given, the more he excelled. Now he is one of the principal leaders in a $125 million operation. In the last three years, he has never been off work sick. He comes in early and stays late, and is one of the most positive employees in the company.

Talk with the employees of any company, and you will soon discover if they work in a caring organization and what type of CEO is at the helm. Leaders who care are leaders who enlarge the lives of others. They care enough to listen. They care to take the time, and will disconnect from their computers to connect with people. They understand that emails are a very limited way of building a culture. They care enough to learn people's names and to find out what their talents and passions are. They come to discover that everyone is talented, original, and has something to offer.

Everyone wants to make a contribution—so find the right niche for them.

## Enlarging the lives of others

Not long ago, I had the good fortune to tour the plant of a client who hired me to help improve the culture of his organization.

As we wandered around, the CEO introduced me to everyone we came across—in the halls, the offices, the labs, and on the shop floors. But he didn't just know everyone's name and title. He made a point, whenever possible and appropriate, of making a brief—and positive—comment about everyone. When he introduced me to the janitor, he told me how this caretaker puts pride into everything he does and that he'll be greatly missed when he retires, after more than a quarter century of service. Every employee smiled as they were introduced and the CEO said something positive about the unique contribution each has made to the wellbeing of the company.

Later that day, while I was interviewing a small group of employees, I asked them to describe their work culture. A scientist who worked in one of the labs spoke first. "It's a culture of high standards and accountability, with the expectation of results," she said. "I am inspired here to bring excellence and pride to everything I do."

There was a pause as she took a moment to gather her thoughts. "But there is something else, something subtler. Something more powerful. Something more important ... The CEO here sets a tone. He isn't just dedicated to the financial wellbeing of the company. He is also committed to the personal wellbeing of every employee. He doesn't just make you want to be a better employee. He makes you want to be a better person."

This CEO understood that a fundamental responsibility of leaders is to enlarge the lives of every employee. People who work for him will tell you that they don't work *for* him; they work *with* him. He attracts people who want to be better people. People want to be around him because the relationship he fosters brings out the best in them. It makes them want to be and do all that they are capable of. When you think about it, the real work of leaders is how they make people feel about themselves. This is what sustains results—beyond the next quarterly financial report.

Caring leaders, leaders who enlarge the lives of others never stop believing in people. How can we know what people are capable of unless we stop, at least periodically, and quit "managing" them and start unleashing their potential? Good leadership is about seeing in others what they cannot see within themselves. Enlarging others is not about perfection or creating an illusion of perfection; it's about imperfectly earning the trust of others through the power of caring.

As a caring leader, you can enlarge the lives of others in these ways:

**Have a sense of your own purpose.** When you show a personal commitment to make the world around you a better place, it uplifts people.

**View leadership as being about presence, not position.** Don't depend on your title to make you a leader. Choose service over self-interest so your work is about helping and supporting people to get what they need. You aren't a leader until you have earned the right to be called a leader by those you serve.

**Care enough to listen.** Care enough to take the time. Disconnect from your computer or cell phone to connect with people. Understand that emails are a very limited way to build a culture. Care enough to learn people's names and to find out what their talents and passions are. Discover that everyone is talented, original, and has something to offer, and everyone wants to make a contribution—if they can find the right niche.

**Live the values that you espouse.** It isn't just about *what* needs to be done; it's also about *how* it needs to be done. Take time to clearly and meaningfully define the culture with a set of values and principles—and hold yourself accountable for living in alignment with these values. Tell stories and celebrate successes. Be receptive to learning. While you can't motivate anyone if they don't want to be motivated, what you *can* do is create a climate where people shine. Focus on people's talents, search for their strengths, and connect them to their own personal values.

## Letting go of fear and anxiety

When fear fuels our caring—when we care in order to feel more secure—we end up with what Mariana Brussoni calls anxiety-based caregiving. The University of British Columbia researcher has studied and written about this phenomenon as it relates to parenting and child development, but the same principle can apply to anyone attempting to help or care for another. Anxiety-based caregiving, Dr. Brussoni says, "is where decisions about childhood and what children need are made based on anxiety, rather than stepping back a bit and thinking about what might be best for child development."

"You're in a playground and you hear, 'Be careful!' 'Get down!' 'Watch out!' Those are things that are based on anxiety, not on stepping back and thinking: What does the child hear when you're saying those things? What the child hears is: 'The world is a dangerous place. You don't trust me to navigate that world. I need you to take care of me; I can't be independent myself.' We give kids too little credit. Often, if you just button your lips and let them get on with it, they actually can be very good at figuring out their limits. They're also good at figuring out each other's limits, and keeping each other within reasonable safety."

When parenting comes from fear, we grow children into adults who don't trust themselves and are over-dependent on others for guidance and approval—especially authority figures. Learning to let go and let others take responsibility for their own pain and their own problems, as well as feel the consequences of their own choices, can be freeing for the person caring and make the caring a whole lot more enjoyable. When you can find a way to let go of the anxiety and over-responsibility for the person you care about, you find that the caring is a little less frustrating and tiring.

Whether you are a parent, a caregiver, or a boss, the following strategies can help you care with less anxiety and help guide others to more self-trust, greater confidence, and increased self-responsibility.

**Become aware.** Know when you are taking on someone else's problem. You can tell caring is creating over-dependence when the caring is stressful. Over-caring likely means you're working harder than the person you care about. It means you're carrying the problem and letting the recipient of your caring off the hook. Remember: caring doesn't necessarily mean *carrying*.

At its core, caring is mostly just "being there." No fixing, no rescuing, no advising, no setting the other straight. While there is often work to do in looking after another, the work of caring is best when you are simply there, being present with and for another. You can't make a seed grow and flourish. All you can do is see that is has sunlight and water and nutrients to grow. When caring becomes stressful, it's a good idea to check and see if you are trying to "grow" for them, or unduly rescue people that don't need to be rescued.

**Learn to accept.** Your first job is simply to listen without an expectation that you have to "fix" anything. If you catch yourself assuming a person's burden, go back to simply listening. Remember that it isn't your job to take away or fix anyone's unhappiness. That's their job. Tune in to a person's feelings. Mature caring that guides people to their own resources and their own truth is first conveyed through the simple act of listening attentively, without judgment.

**Be honest.** Strengthening those you care about and guiding them to their own truth starts with being honest. Most of us have not had adults in our life who have done this, and it's one of the reasons we have such a difficult time relying on our own judgment or trusting our own inner resources.

Suppose, for example, you are in a line at the grocery story with a five-year-old and he says he wants a chocolate bar on the candy rack in front of him. When you tell him, "You don't want that candy bar," you are apt to confuse him. He doesn't know whether to trust himself or you. He's saying to himself, "I do want it, but mom tells me I don't, so who do I believe?" An honest response would be, "I know you want it, but I don't want to buy it for you. If you're hungry, I'll give you a carrot when we get in the car."

**Go inward.** Try to believe that the answers to our questions lie within us. Your job, to be sustainable, is to help those you care about discover what is already within them. Listen and tune in to their feelings, and when they know you understand, it is time to guide them to their own truth.

Simple questions such as, "What do you feel would be the right thing to do?" or "What does your conscience say?" explore a truth behind impulsive feelings. Of course, if people are overridden with emotion, they won't be able hear their own questions. All you can do then is listen and, if needed, set some boundaries. You aren't going to ask a five-year-old if he really needs a chocolate bar while he is having a temper tantrum because you said no. He's not listening. All you can do is calmly and firmly walk him out of the store, put him in his car seat, and take him home.

**Trust others—and learn to let go.** Caring does not mean making people happy, and it also doesn't give us a license to give them heavy-handed solutions. If I don't know what is right for me most of the time, how can I possibly know what is the best decision for anyone else?

No two people have the same life journey. The best I can do is support someone on their path, and trust they will make the right decisions on their own. It can be painful when someone you love is destroying themselves with addiction or depression or even suicide, or making choices that we would not make for ourselves. We simply don't know what is right for another. Be careful about placing your own limited judgments and expectations onto a situation. You only see a momentary snapshot of a person's lifelong movie. What you see and label as destructive may, at some point, become their door into recovery and a new life. Send a person in pain all the resources you believe can help them, and then let go and trust them.

## Gardening

Gerald Weinberg is a friend and a mentor—and a very fine gardener with the heart of a farmer—who over the years has passed on three important lessons to me. Anyone who cares, be they parents, leaders, caregivers, consultants, healers, and/or neighbors, would do well to draw on Gerald's heartfelt recommendations:

**Develop deep roots.** The plants that hold the firmest are ones that develop their own roots. Protect your young seedlings, but the less protection you give them, the hardier the mature plant will be. Caring, to be sustainable, must help people deepen their own roots. "If you give a man a fish, you feed him for a day," the saying goes. "But if you teach a man to fish, you feed him for a lifetime." True caring is not about carrying and over-protecting. It's about being there and, whenever possible, helping develop the internal capacity of the person you care about.

**Find balance in life.** Excessive watering produces weakness, not strength. Too much water weakens a plant because it prevents it from deepening its roots. We all need limits to caring. If you can't say "no," you will eventually be unable to say "yes." Caring without limits or boundaries isn't good for the person doing the caring, or for the person receiving the caring.

**Let things be.** Don't take others' choices personally. In spite of your best efforts, some plants will die. If you plan a garden around the idea that every seed will produce a harvest, you'll be disappointed—and you may go hungry. That's just not the way life works. There are too many variables in farming to predict an outcome, just as there are too many variables in caring and life. Farmers, because they are always working with complex systems, learn to live with failure and not take it personally. A heavy-handed approach won't achieve anything. You may think you know the answer, but you probably don't. There are no easy answers. So just relax. Enjoy standing alongside and loving the people you care about.

# The Art of Tending

The wind, one brilliant day, called
to my soul with an aroma of jasmine.
"In return for this jasmine odor,
I'd like all the odor of your roses."
"I have no roses; I have no flowers left now
in my garden ... All are dead."
"Then I'll take the waters of the fountains,
and the yellow leaves and the dried-up petals."
The wind left ... I wept. I said to my soul,
"What have you done with the garden entrusted to you?"

Antonio Machado, translation by Robert Bly

## Tending the farm

I was raised on a small farm in central Alberta in western Canada by parents who paid careful attention to the environment in which we lived. They taught me that our surroundings are a reflection of how we see ourselves. They put great care in our simple home, our animals, the barns, the gardens, the pastures, and the fences. Summers and weekends were spent repairing, painting, and upgrading such structures as the barns, sheds, and fences—in tilling gardens, maintaining machinery, mowing lawns, trimming hedges, grooming trails, and keeping the horses healthy and in top condition.

I learned early in my life to put effort into continually improving and caring for the world around me. It was about tending. About pride. About caring.

Not long ago, after a visit with our brother, my sister and I stopped to visit the old homestead for which we had such fond memories. As a family, we had worked hard to maintain the place, and with work came much joy from working together, riding together, and playing together. We hadn't been back there since the homestead was sold in 1984.

What we found was more than thirty years of neglect. Weeds in the yard grew up to our waists. The pastures and fences were completely run-down and neglected. What used to be a beautiful retreat center had deteriorated to a dilapidated, collapsing, unrecognizable shack. There had been virtually no upkeep to the property or the nearby trails in the forest for decades. Unpainted, derelict, and rusted buildings, broken and rotting windows abounded. We knew not to bring expectations to our visit, but what we discovered was unbearably sad. All we could do was stand and weep.

The lack of caring was so unbelievably painful given the way we'd been taught to tend. Kate and I did experience some joy and gratitude from reminiscing about our good upbringing, the solid values we'd acquired, and our wonderful memories, but we also left with broken hearts.

Caring takes work. It takes some effort to tend to a relationship, a home, a garden, or any part of the environment that surrounds us. Caring for our own houses, like caring for others, is not always comfortable. It takes work to sustain what we love.

## The law of entropy

Tending is about basic physics. The second law of thermodynamics—entropy—states that anything left to itself will, over time, lose its energy and break down until it reaches its most elemental form. Anything that is not intentionally renewed will be continually in a state of decline. Neglect your body and it will deteriorate. Neglect your car and it will depreciate. Neglect your mind and it will atrophy. Neglect your soul, and you will soon be living an empty, depleted life. Here are some indicators of a neglected personal life, a life without tending:

- You have no personal vision or sense of purpose beyond your own self-interest.
- There's no attention to bringing value and care to the relationships around you.
- You have formed no health habits, and have taken no consistent action toward tending to your physical, mental, and spiritual wellbeing.
- Most of your life consists of sitting in front of a computer or the television.
- You live a hurried, busy, frenetic existence.
- You have a prevalence toward addiction and addictive behaviors.
- You regularly experience low energy, depression, and apathy.

We all know someone who has allowed their career, creative self, mind, relationships, house, or health to deteriorate over many years. While without tending, our lives and those we say we care about will decline, entropy also opens the door to new possibilities. If we are attentive, returning to a more elemental state can allow for reconsideration, new growth, and new vision.

Caring is the interception of entropy. Intercepting entropy around you begins with intercepting entropy within you. While rotting wood, broken windows, weeds, and overgrown vegetation are signs of entropy in and around a house, here are some indicators of entropy that I have seen in organizations:

- There's a dark tension among people.
- People have no time for celebration and enjoyment.
- There's a void of rituals (no recognition of birthdays, achievements, life transitions, and so on.)
- People have difficulty with words like responsibility, service, and trust.

- People see customers as impositions on their time rather than as opportunities to serve.
- "Getting the job done" takes priority over meeting the needs of others.
- There's an atmosphere of entitlement and self-interest instead of gratitude and service.
- Problem makers outnumber problem solvers.
- Leaders seek to control rather than to trust.
- Pressures of day-to-day operations push aside a commitment to vision and values.
- A loss of confidence in judgment, experience, and wisdom is present.
- People forget to say "thank you."

While there's no immunity from entropy—since everything physical eventually breaks down and dies—you can interrupt it, counter potential deterioration with renewal, and slow the process. All things need attention and care. "Use it, or lose it," the maxim goes. It's no use blaming bad bosses, an ailing health care system, or your marriage partner. Recognizing a state of entropy is an opportunity for renewed growth.

## Tending for leaders

Good leaders, regardless of their title, ward off entropy through tending. Good leaders are concerned about results, but they also tend to the wellbeing and growth of the people they serve. Here are some ways that, as a leader, you can stave off entropy:

- Tend to those you serve by attending to their needs, aspirations, and dreams. This doesn't mean you have any obligation to please people or take responsibility for their happiness. It means, instead, to bring a service mindset to the work of leading—a commitment to a cause beyond self-interest, a co-participant in achieving the vision and living the values that brings us to work every day, a pledge to people's growth, and using your position to access the necessary resources to make this happen.

- Infuse the organization with energy from the outside; bring in new ideas, relationships, and new ways of thinking about the problems.
- Clarify and communicate vision in fresh ways.
- Stay in touch with the people you serve: take time to connect, listen, call people by their name. Remember birthdays, children's names, and interests. Write a handwritten thank you card. When it comes to caring, the little things *are* the big things.
- Express recognition and appreciation, often and relentlessly.
- Inspire the organization with your passion—for excellence, for people, for the work you do.
- Take time in conversations and team meetings to answer these questions: "What is entropy? How might entropy be evident here?" Discuss and explore the idea that "all things need watching, tending to, caring for."
- Replace entitlement and self-interest with gratitude and service.

## Everyday tending

Each of us in our own way can lead our lives with a higher degree of entropy interception or tending. Consider these questions for reflection and action:

**What, in your life, do you claim to care about**—yet is neglected through a lack of tending? Even painting a room in your house or cleaning out some clutter in the garage can awaken renewed energy.

**What creative ways have you found to counter entropy**—either in your life or in your workplace? If you aren't mindful and intentional, the weeds of entropy will begin to consume your energy.

**What needs appreciating in your life?** What relationships need your encouragement, attention, gratitude, or tending?

This could be close friends, a spouse, children, or even your own body. What you appreciate, appreciates.

**What are you doing to care for and tend to the needs of your soul?** What does your heart yearn for? What calls to you? What do you most desire?

**We have all been entrusted**—to a greater or lesser extent—with certain gifts, relationships, belongings, even our society. The Machado poem in this chapter's epigraph is about the many losses we experience in life. The older we get, the more gardens have been entrusted to us, and the more we seem to abandon. Be careful that you don't get so many gardens going in your life that you lose contact with the few that matter most. What have you done with the garden that was entrusted to you? What act of tending can you do today?

❧

Who knows what the owners of our little farm were attending to instead of tending to the property that we had so loved. Who knows what hardships or troubles they may have encountered. No one can judge the life of another.

Of the many voices today clamoring for your attention, what voice are you listening to? What are you paying attention to? What is calling you to action? Finding the right balance and proper consideration for what needs tending in your life is a matter of continual attention.

# Caring for Nature

The sharp-hoof'd moose of the north, the cat on the house-sill,
    the chickadee, the prairie dog,
The litter of the grunting sow as they tug at her teats,
The brood of the turkey-hen and she with her half-spread wings,
I see in them and myself the same old law.

Walt Whitman

## Stewardship

Behind our home lies a pristine valley designated as a nature conservancy. The valley and escarpments of the creek that runs through the protected land are representative of Foothills Parkland. The stream edge and floodplain is known as Aspen Parkland, a transitional biome between prairie and boreal forest that supports a variety of wildlife including deer, coyote, badger, red fox, lynx, mink, weasel, rabbit, beaver, red squirrel, and porcupine. The creek supports such shorebirds as killdeer, snipe, sandpiper, pipits, great blue herons, and many species of waterfowl including Canada geese, mergansers, and a variety of ducks. The creek and valley are also an important hunting area for osprey and bald eagles. As stewards here, we are a part of a community effort to protect and conserve the beauty of these lands for the future.

The creek—a critically important habitat for spawning rainbow trout, brook trout, cutthroat trout, as well as whitefish—has become a swimming hole for some local townspeople, and the cliffs a means to jump into the creek. People trespass through our properties to get to the water and, once there, they climb the escarpment which is now rapidly eroding. The area is riven with random trails. Wildflowers and prairie grasses get trampled underfoot. During summer months, we now spend time in the evenings along the creek and bordering land, picking up empty beer cans, broken glass, and garbage, and attempting to educate trespassers about the value of this land. What disheartens us most is that many of these people don't care about this precious place. They *use* it, rather than value it.

As a steward of the nature conservancy, I feel protective of this place. It's possible that my protectiveness comes from a selfish impulse. Still, I want to safeguard this beautiful place and the habitat it supports. I aspire for others to see it as a precious piece of wilderness in a similar way that I do.

I'd be happy to share it with others, even trespassers, if they just showed it some reverence and respect.

—~—

Stewardship is holding something in trust for another. The implicit notion of a deep caring for the land, of feeling a sensitivity and compassion toward the environment that surrounds us, was deeply engrained in me as a child.

Hiking in the wilderness as a boy scout with my father (a scout leader), he taught us to "always leave the place you visit in better shape than you found it." This axiom has extended beyond camping and hiking to a motto for the way I want to live my life.

Perhaps the seed of respect and care for nature was planted in me when I was twelve years old, and I bragged to my brother about how I'd killed a blue jay with my 22-caliber rifle. My mother overheard our conversation and, in her shock and dismay, simply stood behind the kitchen counter and wept. She didn't have to say a word. Her sobbing said everything. What I'd done was not acceptable. Still, at that young, self-centered stage of my life, I couldn't understand why she was so upset. Now, years later as I reflect on this, I can't understand how I could have killed a blue jay.

I learned much of my reverence for nature, and thus for life, because animals were so much part of my upbringing. Watching the birth of foals, raising chickens and litters of dogs and kittens, nurtured a love of life within me. I recall one time my father and I went hunting when I was still in high school. He shot a grouse and it landed on the ground, and then flopped around helplessly as we approached it. With a crank to its head that broke its neck and put the grouse out of its misery, Dad picked it up by the feet to carry it home to prepare for dinner.

He handed me his shotgun. "I'm done with hunting, son. The shotgun is now yours."

That was the last thing either of us killed with a gun.

## Nature's gentlemen

On a plaque mounted on large stone, below an ice lake in the Yoho valley, are these words: "This plaque is a tribute to Lawrence Grassi 'truly one of nature's gentlemen' who built many trails in the Banff-Lake Louise area, including this trail and these steps, so that those who follow might more easily enjoy the mountains he loves." This tribute was lovingly "erected in gratitude" by the Alpine Club of Canada.

I always imagine Lawrence Grassi—the miner and mountaineer who was so devoted to artfully putting in trails through rock slides, narrow crevices, and the edges of steep precipices, who nudged and coaxed monumentally heavy rocks into place as footstones to preserve the fragile landscape—as a person who cared. He cared about the land. He cared about nature. He cared about the people he left these trails for. He followed my father's axiom to "always leave the place you visit in better shape than you found it." I have no doubt my father would have called Lawrence Grassi a very good steward.

Allan Savory is a former wildlife biologist, farmer, and politician from Zimbabwe. He has dedicated his life, through the Savory Institute and with holistic management, to empower people to properly manage livestock to heal the land. Allan's friendship and commitment to stopping land desertification around the world has inspired me and made a difference in my life. He, among others, has taught me that the relationship between how I treat myself, how I treat others, and how I treat the land are inseparable. We are not compartmentalized. We are one indivisible, interdependent whole. Every decision we make in every moment affects the whole planet.

Allan once shared his thoughts on caring. "The subject of caring amazes me because it is so vital and so seldom mentioned other than in a hollow sense. 'I care for my family' is one example. Caring comes up so often when I am interviewed, as is occurring increasingly."

"When people learn about my holistic management recommendations and their vital importance to humanity's survival, they also find out about the unbelievable efforts to vilify me, my character, and the work I do. These efforts come from governments, universities, Nobel Laureates, major environmental organizations, ranching organizations, and individuals who have plagued me for more than fifty years. Inevitably people will ask me, 'What has made you able to withstand so many years of opposition without quitting?'"

"I've long pondered this question myself, because I know nothing short of killing me would make me give up what I do. Even some whom I love deeply in my close family have put pressure on me to give up my deep convictions and live what they consider a more normal life, because they were suffering. I cannot do this. Friends who for periods stood shoulder to shoulder beside me have all too often given up. They have even betrayed me by doing further damage—at times more than my opponents—so much so that I came to understand the old saying 'never rely on a weak man.' This has made me think deeply. Eventually I've boiled it down to one word. The one word is caring."

"When you reach a point where you care strongly enough about something, you will do whatever it takes, even give up your life if you have to, in order to achieve it. In my twenties I came to realize that I cared about wildlife, the environment, and my nation, which meant I cared about my children and everyone else's children more than anything in my life. I reasoned that if I was prepared to be in the army fighting for my country, then I should be equally prepared to give my life for what I personally care about. I was always a determined sort of child. From the day I reasoned these things out for myself, it became clear nothing short of death would stop me."

"This made it relatively easy to give up my job in a bureaucracy, when I was blocked from doing honest science, and start supporting myself and my family in any way I could. It made it easy to accept mistakes along the way and not make excuses for my failures; it made it easy to learn from others without ego blocking my way; it made it easy to question my training; and so on, endlessly. Caring deeply enough is all I need to never think of quitting, even in my darkest days. I don't want to overdramatize it, but that is simply how I feel and what has kept and will keep me going until my last breath. It is a wonderful world and a marvelous life, and each of us has a very short stay. I care about this world."

Allan's passion for the land, for this world, and for the principles that he stands upon, is evident in how he lives his life. His caring reminds me that being a good land steward is critical. Which is why I get very frustrated with trespassers who seem to lack caring. This creates a paradox. I am aware that in my caring for the land, there is an opposing lack of care toward these trespassers. On the one hand, I care. On the other, I judge. Many of those I criticize are simply enjoying themselves and are unaware of the effect that their enjoyment has on others.

This is what can happen to our caring. It can become blind. This seemingly natural human tendency to turn caring into a personal passion, and passion into a battle, has caused much destruction in the world. Caring can elicit conflict when you care about something that clashes with what someone else cares about. For my part, I believe there must be consequences for trespassers who blatantly disrespect and destroy land, who build fires that could raze precious and fragile forests, who litter and cause damage. Yet I know what is called for is caring, seeing the positive intent in those trespassers I judge, perhaps opening a relationship that could lead to a better understanding between us. Caring asks me to think deeply about my actions and reactions, and bring a higher level of awareness to the conflict. It is only through caring that I'll earn the trust of and potentially influence those I am judging.

Sometimes caring for nature means stopping and slowing our lives down. Tread softly. Respect the earth and take care not to damage fragile places. Notice and appreciate what's around you. Catalogue the richness. Call things by their proper names, the trees, the wildflowers, the mammals and birds, because naming something will make it dearer to you. Or just feel the wonder of being in the sacred presence of nature.

What are you doing to be a good steward? How are you caring for the precious environment that is the basis of our survival?

# Taking the Time

In America you have the clock; here we have the time.

Eastern proverb

## Important times together

I held tightly to my dad's huge baby finger. He opened the door for me and we walked together into the familiar gymnasium. The place smelled like my grandmother's house. It was dark and stuffy, with pale yellow paint coating the walls. The hardwood floors creaked with each step. Every Saturday morning, we would come here together, just Dad and I, always the first ones to arrive, and as usual find the stale, old facility full of tumbling mats, climbing ropes that went to the ceiling, a balance beam, an old torn up pommel horse, and—Dad's favorite—the parallel bars.

I don't think my father knew much about this thing that, today, we call "quality time." All he knew about was taking the time to do whatever was worth doing. Sometimes it was quality. Sometimes it wasn't. Dad began bringing me to the local YMCA every Saturday morning before I was old enough to go to school. He'd been one of Canada's top gymnasts in the 1940s, and my father had a passion for the sport that he wanted to pass on to me.

While it wasn't so obvious to me then, Harlie Irvine's appetite for exercise, his eloquence, ease, and grace of movement on the bars—combined with his finely tuned muscles—were pretty amazing. When my friends would come over they would be captivated by the fact that my father could walk around the house on his hands.

For some reason, this feat wasn't anything special to me. His most precious talents were so close to me that I didn't know they were there. At the time, I didn't recognize my father's gift, nor did I have much appreciation for the degree of discipline and perseverance it took to develop that gift. It was just who he was. His ability to do a handstand on the ladder of our local swimming pool, or to stand on one hand, or to somersault from a standing position, all seemed so ordinary that I didn't pay much attention to it.

Joining Dad at the gym, and in nature, is how we connected in those early, formative years. Athletics was his language. Sport was how he spoke to me. Dad was also a great outdoorsman and my scoutmaster. We fished, canoed, and camped together. "Be prepared!" and "Leave this campground cleaner than you found it," are two scouting mottos that have had lasting impact in all areas of my life. Harlie was also a man of deep faith with strong spiritual roots. Every Sunday we would drive an hour to church. I don't remember much about what I learned once we got there, but I do remember the time spent with my father getting there. During those long car rides, we'd sometimes listen to Earl Nightingale on the car radio, or I'd hear about Dad's philosophy of life or about his faith. I remember him opening up a few times about his struggles with the demons of depression or his bouts of insecurity and fears. Most often we would sit comfortably in silence. These times weren't usually very profound or insightful and I didn't necessarily feel particularly close to my father. But they were important times together, nonetheless. It was on these rides to church that Dad taught me to drive. I would not have been able to recognize it then, but I know now that these were consistent, unfailing occasions that my father would show me, in his imperfect, simple way, that he cared.

As my track coach in high school, my father inspired my future dream to make the Canadian team at the 1980 Moscow Olympics (that were eventually boycotted.) The training regime we developed started with a run at 5:00 a.m. If I wasn't up five minutes after the alarm rang, he would sometimes come and sit on the end of my bed and give me an encouraging, yet stern, lecture. I can still, to this day, hear the persuasive tone in my father's voice forty years later.

"The purpose of having a dream is not to achieve your dream," I can hear my dad say. "The purpose of having a dream is to become the kind of person it takes to achieve your dream. It isn't about a target, it's about the direction you are headed. Very few people will make the Olympics, and fewer still will stand on the podium, but anyone can be *the kind of person it takes* to make it to the Olympics—and you'll never be that person who makes it to the Olympics if you can't put two feet on the floor in the morning when you don't feel like it." It was instances like these that engrained in me that people who care are people who take the time.

My mother took time with me in a different way. Joyce was a philosopher and a teacher. Her sharpness lay not in her body but in her mind. She took the time to nurture us with her insights and perceptions. She held intellectual discussions, shared her wisdom, and invited good friends over to enrich us and tell their stories.

Like my father's physical prowess, I took my mother's wisdom for granted and did not fully appreciate her until much later in life. As a psychotherapist, Joyce brought family systems thinking to western Canada in the 1960s, and she had an incredible impact in many people's lives. In my travels, I still hear of the influence she had on people through her workshops. It was from my mother I learned to follow my heart and never lose sight of wonder.

Not a day goes by that I don't think of my parents and reflect upon their caring influence in my life, or the time they took to show their care for me when I was growing up. They certainly weren't perfect. They had their share of shortcomings, as we all do. They didn't give me everything I wanted. But they gave me everything I needed. With sadness, gratitude, and joy, I am grateful for my upbringing in its entirety.

A few weeks after Joyce's death in 1999, we found this astonishing entry in her journal: "Every parent, no matter how hard they try, will be both a blessing and a curse to their children. My hope is that my children will appreciate the blessing, if not immediately, then later in life, and perhaps more importantly, my hope is that they take the curse and, like an oyster irritated by a grain of sand, over time, use it as a catalyst to build layers of character and understanding—thus producing a pearl."

## Caring takes time

My parents' influence in my life continues to reverberate through me and, in turn, through the people I love and care about. My parents' gentle love and wisdom, and the time they took to share what they had and who they were, has embedded in me a vision of what is possible.

Caring takes time. An artist who cares about his craft takes the time to develop it. The athlete who cares about her performance takes the time to train and get better. New lovers take the time. Employers who care about their employees take the time to listen to them, get their input, and learn from them, and ensure they get the support they need to succeed. Friends who care make time for each other. Parents who care make time for their children.

Philip Simmons thought a lot about time in the last decade of his life. A husband, father, climber of mountains, writer, and English professor, he was thirty-five years old when he was diagnosed with Lou Gehrig's disease or ALS. In *Learning to Fall*, Simmons wrote about coping with his terminal diagnosis and his struggles to make peace with dying, and about taking the time to explore the mysteries of everyday life. "Busyness is often a distraction, a way of avoiding others, avoiding intimacy, avoiding ourselves ... We want to know we matter, we want to know our lives our worthwhile. And when we're not sure, we work that much harder, we worry that much more. In the face of our uncertainty, we keep busy."

With a young family to live for and not many years left to spend with them, Simmons forced himself to stop and pay attention. He noted just how hard and yet how worthwhile it was to take the time to experience life moment to moment, and pondered what it was that "restores us to a better version of ourselves."

"Perhaps it's a question of grace," Simmons writes. "A reflected sunset flares in the windows of a skyscraper, a sheet of newspaper takes flight down an empty street ... a world made luminous with wonder. We can't summon such moments, but we can open ourselves to them when they arrive ... Our attention is arrested, quite literally stopped, and the world seems to say to us: 'Don't just do something, stand there.'"

Busyness doesn't allow much room to grow. A garden can't flourish in the midst of continual cultivation. Stillness is needed for roots to take hold. We all need time away, time to reflect, to just be. Caring requires a slower pace, a realization that life is more than an accomplishment of tasks or a triumph over our "to-do" lists. Caring is about time. Not perfect time, not necessarily "quality" time, but simply making the time to be present as best we can be.

Maybe when we actually slow down and take the time, we gain what is most precious, maybe what we were seeking all along.

## Too much rushing

Robert Levine has been studying time as it is experienced in various cultures. Levine measures three different variables: the time it takes to buy a stamp in a post office, the speed at which pedestrians walk across the street, and the accuracy of clocks in a bank. What he discovered was that there are cultures where punctuality and precision are rewarded, while other cultures are slower and less precise. Western society is the fastest; Brazil, Indonesia, and Mexico are the slowest. Levine doesn't make a judgment that some cultures are necessarily "better." There are, after all, advantages and disadvantages to both slow and fast cultures. What's fascinating is that, in cultures where the pace is hurried, not only do people feel less appreciated and less cared for, but cardiovascular disease is more widespread.

What worries me is the possibility that we've created a world that is much more economically and technically efficient, but much less satisfying and caring to live in. I care about caring. It's my life's work to create more human and caring organizations, and to inspire people to care enough about themselves and the world around them so they will be more fully themselves.

Technology allows us to communicate and take action at light-ning speed and in ways our ancestors never could have imagined. But how does technology help us improve the quality of our connections and the quality of our lives? Is technology helping us be more caring, or are our devices driving us in a way that is no longer human? Has speed become more important than anything else?

Much emerging research is telling us that the more we hurry, the less we are able to connect, and the less we connect, the less we care. We can list examples of technologies that enable connections and en-rich our lives and, in certain instances, even make significant changes in the world, so maybe the question is more *how* we use our technol-ogies. Putting a value on *real* time over *screen* time. Not always taking shortcuts, because maybe doing things the long way could be worth the journey. Stopping once in a while to, you know, smell the flowers. Everyone communicates, but how many take the time to go deeper? How many actually make a connection?

Sometimes doing things the long way can be as simple as plant-ing a few seeds in a window pot, or taking the stairs instead of the elevator. Maybe it means giving ourselves a little more time between meetings and appointments, or taking the time to connect with peo-ple and asking them about their lives. When we rush our lives too much and without pause, we may think we are accomplishing a lot, we may even get high on the pace, but we can start to separate from life and the world around us. Eventually, the breakneck pace becomes unsustainable.

## The slow movement

It's amazing what a little slowing down can do for us. Since the late eighties, there's been a growing worldwide curiosity and hunger for slowing down. The Slow Movement advocates a downshift in the frenetic pace of our lives. Author Carl Honoré says, "It is a cultural revolution against the notion that faster is always better. The Slow philosophy is not about doing everything at a snail's pace. It's about seeking to do everything at the right speed, the speed for which we were designed as humans. Savoring the hours and minutes rather than just counting them. Doing everything as *well* as possible, instead of as *fast* as possible. It's about quality over quantity in everything from work to food to parenting."

How does the Slow Movement relate to caring? It places a premium on human connections and a more human pace. In a world where we've come to expect instant everything, sometimes the answer is: there is no shortcut to caring. Things take the time they take. If you have any doubt that caring requires a slower pace, try to show caring to a small child when you are in a hurry and late for an appointment.

Too often we place a high value on speed and efficiency, on jam-packing our schedules, or on going from one event or meeting to the next as quickly as possible. Or we get stuck staring at a screen, sitting in one place for hours at a time, ignoring our body's natural instinct to move. Could it come down to doing things at a more human pace? What if we were to take the time to actually see what's around us, to use our five senses and our bodies in the way they were designed? How many people take the time to sit and read books to each other anymore? To gather around the piano? Why don't we make more things by hand, the way we learned to as children? One of the gifts of grandparenting, I've noticed, is it helps a person slow down and return to that child-like wonder that exists in each of us.

To understand the effect of hurriedness on a person's ability to express caring, there's a classic social psychology study conducted by researchers who were interested in how situations affect helping behaviors. John Darley and Daniel Batson, psychologists from Princeton University, studied a group of theology students who had just listened to a lecture on kindness, and then had to move, one by one, to a nearby building for their next class. On the way, they met an accomplice of the experimenters. This person was down on the floor, pretending to have fallen and hurt himself. Most of the students helped him. But when they were pressured and had to hurry from one building to the next, the Good Samaritans among them dwindled rapidly. One of the priests, in his hurry, even stepped over the unfortunate crying actor and headed straight for his destination. It's more difficult to be caring when we are in a hurry.

## What grandmothers know

A generation ago, a young child wrote this poem, "What is a Grandmother?" These words—that could just as easily have been written in the context of our current, frenetic world—speak simply and honestly about the caring quality of this thing called time.

> A grandmother is a lady who has no small children of her own. A grandfather is a man grandmother. He goes for walks with us and talks about fishing and tractors and stuff like that.

> Grandmothers don't have to do anything except be there. They are old and shouldn't run or play hard. It's enough that they drive us to the market where the pretend horse is and that they have lots of quarters ready. When they take us for walks, they like to slow down past pretty leaves and caterpillars. They don't say "hurry up."

> Usually grandmothers are fat, but not too fat to tie your shoes. They wear glasses and funny underwear. They can take their teeth and gums off. Grandmothers don't have to be smart. They only have to answer questions like, "Why doesn't God get married?" and "How come dogs chase cats?"

> Everyone should try to have a grandmother, especially if you don't have a television. Grandmothers are the only grownups who have the time.

## That human connection

In our quest for efficiency, we can lose our humanity. We become human *doings* rather than human *beings*. Efficiency in our world may be important, but efficiency without humanity is drudgery. Efficiency is for systems, not for people. We live such busy lives that we even schedule our time to efficiently buy our groceries, fix our car, and buy lunch—and in the process we can lose our connection with the cashier at the grocery store, the mechanic who services our car, and the restaurant server at lunch. Rather than human beings, we turn people into objects, into "roles" that we encounter in the course of the day, service oriented automatons that "efficiently" meet our wants and needs.

We've all experienced what I call assembly line efficiency. This is when we take a number at the end of a bureaucratic line and get slotted into a system that removes any sense of our humanity. No civil manager wakes up one day with the intention to create a process that is inhuman. Somebody probably just wanted to make things more streamlined and cost-effective. But as a person inside these inhuman and disconnected systems, and as we live our busy lives, let us remember the importance of s-l-o-w-i-n-g down and making contact. Maybe it's time to look up from our lists and tiny screens, at least every so often, and simply notice the person in front of us, the person an arm's length away.

A smile. A question that shows interest. A touch that connects. It's caring that bridges the gap of isolation.

# The Caring Muscle

> We cannot teach people anything; we can only help them
> discover it within themselves.
>
> Galileo Galilei

## Caring by doing

You can learn about healthy living in a classroom, but if you actually
want to get in shape, you have to get to the gym. You don't assess a
person's strength by what they claim they can lift. You assess a person's strength but by seeing how much they *actually* lift. In the words
of Henry Ford, "you can't build a reputation on what you are going
to do."

We learn by doing. We never find out what the Good Samaritan
had to say after he was moved to act, or what emotional reaction he
may have had to the people he showed caring for. All we know is
that he took the right action. Caring is more than an emotion. It's
more than empathy or compassion. In the words of my friend, the
Canadian artist Murray Phillips, caring is a creative *response* to a hurting situation. Caring is empathy in action. The good news is that we
don't *have to* wait for the feelings to emerge in order to care. Action
can come before the experience of caring for someone. It behooves us
to decide and to act. Through practice, we'll ultimately unlock the
capacity to care.

If we couldn't learn to be more caring, then there would be no
reason to ask people to care. Asking people to care implies that it's a

learned thing, right? We learn to draw by going to drawing classes, by practicing sketching in ways that may not come easily for us. Soccer camps improve ball handling and dribbling skills. Maybe a course in caring could include an assignment to plug a stranger's parking meter, to let someone in traffic move in front of us, to help a local business by referring a customer, or to hold our dear aging mother's hand when she tells us about her childhood.

Just know that it is possible to learn to be more caring.

## Enlarging your "caring capacity"

There's a drug called tolcapone that was discovered in a 2015 "compassion pill" study at University of California Berkeley and San Francisco to change the social behavior of study participants, and make them more caring. Participants played a simple economic game in which they divided money between themselves and an anonymous recipient. After taking tolcapone, they divided the money with the strangers in a fairer, more egalitarian way than when they received a placebo.

The drug apparently makes people care. By changing the participants' neurochemical balance in the prefrontal cortex of their brains—the area responsible for personality, social behavior and decision-making—the pill was found to increase a person's ability to sense the pain in others. In essence, it produced feelings of empathy in the participants and thus enabled them to artificially produce feelings of kindness.

"But does this artificial altruism really count?" ask Craig Kielburger and Marc Kielburger. "Or is it the emotional equivalent of Lance Armstrong's Tour de France fixing?" The brothers Kielburger call it "compassion doping." To me, this drug seems questionable. Like cheating. While the world could undoubtedly use a super-size dose of loving kindness, performance enhancers to increase caring aren't necessarily the answer.

Action, ultimately, is the gateway to caring. Even if you don't feel very caring, you can act your way into the feeling, if it's the right thing to do. The action leads the feelings. Let action kick-start your caring response to others. Learning to "act" in a caring way, even before you "feel" like it is a possible strategy for us when we are around people or situations where caring is tough. Caring actions toward my brother, even on the days when it was uncomfortable to be there, resulted in a feeling of compassion toward him. Maybe behaving our way into caring is like my friend Scott with his listening face. When he put on a caring and attentive expression, with the *intention* of listening, eventually he exercised his way into being a better listener.

We may not have control over our instincts and the ways we respond emotionally. However, we can govern our intentions and direct our actions.

Caring, while it's in us, can also be both hidden as well as developed. The selfless desire to alleviate the suffering of others is something that even rats and chimpanzees experience. In studies, these animals will attempt to rescue a lab mate in distress. As for humans, there's evidence that caring and cooperative behavior predate speech and contribute to the evolution of intelligence. This could be why babies seem hardwired for compassion, and why toddlers are prone to spontaneous acts of helpfulness. Meanwhile, adults are prone to road rage. Why? Maybe because caring has been socialized out of them, or maybe they haven't had enough practice using their caring muscle.

We're compassionately challenged, point out the Kielburger brothers, but we are not permanently indifferent. Anyone can rekindle the compassion they felt as children. While it is unlikely that it can be "taught" like a mathematic formula or a business process or a technique, caring can certainly be learned through repeated practice.

Our ability to be caring can erode with neglect, just like physical fitness. There's another adage that has to do with physical training, "use it or lose it." Studies have found that suppressing our instinct for kindness, say, walking indifferently past a homeless person, might make us less attuned to the distress of others. And this depletes our compassion even further the next time around.

If you wish to find ways to attune yourself to others, Appendix G contains ten caring practices for strengthening your caring response.

Just know that the capacity and impulse to care is in you. Even if you don't think you had very caring parents, even if you came from an uncaring, drug-abusing home, even if you were raised by adults who abandoned or abused you, the caring muscle within you can be unlocked. Just like strengthening any muscle, the key to caring is just to do it. Consider it your daily practice.

# Health and Wellbeing

Health is the greatest possession
Contentment is the greatest treasure
Confidence is the greatest friend
Presence is the greatest joy

Lao Tzu, 600 BC

## What the body knows

From my preschool days on the parallel bars and the tumbling mat with my father, to an early pursuit of physical education in university, to decades of competitive running, and now as a student of yoga and meditation, I've always been interested in health and how to improve it. Most of what I have learned about it has come through my own study, and my experiences with injuries and illness. I call myself my own research institute.

The older I get, the less sure I am about more things and the more sure I am about less things. One thing I am surer about is the wisdom of the human body. The body knows. Our work is to learn to pay attention and follow its promptings.

My awareness and experience with health extends beyond mere physical health. As a former family therapist and current consultant to organizations, I've observed unhealthy families and cultures, and watched the effect of toxic environments on people. I've learned that even if there are both unhealthy and healthy systems, there really is no such thing as a totally "dysfunctional" family or organization. Every family, like every organization, has elements of health and elements of dysfunction—each to varying degrees. There are no complete malfunctions and there are no perfect systems. There is also no standard of "normal."

Normal means you just don't know them well enough yet. The key is to pay attention and embrace both the light and the dark.

Our reaction to a bad boss can make us sick. Staying in a poisonous organization can contaminate us. Living in an unhealthy family can drive us to madness. On the other hand, a healthy environment can inspire us. A healthy workplace can help fulfill us. A healthy family can help us be a healthier person. Recognizing the unhealthy aspects can inspire us to choose to not duplicate them and to work toward greater vitality.

## Some of what I know about health

"Health" is different than "fitness." These two terms are often used interchangeably, but they are not the same. It's very possible to be healthy and not very fit, or fit and not very healthy. Many "fit" athletes have been known to die of heart attacks. Conversely, I've known healthy people who can't necessarily run very fast or bench press much weight.

There was a time when I could run near six-minute mile marathons, but I couldn't sit still for six minutes. Riddled with insecurity in those days, I was "fit" but I wasn't very "healthy." I competed at a national level in track while simultaneously suffering anxiety attacks and severe, life-threatening asthma. How useful is it to have strong arms and shoulders and have an unhealthy liver? How worthwhile is it to be hyperconscious of your diet if you are up all night with anxiety, stress, and hypertension?

I've often wondered if a relaxed person who doesn't pay much attention to what they eat, who doesn't have any kind of a structured exercise regime, but sleeps in, may live longer—and maybe even better—than an uptight person who is obsessed about their diet, is up at five every morning to run, and works zealously into the night. Staying relaxed, having a steady mind that maintains equanimity in the midst of ups and downs, learning to not take things so personally or seriously, maintaining perspective, and learning to lighten up are qualities of health that are sorely undervalued.

Fitness is a physical ability to perform an athletic activity. In a world that reveres appearance, quick fixes, and youth, fitness is highly valued and often used as a standard of measurement. Health, on the other hand, is when all the body's various systems—nervous, muscular, skeletal, circulatory, digestive, urinary, lymphatic, endocrinal, hormonal, reproductive, respiratory, immune—are all working in harmony and optimally. Health is a dynamic condition of wholeness, vitality, and balance that allows us to move through life with immunity from the harm of damaging influences, and be engaged in life with energy, ease, and resilience. It's about having the energy to do what we are meant to do with our lives.

We can influence our health, even if we can't control it. Health habits greatly influence quality of life. Freedom from pain is one of life's most cherished blessings to seek, especially chronic, debilitating pain. However, pain is also part of the human experience. It may be a symptom of ill health, or simply part of being human. Regardless of how we manage our pain, it's always good to look at the pain from a broader perspective and ask, "Why is it here?" Learning to befriend pain is a way of learning to listen to the body and can lead us to understand more about ourselves. It can open a door, if we listen carefully. It's about learning to work with pain, rather than working on it. Pain, in a strange sort of way, can be an ally to you if you suspend, even temporarily, the immediate, natural impulse to eradicate it. Instead, experiment with taking the time to listen to it and hear what it is saying to you. You may be surprised.

If we aren't mindful and intentional, health can be like a good friend we take for granted. We don't realize what we had until they're not there anymore. As the old saying goes, "When you have your health, you have a thousand wishes. Without your health, you have only one." Health is a precious and precarious possession, a gift truly worth seeking.

# Different paths to health

This past year, while scrambling down Mount Yamnuska, at the foot of the Rockies outside Banff National Park, I miscalculated the depth of the scree and slid several feet on hard rock with my left knee buckled under my right buttocks. While I knew I had twisted my knee, the pain didn't set in until later that night when I could hardly bear to stand on it.

Over the next few days, the pain subsided, but I had my physician assess it. Medial collateral ligament partial tear was the diagnosis. Rest, he told me. Don't annoy it. Back off, and the joint will heal on its own. After six months of rest, my knee was worse. Surgery was posed as an option, but at age fifty-nine, the prognosis of surgery wasn't positive, so I spoke to my yoga teacher about alternative ways of looking at my situation. She referred me to an acupuncturist who works in the field of Traditional Chinese and Eastern Medicine. At our first meeting, the doctor explained that his approach to health was a balance of clarity of mind, freshness of spirit, and strength of body. He believed that true health would result from a sense of ease and joy in a person's everyday life.

The doctor continued with acupuncture and, while applying the needles, talked about the stress in my life. He explained how even the best hockey players have to get on the bench frequently during the game. They have to completely relax and let go.

The "fight or flight" stress response is meant to be a reversal of the natural state of rest. Instead, I had things backward. My natural state had been stress. And now, while my knee yelled at me for a reversal, I merely tried to "squeeze" relaxation into my frenetic days. I wasn't actually resting. I wasn't letting go.

This pain in my knee was a gift—a message from my body—to help me reexamine my life and to realize that I needed to start to relax more. Anyone who knows me knows how intense I live my life. While I appear healthy on the outside, I am a work of healing in progress. Working with the pain from a broader, holistic perspective, improved my health. Surgery was inevitable, but I'm healthier because I have learned from the whole experience.

Everyone is unique, and there is no one right path to health for everyone. I know there are certain foods and substances that, for me, activate addiction and fuel depression. Yet I can't prescribe these as health habits to anyone but myself. I am the kind of person who thrives on structure, while others I know thrive on not having structure. Some, like me, have a sensitive nervous system, while others have a natural propensity to stability. There are certain foods and activities that I personally need complete abstinence from, while for others, it's more about moderation. Health is knowing ourselves, being honest with ourselves, and living accordingly. Again, the body knows if we stop and listen.

Needs change over time. I knew a woman who was a vegetarian for more than thirty years. One morning she woke up and knew within herself that she needed to start eating meat. She was healthy as a vegetarian, but her needs changed. Just as there is no one path for health that is right for everyone, it's important to be sensitive to our changing needs as we age, evolve, and emerge into each new stage of our lives.

## Here is some of what I know about exercise

During the past few years, I have found that being out of breath and tiring myself out is not necessarily self-caring. So I don't push myself in exercise the way I used to. Knowing my Type A temperament, I find it healthier, especially as I age, to bring less ambition into exercise, and to experiment with a broader range of experience. Now that I am entering my sixties, my new motto is to find a pace that I can stay at for the rest of my life. I'm not sure if this will be possible, but it is a worthwhile goal.

Applying nonviolence to my body is integral to my journey of self-care. People who exercise tend to be healthier than people who don't exercise. But if we over-exercise, if we strive to get fit at the expense of our health, we can end up with the same symptoms as the people who don't exercise! In other words, signs of over-exercising can be essentially the same as signs of not exercising. See if you recognize any of these indicators of under—and over—exercising:

- Low energy
- Chronic fatigue
- Decreased immune system

- Increased susceptibility to illness and injury
- Mood swings and depression
- Circulatory or cardiovascular issues
- Digestive problems
- Blood sugar or insulin imbalances
- Hormonal imbalances

Remember not to abuse your body. In other words, try treating it with the same respect and reverence a musician has for their musical instrument. For a list of ten simple rules for finding and sticking with an exercise program that will keep you healthy, see Appendix H at the end of the book.

# Cultivating a Practice of Self-Care

To be idle requires a strong sense of personal identity.

Robert Louis Stevenson

## Self-care is an ethical issue

I don't remember a great deal from my lifeguard training back in high school, but one lesson has remained with me over the last forty-some years. "People tap into an overwhelming strength when they are drowning," our instructor adamantly pointed out on several occasions.

"What's vitally important is to never, never, never, in the work of saving a life, *put yourself* at risk. Make sure you take care of yourself, so you can take care of those you are saving."

Even though this idea of "never putting myself at risk" was embedded in my mind as an aspiring lifeguard, I didn't connect it to my caring work until much later in life. What I've learned since those days is that, if I'm not careful, the work of caring—and subsequent leading—can wear me out and break me down. Like a drowning swimmer, people suffering and in need of caring have increased strength to draw on that can suck the energy and life out of the person doing the caring.

Whether you are a physician or a health care professional, caring hour after hour for your patients, or a psychotherapist working with people in pain and trauma, or an executive leading a division within your company, or an owner of a company responsible to your shareholders, or a customer service representative caring for customers, or a parent of young children or teenagers, or a family member caring for an aging parent or a dying loved one, or a teacher attending to the needs of the young people in your classroom all day long, you pay a price when you consistently put the demands and needs of others ahead of your own.

If you find that your focus on caring is hurting you or the people and world around you, then perhaps it is time to rethink your approach to being there for others. I know the cost of caring without self-care from first-hand experience. When I don't put personal time on my calendar first, I pay a price. When I don't have a disciplined, sustained habit for taking care of my physical, spiritual, and mental health, my energy and overall wellbeing suffers. When I allow the needs of others to crowd out and suffocate my own needs, my relationships suffer. When I spread myself too thin, when I promise too much, when my expectations are too high, my health and quality of life starts to suffer. Caring, without self-care, will sooner or later inhibit our ability to care for others.

A group of nurses once hired me to speak on the topic, "Self-Care is an Ethical Issue." It was a fitting theme. They understood that self-care is more than a luxury. Self-care is a responsibility. If we don't take care of ourselves, we eventually won't be able to carry the responsibility of caring for others.

So why don't caregivers take better care of themselves? What I've learned is that, just as there is a price to be paid for a lack of self-care, there can be a downside to self-care. You'd think that it would be all positive to work less, rest and relax more, and take a break from caring, and to live life in greater alignment with what is truly essential for you. But a life of ease isn't easy. I have taken on caring as a way to define myself, to the point that when I take a break from caring, all kinds of uncomfortable emotions surface. I get anxious. I feel guilty. I worry that I'm not doing enough, that I'm not contributing enough, that I'm not caring enough.

Rather than face these emotions honestly I plunge back into a variety of activities to prove my competence: reading and researching too obsessively, exercising too intensely, achieving too compulsively, and caring without self-care.

Good self-care for so many of us is about breaking a pattern, being willing to face the fears that have made us caring people, and developing our sensitive natures that, paradoxically, make it so difficult for us to care for ourselves. Learning to be self-caring may mean facing these fears and the inhuman guilt we have so these emotions don't control our lives. Instead of frenetically keeping busy in order to mask our emotions, self-care is about learning to punctuate our day with pauses. It's about learning to savor and enjoy life with all its warts and bumps, developing self-acceptance, and embracing the blessings of an imperfect life.

No matter your personal definition of self-care or what your self-care consists of, it will likely involve stepping back and reflecting on what matters most in your life. It may entail going within, following your heart, and being honest with yourself and those you care about. Eleanor Roosevelt, a profound leader and caregiver in her own right, once said, "Do what you feel in your heart to be right, for you'll be criticized anyway."

Or as Polonius said to his son Laertes, who was in a hurry to get on the next boat to Paris and did not know he would never see his father again, "This above all: to thine own self be true." What is often skipped over is the line that comes next. "And it follows, as the night the day, thou canst not then be false to any man."

Take care of yourself first. "Put your personal time on your calendar first," Geoff Bellman says. That way you'll be in a position to take care of others. Above all, actively set intentions for yourself—be honest with yourself and others about your needs, your desires, your fears and dreams. From this place, true caring can emerge.

## A self-care system

Caregivers and caring leaders must have what I have come to call a Self-Care System: a detailed process for sustaining and renewing, on a regular basis, your physical, spiritual, and mental energies. Because we are all unique, there is no one prescription for a self-care system that fits everyone. But, like a track athlete who requires adequate recovery in the midst a rigorous training, caregivers need an intentional, disciplined, consistent process of self-renewal.

A self-care system can be a regular exercise regime. For others, it's daily prayer and meditation. It can be about preserving your sense of purpose, or creating a sanctuary where you go within and hear yourself think. For some, it's about creating boundaries around your work, turning off technology, or maintaining a Sabbath ritual. A self-care system can be as simple as turning off the television and relaxing before bed, settling in at a regular time, and getting a full night's rest on a regular basis. It could be about having consistently good eating habits, or making time to relax and be around friends that uplift you. For some, it's about learning to be less critical, less perfectionistic, and more accepting of yourself. Deciding to spend less money and live below your means to avoid financial stress is another valid self-care system. Having a Personal Planning System and starting your week by planning for personal time is a kind of self-care.

While self-care systems can be varied and tailored uniquely to each person, the common threads are discipline, consistency, and regularity. It isn't so much about pampering yourself, as it is about developing conscious habits that result in self-respect and health and inner wellbeing. Self-care is not always comfortable. It isn't always easy to put on your walking shoes and get outside after work, but you'll invariably feel better when you do, and you'll especially feel better when you are done!

Creating a rewarding, healthy, and vital self-care system for yourself gives the caring in your life an opportunity to arise from overflow rather than emptiness. Having a self-care routine and establishing healthy boundaries that create a sense of wellbeing are vital to a sustainable caring journey.

As you make self-care and personal renewal a priority in your life, it's important to distinguish between self-*care* and self-*centeredness*. Self-care means taking care of yourself so that you can take care of others. Self-centeredness, on the other hand, is taking care of yourself so you can take care of yourself.

At the end of the book, in Appendix I, is a Self-Care Inventory to help you establish a snapshot of your current self-care status, and—if appropriate—provide a few ideas for creating or sustaining your own self-care system. It's an inventory you can return to when life gets overly frenetic, stressful, or busy, or when you allow the demands of others to bury your need for self-care. Discipline, consistency, and regularity can be hard! But making time to renew and tap into your personal sources of inspiration are essential for when the work of caring becomes demanding.

Taking care of yourself is not selfish. It's life-giving.

# Finding Beauty in the Beast— Caring Through Darkness

We have to learn to be our own best friends, because we fall too early into the trap of being our own worst enemies.

Roderick Thorp

## My journey through depression

No two people experience depression in the same way. Depressive disorders come in different forms, as do other illnesses such as cancer, heart disease, and diabetes. There are major depressions and persistent depressive disorders. There are bipolar disorders and seasonal affective disorders. There is psychotic depression, premenstrual, and postpartum depression. Some kinds of depression are primarily genetic or biochemical, and the sufferer will respond only to drugs. Some are predominantly situational and will benefit from inner work, self-awareness, a change in thinking, and new choices.

If you or someone you care about is suffering from depression, you would do well to start with a good thorough assessment by a reputable health care professional or psychiatrist that you trust.

What I share with you in this chapter is my own personal journey through the darkness of depression. It has taken me a long time to acknowledge and talk about this publicly, in part because it was engrained in me that depression was a weakness. But as I acknowledge and have a little more kindness toward my depressive nature, the load starts to lift. If you struggle with this malady, or are drawn into the shadows of someone you care about, my hope is that my story will inspire you to be a little more caring toward yourself through the darkness. Regardless of how depression may manifest itself in your life, caring is the only way into the light.

From the time I entered adolescence until I was about forty years old, I found myself intermittently consumed with the subtle and excruciatingly painful darkness of clinical depression. There were episodes when I couldn't muster the will or the strength to get out of bed, and I felt alienated from all of life. Amid these depressive spells there were also some manic periods where I would over-work to the point of exhaustion, over-spend into unmanageable debt, over-exercise to the point of injury, and over-eat to cope with life.

During these times, I was insensitive to the needs and feelings of those close to me and blamed others when things didn't go my way. I know now that these responses to life were a protection against my own feelings of inadequacy and the fear of being ordinary. If I could be the best, then maybe I wouldn't feel so invisible.

It is so easy to be seduced by a celebrity culture that defines your worth by material possessions, achievement, or number of "likes" you get on Facebook or Instagram. I also understand how entitlement and admiration-seeking seem like the right ointments to soothe the ache of inadequacy. Being ordinary just wasn't good enough for me. I had to be extraordinary to be enough. But I was never extraordinary enough to not feel invisible. So I kept striving, endeavoring, achieving, yet never fully knowing what enough actually felt like. The ambition would eventually lead to despair and subsequent hopelessness and despondency.

Between the extreme mood swings were extended periods of what I call *functional* depression, where I was able to show up for work and maintain personal responsibilities, but underneath, a sense of impending doom seemed to surround me. During these periods I was irritable and moody to people close to me, and couldn't get hopeful or happy about much of anything. Getting up in the morning required a lot of effort, and normal conversations were often a struggle. Making simple decisions seemed impossible. I was forgetful and preoccupied, and it was difficult to concentrate on what was in front of me. Upon awakening, my first thoughts were of my failures from the day before. I felt like I couldn't do anything right, and had recurring thoughts of how I would do myself in to relieve the hopelessness.

It was dark during these periods, even when the sun was shining. Even if in heaven, I would be in hell. I would often feel like I was drowning or suffocating, and I would get easily agitated as a way of attempting to handle unacknowledged anxiety.

William Styron in *Darkness Visible* describes such times well. "It was not really alarming at first, since the change was subtle, but I did notice that my surroundings took on a different tone at certain times: the shadows of nightfall seemed more somber, my mornings were less buoyant, walks in the woods became less zestful, and there was a moment during my working hours in the late afternoon when a kind of panic and anxiety overtook me …"

There were also relatively stable, successful times for me when the depression seemed to go into remission. In between the depressive episodes I was able to complete a post-graduate program in social work, build a successful business, and compete as a long-distance runner. I know now, however, that during these periods, depression, inadequacy, and fear were actually fueling much of the ambition. I was successful in the eyes of many people except myself. Over time, the periods of reprieve shortened, and the intensity of the depressive episodes increased. Even when I didn't feel depressed, I was difficult to live with and my relationships reflected my inner life: volatile, intense, remote, and erratic. In search of a reprieve, I was also consumed in those days, with self-help books, personal development workshops, and self-analysis. Besides a half dozen kinds of psychotherapy, I tried vision quests, sweat lodges, crystal healing, and a myriad of other alternative "remedies" that promised answers and relief. Although I never experienced any kind of sustained recovery, all these efforts, with their new awareness, at least left me with a residue of growth.

While I was working as a therapist, I was able to escape from the misery and the despondency—at least most days—by helping others.

And while I was able to connect pretty easily with clients who were also depressed, anxious, and confused, at the end of the day, I would sit in my empty office feeling completely hopeless and unable to see the good I had brought to anyone. I coped with the emptiness by working longer hours to flee from the anguish of being alone with myself.

After my father died and my marriage broke up, I was finally desperate enough to seek help from a competent psychiatrist who looked at both the biological as well as the psychological origins of the depression. I gained insights about myself and the origins of my depression, and I learned that I'd inherited a propensity to manic depression from my father and that depression and self-punishment were my responses to the trauma of living with the instability and rage inherent in my parents' relationship. Yet even amidst the clinical depression diagnosis, medical intervention, and psychological attention, the intensity and duration of the depressive episodes increased over time.

Today, while not cured of depression, at least I am free of its worst symptoms. While the tendency toward depression remains with me, it's been more than twenty years since I have been locked in depression's grip. The journey has been long and arduous, as well as rewarding and fulfilling. Caring has been, and continues to be, what has made all the difference. While it may not be sufficient, caring is absolutely necessary on this journey. I have been blessed to have caring people to walk alongside me. But caring is not just about the people *in* my life. Caring is also about the whole approach I take *to* my life.

## Having someone to walk with me

Depression manifests itself differently for everyone, and so the many roads that lead out of depression are numerous and varied. For some it comes through hospitalization and intense medical intervention in order to stop us from hurting ourselves and others. At times, a caring and wise psychiatrist or therapist intervenes at just the right moment in just the right way to kick-start a new direction. Sometimes a close friend, mentor, coach, or recovery community will guide us through the dark terrain. Depression is about *disconnection*—from ourselves, from others, from the world around us, and it is *connection* that is integral to recovery. My journey has included all of these paths while finding my own internal guides, inner resources, and strength.

My caring wife Val, who continues to walk with me through this journey, discovered my depressive tendencies only after we were committed to each other. She, among others, has taught me that caring doesn't mean fixing. If you are dealing with someone close to you who struggles with depression, remember that it isn't your job to fix anyone's depression or ultimately prevent anyone's suicide. Caring is about leaning into the discomfort and the ambiguity and the pain, and holding open a space where the person you care about can find their own way. I have found, that for me, *healing* and *recovery* are more helpful responses to depression rather than *fixing* and *curing*. Depression is like grief in that it is not a "problem to be solved," but rather a force to be worked with.

Depression is a family disease. It impacts our loved ones as much as it does us. When we hurt ourselves, we inflict pain onto someone near us. It was when I began to realize that Val was going to take care of herself and was merely going to guide me to some resources and support, that I knew I must make my own choices. Val knew how to say no and she knew she was not capable of taking me through to the other side of the darkness.

Having my wife step back from me when I was depressed was agonizingly frustrating (and painful for Val), but paradoxically it opened the door to healing, empowering me to seek my own guides and my own recovery community. This approach was liberating. It took the pressure off our relationship and allowed for mutual love and respect rather than one based solely on caregiving. Being too enmeshed in a relationship can actually contribute to the depression. I knew I was sucking the energy out of the person I loved most in my life, and my guilt about this was driving me into further despondency. You can get sucked into to the depression of others, just like you can get sucked in to your own depression. Being enmeshed with the illness—whether it is in yourself or in others—is part of the problem. Learning to step back and separate yourself from the depression—whether it is in yourself or in someone you care about—is part of the solution.

Although it is risky for loved ones to let go, it's just as risky to hang on. Just remember that no one is responsible for the choices another one makes in their life. Depression may be that person's journey. The caring journey of a close family member is to *care* without being *consumed*. Once again, care without carrying. Val has been there for me, but she does not allow my depression—either intentionally or unintentionally—to become manipulative.

## I am not my depression

A caring approach to depression is one that encompasses all aspects of being human—your mind, your body, and your heart. Depression in the mind is an example of neurodiversity: people who have brains that are wired in a different way. You can learn to separate yourself from your thoughts, and counter a tendency toward pessimism by changing the channel of negative thinking to gratitude and optimism. Depression is also in the body. I inherited my father's bipolar tendencies. It seems to be in my DNA.

Depression can feel all-encompassing and suffocating, but it's vital to remember that depression is never the totality of you as a person. Healing starts when you can separate yourself from your depressive thoughts and see them through new, more caring lenses. My youngest daughter spends time working alongside people who have disabilities. She has taught me that there are no "disabled people," only "people with disabilities." We all have disabilities, just as we are all "differently-abled." There are no "depressed people," only good people who suffer from depression. The distinction, for me, is vital. There may be a depressed part of you that seems to be ruining your life, but there is much more to you than your depression. Facing the demon isn't usually as frightening as it appears. It can be liberating and lifesaving.

Depression is also in the heart. When I succumb to the demands of others and disconnect from my soul, depression will begin to surface. Am I living my own dreams or someone else's agenda? What in the world is calling me? What is my sense of purpose? What does my heart yearn for? Discovering and connecting with my soul is what depression asks of me. Depression, I know now, is a force trying to move me toward growth and completeness. Instead of seeing depression as a dysfunction, it's been good to listen and pay careful attention to what this voice from my soul is seeking. While prescribed medication can, at times, provide some vital scaffolding during the reconstruction of the soul, it can also be too easy to pop pills for everything that ails you. You can turn yourself over to medicine without ever questioning what your heart is trying to tell you. When you attempt to right your physical ills without making the necessary psychic corrections, the body eventually takes its revenge.

## The dark night of the soul

Joseph Campbell was once inspired to write these words:

> The dark night of the soul
> comes just before revelation.
> When everything is lost,
> and all seems darkness,
> then comes the new life
> and all that is needed.

Depression is both a curse and a blessing. The curses seem more obvious. The darkness. The pain. The suffering. The lack of hope. The self-criticism and destruction we put ourselves and others through. Then there is the judgment we pile on to ourselves—we *should* be stronger than this!—which inevitably drives a darker, deeper knife into the already depressed mind. It can be depressing to be depressed! It can also be depressing to be around someone who is depressed.

The blessings of depression are not so apparent. But when viewed through the lens of caring, we may discover gifts such as a capacity toward compassion and empathy, creative and artistic abilities, tenderness, an increased capability for introspection, and a deeper understanding of the human condition. Indeed, some of the greatest human achievements have been made by people who are known to have depressive wiring. Through caring, we can define our condition by our *strengths*, rather than our weaknesses. Because I have suffered the horror of depression, I am able to tune in to the pain of others with greater empathy and kindness. I simply would not be the person I am today, nor would I be able to do the work I do today, without having gone through hell and back and learned how to face and tame this beast.

The most important blessing of depression, however, is that of mindfulness. Coming to grips with this malady has forced me to be attentive to the impact of my choices on my overall wellbeing. I was once told by a doctor that the key to a long and healthy life is to be diagnosed with a chronic, life-threatening illness and have to take care of it every day, your whole life. At the time, he was referring to diabetes, but the same could be said for depression. To prevent this condition from taking over and destroying me, I need to be extraordinarily vigilant about the amount and kind of rest and exercise I get, what I eat, the kind of people I associate with, the stresses in my life, and my workload. Caring for my depressive nature means being accountable for having structures and disciplines in place that lead to a healthier life.

Traditional societies seem to have known the value of depression, where the people who suffered from it became the Shamans—the healers—in their tribe. Today, we put those with acute depression in a psychiatric hospital. While a thorough diagnosis can be helpful to know what you are dealing with, the mind-set of pathology and intolerance, if we aren't careful, can actually contribute to the problem we are trying to remedy. Maybe instead of asking how to do away with our gloom, the braver idea is to remain attentive to it. If we welcome our personal sadness, we may recover a sense of meaning in our lives and possibly even contribute something valuable to the world in the process. With gentle, caring acceptance, the land of depression can be exceedingly fertile soil.

Sadness isn't bad. In a society hell-bent on happiness, we are told that happy is good and sad is bad. This can get confusing. Sad, we are told, has to be "fixed," which means reaching for something that gives immediate (and often short-lived) gratification and comfort. Instead of trying to "fix" your depression, befriend your deeper self, cultivate a sense of self-acceptance, and move through your depressive periods with a realization of the blessings of being human.

In order to realize any of these things, a caring, insightful community is needed to support you through to the other side. Depression is a lonely journey, but it cannot be done alone.

I have gained both support and strength in my own darkest hours from the thirteenth-century Persian poet and Sufi mystic Rumi—and often from reading his poem "The Guest House."

> This being human is a guest house.
> Every morning, a new arrival.
> A joy, a depression, a meanness,
> some momentary awareness comes as an unexpected visitor.
> Welcome and entertain them all!
> Even if they're a crowd of sorrows, who violently sweep
>     your house
> and empty it of its furniture,
> still, treat each guest honorably.
> He may be clearing you out for some new delight.
> The dark thought, the shame, the malice,
> meet them at the door laughing, and invite them in.
> Be grateful for whoever comes,
> because each has been sent as a guide from beyond.

By learning to somehow appreciate even some small aspect of this crowd of sorrows that comes to your door or has lived with you for some time, hope is born.

Depression—in some form or another—seems inevitable for some of us, so it can be useful to think of it as a refinement. Fine leather comes from being tanned. Wisdom can come from suffering. In the end, depression grows our soul rather than leaving us feeling a victim of life. Depression opens up greater possibilities—to know how to care more deeply and live more fully.

Learning to be there for others is integral to the depression recovery journey, especially in the context of a community that helps you understand boundaries, motives, and limitations, and is part of the healing. Dr. Karl Menninger, the eminent psychiatrist, was once asked what he would recommend if someone were having a nervous breakdown. He said he would tell them to leave their house, cross the railroad tracks to find someone in need, and help them.

Dr. Menninger has it right. Helping others heals your soul.

As I look back over my life, I see that the moments of great failures, great suffering, and great trauma actually were incidents that helped to shape the life I have now and the person I have become. Those moments may have looked and felt like irreparable crises, but through the light of time's perspective they were but learning opportunities.

Like the young maiden in the fairy tale Rumpelstiltskin who was locked in a room full of straw, we often do not realize that the straw all around us is gold in disguise. Depression, when faced with honest self-acceptance, compassion, and a caring community, is the very place we discover our wisdom. Look deeply and find the gifts amidst the suffering. A wise Wyoming rancher once explained it to me this way. "You'll always find a crocus in the cow pie." Beauty in the beast!

# Care of the Soul

I think that if you let me,
I'd treat you like the sky,
I'd join up all your insecurities
And bundle all your flaws.
I'd create a new constellation
And search for it endlessly.

A.J. Sanders

What in your life is calling you,
When all the noise is silenced,
The meetings adjourned ...
The lists laid aside,
And the Wild Iris blooms
By itself
In the dark forest ...
What still pulls on your soul?

Rumi

## Making room

I have a friend in Boston whom I've talked to on the phone almost every week for more than twenty years. Whenever I travel to Boston, George will pick me up at the airport and make time for me. We go out for dinner to his favorite Greek restaurant. He accepts, affirms, and encourages me to be who I am. I never feel judged: only supported. He's not afraid to be honest with me. He makes a place for me where I know I belong.

My sister Kate is the same way. Whenever I call her, she makes room for me and gives me undivided attention. When we are together, she makes the time to be present. She listens to me, and somehow conveys that same sense of belonging.

## A place to belong

My wife Val and I make a place for each other to belong. Even in my darkest hours, I know I belong. When I don't love myself, I know I am loved. Language cannot accurately explain what it means to have another human being care about you, what it means to have a place to belong. Sometimes the closest we can get is to read a poem, a gift that speaks to me deeply—like these few lines of poetry my daughter Hayley shared with me, written by A. J. Sanders, a young UK poet:

> I know you don't see yourself,
> the way I see you.
> And you still argue,
> when I call you beautiful.
> But all the things you can't stand
> about yourself,
> are all the things I can't
> go a day without.

We all need to find—or create—a place where we know we belong. It can be place in our outer world or a space within. Either way, we need a place that speaks to our soul. Caring is about creating that place. I return to and frequent businesses that give me a message that I belong. This is one of the reasons I have always supported independent bookstores. In almost every case when I walk into a privately owned bookstore, I feel as though I have come home.

How often do we stop to connect with our sense of belonging, our need to belong, and our capacity to create places where people actually know they are a part of something? It's human nature to seek belonging. We seek to replicate the experience of being loved or to find ways of being loved that we never had in our youths and childhoods. Because this need is instinctive, we don't always make the right choices. We choose friends with destructive tendencies, we choose affiliations that are exclusionary. Or we end up belonging somewhere because of old habits, without questioning, because it's what our closest associates have always done.

When I was a family therapist, parents would usually present a list of the areas and activities that caused problems with their kids, and I would ask them, "How much time do you spend with your children when you are not trying to 'get them to do something,' when you don't expect anything from them, when you are simply creating a place where they feel they belong?"

Inevitably, in the most troubled families, their minds would go blank. There was no space aside from lecturing, reprimanding, directing, or ignoring. There was no sense or experience of belonging.

If you work in customer service, what are you doing to take the time to listen, attend, connect, or tune in to your customers' emotions and needs? Are you just selling stuff, or have you created a space where your customers feel a part of something? If you are a parent, are you merely directing your children, or have you made a place where they belong? If you are a friend, a companion, a spouse, or a lover, are you creating a space for the person you deeply care for to belong? If you are a leader in an organization, are you creating a place where people have a chance to be their best, to realize their potential, to be recognized for their achievements, and to be acknowledged and appreciated for their contributions? Are you making a space where your staff feel they have a reason to come to?

I was in a dark and despondent mood not too long ago, fighting internal demons that were trying to erode every bit of goodness inside me. I woke up to these words on my computer screen.

It's always darkest before dawn,
your world is weary,
when all is dark,
when dreams die and fade away,

and all of life is stark,
take heart in gentle love,
for she waits in the wings,
and where she walks,
fairies dance and angels sing,
though you cannot see her,
she weaves a silken touch,
leaving footprints in the sand,
sprinkling spells and such.
lighting the dampened corridors,
the dark corners of your mind,
leaving you breathless,
bewildered by her kind,
goodness glints in her eyes,
hope is in her arms,
and all you've ever dreamed of,
rests sweetly in her charms.

My wife Val had taken the time to choose these beautiful lines of poetry, attributed to J. Blagojevic, and leave them for me where I would find them, knowing me, and knowing how much the words would mean to me, and how they would uplift my spirit.

As important as it is to live in a place where we belong, and to work in a place where we belong, belonging isn't something that is done "for" us or "to" us. Belonging is knowing to give to others what we expect from them back. Caring teaches us that the best way to make a place for ourselves to belong is to make a place for those around us to belong. What we give to the world will come back. Belonging invites belonging.

## If you don't go within, you'll go without

Sharon, a health care executive, arrived to see me wearing a thin shell of composure. As usual, she had on a crisp business suit and wore makeup, but beneath these was a woman who was tired, sick, in pain, carrying extra weight, and deeply sad.

As a child, she had lived with a father who was a raging alcoholic. In order to cope, Sharon, the oldest of five siblings, had done her best to make herself invisible to herself, instead throwing herself into caring for others by becoming highly attuned to the emotions and physical needs of her mother and four siblings.

For months, Sharon now explained, a rasp audible in her voice, she had been fighting a viral infection she couldn't get rid of. She had been seeing a chiropractor to deal with a degenerated lower disc problem that made sitting excruciatingly painful and getting to work most days almost impossible. And every other weekend, she lay on her back in a dark, cool basement bedroom recovering from a migraine headache.

Gradually, Sharon opened up about the pressures she was under at work: managing a large health care division, staffing and administering the sites she was responsible for, dealing with union demands, overseeing budgets, and ensuring that the managers within her division remained healthy and competent. She then told me about various other demands in her life—minimizing the actual strain they placed on her—including caring for aging parents and in-laws, helping her kids with difficulties in university, and dealing with her stepchildren.

After listening for some time, I asked, "Sharon, what are your hopes in working with me?"

Tears welled up in her eyes. "I need to make some changes in my leadership and in my life, but I just don't know where to start."

She had forgotten how to care for herself and was afraid to even begin.

I'd known Sharon for many years now. She had been in my leadership development programs and was one of the most caring leaders a person might meet. Yet, like so many caregivers, she defined herself by her capacity to be caring toward others, while at the same time losing a connection to her authentic self.

In our coaching sessions, Sharon began opening up about her past, and the tumultuous volatility and instability of her early life with an alcoholic father. Through our time together, we discovered how Sharon had sacrificed her own feelings and needs to respond to those around her. Because of fear, she'd made her sense of herself invisible. Yet at the same time, as she neglected tending to her own needs, she was able to discover an innate desire and capacity to tend to others, and had found great solace in caring.

Looking after others at the expense of ourselves may look like caring, but in Sharon's world, it was more like *pleasing* or *sacrifice*. When it arises from being wounded, *caring* for others can become *carrying* others. When our motive is to override inadequacy, unworthiness, and insecurity, caring can lead to unacknowledged resentment and, eventually, self-punishment that takes the form of burnout and exhaustion. We all share a common, compelling yearning to be seen, to be known, and to be loved, but when caring is used, knowingly or unknowingly, to fill this empty yearning, the consequence can be an anxiety-based compulsion to care, something we are *driven* to do, rather than an expression of the love that flows through us with ease.

"Hell is life drying up," wrote the American mythologist Joseph Campbell. When we lose our connection to the wellspring that nourishes our caring, helping others can deplete and exhaust us. If we do not stay connected to our soul, then those vital tasks that sustain us are pushed aside and we become a slave to the tyranny of the urgent demands around us.

It's an old human habit to run faster when we have lost our way. Sharon, in her desire to improve the world, had lost her way in the world. Her sense of herself and her body had deteriorated to the point that she was struggling to maintain her current workload and her personal commitments. This unseen, automatic desire to use caring to make her more visible and to validate her own worth had unintentionally caused her to drift away from herself. Being unable to say no to other people's needs, her body, in an effort to lead her out of the darkness and back home, was saying no for her.

When we are lost, the first step is to stop and get our bearings. Sharon knew all too well what others around her needed: she was frenetically consumed by taking care of these needs. But she drew a complete blank when asked, "Sharon, what do *you* need?" In her efforts to care, she had lost touch with her soul's desire. She had lost touch with her internal compass.

Over the ensuing months of coaching, Sharon began her restorative journey. She learned to listen to and care for her soul. Her first step was to allow herself to carve out personal time in her busy schedule. She began a daily practice of meditation, and she scheduled time for solitude and silence and to attend to the voice within. Seeking her own truth, rather than being driven by the world's expectations, Sharon bought a journal and now takes time to write in it most days. She is learning to listen more carefully to the voice of her soul, those quiet promptings from within, away from the demands of the world. She has created a simple sanctuary in her home, with special photos and phrases that inspire her, where she can go without technology to interrupt her, or anyone expecting anything from her. Some days, she hears nothing but the voices in her head, the voices of a world clamoring for misguided attention. But by learning to be still, her intuitive self is slowly emerging and guiding her. She is learning to be comfortable with herself, and more self-accepting.

Just as important, Sharon has begun caring for her body, beginning with incremental changes in her life. She has stayed, at least for now, in her executive role, but she is learning to set limits and sometimes say no, and to not carry the world on her shoulders. She also knows that if, in the future, the load gets too heavy, she can always go back to front-line nursing, where her heart is. She is leaving her Blackberry at work and spends time in the evenings going for walks with her husband instead of answering emails. Having examined the link between her own burnout and her need to overprotect her family, she is learning to care from a place of strength as a mature adult, not from a place of weakness and invisibility, as a way to prove her worth. On this path of recovery, she is remembering that caring is meant to be an act of love, not a burden.

---

I don't want to make Sharon's transformation sound easy. It's taken months of reflection and mindful effort. She has not been cured, but *is* healing. Within herself, she's uncovered a bedrock of emotional and spiritual strength. Leonard Cohen says it this way, "Forget your perfect offering. There is a crack in everything. That's how the light gets in." By appreciating this capacity in herself to care so deeply and carefully, through having been wounded long ago, she is able to value and direct her gift of caring more fully toward herself.

Sharon may never completely shake the coping strategies she learned as a child, this impulse to put others' needs before her own. As E. B. White, the American writer and long-term contributor to *The New Yorker* magazine, once said, "I arise in the morning torn between a desire to improve the world and a desire to enjoy the world. This makes it hard to plan the day." Yet, like reacquainting herself with a long-lost friend, Sharon is learning to stop and savor life by listening and caring for her soul. She understands that the hard nugget she earned from being wounded is ultimately a gift. On the journey, she is discovering that caring means first enjoying the world, and through that joy she can actually, and often unexpectedly, improve the world.

Sharon is also learning through a supportive, caring community to let go of her addiction to perfection, and is enjoying the blessings of an imperfect life. She is facing her fears of being still and unproductive at times, and takes at least a day each week to be what she now calls "unbusy" and "unproductive," when she simply putters and relaxes.

If we don't go within, we will go without. It's a long voyage home after we have become lost. But the journey is possible—with careful attention and vigilance.

# In Search of Caring

Our lives begin to end the day we become silent about things that matter.

Martin Luther King, Jr.

## How can I care?

As the long journey of this book draws to an end, Hal continues *his* journey. He has little quality in his existence now, except for the love that surrounds him from his devoted wife Dianne, his children, and the rest of us who care so much about him. He also has Dez, a moody black cat that sleeps next to him.

Hal has long since lost his capacity to be a doctor, the field that was the core of his life for so many years. His eyes, however, will brighten at a conversation about our health care system, or the topics of anatomy and physiology. He can no longer enrich his beautiful mind except through listening, in very short stints, to audiobooks and good music. Once a gifted amateur photographer, he has been unable to take pictures for months. In the early stages of adjusting to his illness, Hal would often be found at this computer filing his images, maintaining contact with the art that he loves so much. But now he is no longer able to focus enough to work on the computer. While he loves his grandchildren deeply, and they will excitedly climb up on his wheelchair to sit on his lap, their energy soon wears him out. He is still able to be at home, though, and feels most fortunate about this blessing. His body is essentially now paralyzed entirely on the right side, and it continues to swell from his anti-seizure medication. The seizures are becoming more frequent. But his appetite remains good, and, with a little help, Hal is able to feed himself with his workable left hand.

Long dedicated to educating future generations of physicians, Hal has been intensely involved in training and mentoring medical students in rural medicine during his long career in the town where he lives. In honor of Hal's determined presence and his contribution to rural medicine, the University of Calgary Faculty of Medicine created the Dr. Hal Irvine Community Focus Award, to be presented to physicians who demonstrate dedication through their service and personal commitment to improving the quality of life in their community.

My brother would never have sought to have an award named after him. In fact, in his own modest way, he was embarrassed to hear of it. What matters to him is the virtue of human goodness.

There is incredible power in what may appear to be a simple gesture. All we have to do is ask "how can I care?" with an open heart, a willingness to listen, and the courage to take even a small action. This is Hal's legacy. It's why I wrote this book.

Caring matters to me, and I believe it matters to the world. It all begins with a single caring action—like when Amelia Curran made her way to Hal's hometown and paid him a special visit.

## A special concert

Even with her long list of accolades—a Juno award winning singer-songwriter with a "velvety-smooth" voice, often compared to Leonard Cohen, and so on—Amelia Curran, who hails from St. John's, Newfoundland, remains one of the most down-to-earth performers you can meet.

Hal comes alive when Amelia's music is playing. Growing up, he was a fan of Leonard Cohen and he's developed the same affinity for Amelia and her work. Both her words and her music have never failed to lift his spirits. One of his few remaining pleasures has been to listen to her recordings.

Amelia was scheduled to perform in Hal's hometown in the central Alberta foothills, in the same out-of-the-way community where Hal has practiced medicine and served others all these years. He was so excited that Amelia was coming to town and had anticipated being able to hear her in person. Dianne immediately went out and bought tickets, some of the first to be sold. But as the date got closer, the reality of Hal's situation settled in more and more deeply. He was simply too weak to go out in public.

His good friends and the organizers of the concert asked Amelia's agent if she would consider doing something very unusual. "We know about Amelia's demanding schedule. She is arriving directly from the airport and is leaving for London, England the next day. But we have a special friend who is a huge fan of Amelia's music, and, with brain cancer, he is too ill to attend the concert. Is there any possible way that Amelia would consider coming to Hal's house to meet and play for him beforehand?"

At four o'clock, on the afternoon of the performance, Amelia Curran arrived on Hal and Dianne's front driveway in an old red pickup truck with a border collie in the back. She'd come directly from the airport, an hour-and-a-half drive. After reaching in the backseat for her guitar, her driver brought her to the front door. With a gracious and caring heart, this rising star of the Canadian music scene had made her way from St. John's, Newfoundland to a tiny town in Alberta—and into my brother's living room. She gave Hal the best little concert of his life. She came for no other reason than because Hal's good friends had asked her and because she cared.

There were four of us in the room that day. Amelia's mini-concert was unspeakably moving. I still get emotional recalling how she sang and strummed her guitar in the quiet of the afternoon. Amelia was so utterly genuine. She even confessed how shy and awkward she felt not being able to hide behind a huge crowd, not knowing, in those pauses between songs as she struggled in her own human way, what to play for us next.

"I'd rather play for a hundred people than four," she said honestly, with a touch of humor.

Despite these admissions of awkwardness, it was clear Amelia is a gifted musician. She put us at ease with her warmth, grace, humility, and beautiful voice. I learned later that Amelia has been outspoken about mental health issues and about her experiences with depression. With the help of various St. John's friends, health care professionals, and a handful of local celebrities, she even produced a music video (titled "This Video") to help combat the stigma around mental illness and promote better access to health care. It was no surprise then, that she generously took time out of her schedule to grace us with her presence.

She certainly made a difference for this family. For the rest of his days, Hal's eyes will light up whenever anyone mentions Amelia Curran.

## Bits of good put together that overwhelm the world

Last night, instead of sleeping, I lay in bed thinking rather bitterly about life and its ironies. Why should such a horrible disaster come to a man who has given so much of his life to the world around him? Throughout his thirty-one-year career in rural family medicine, Hal has lived and believed in the value of caring. He's cared deeply for his patients, for his colleagues, and for his community. He has cared about his work. A compassionate and skilled physician, Hal has delivered the kind of service to his patients that he himself would want—and now he is receiving it all back from his family, his colleagues, and his community who love him so much. How can a person who gave so much spend the last years of his life in such a helpless, deteriorating state?

As I lay in sadness, my mind drifted to a scene three years ago, when a fire decimated a scenic mountain pass in Banff National Park not far from our home. Soon after the fire, I hiked with a friend through the trails that wove through the blackened slope. A hillside that had once been shrouded in majestic pine, spruce, and fir trees now bore only smoldering stumps and ashes. It was a bleak picture indeed, compared to the beauty that had once been there. And yet, amid this terrible desolation, we discovered there were young green seedlings emerging through the grey, bitter ash.

Fire is the mechanism by which a forest regenerates itself. Many species rely on fire to spread their seeds. The jack pine produces resin-filled cones that are very durable and remain dormant until a fire occurs and melts the resin that allows the seeds to germinate. The heat from burning trees bursts open the cones and releases seeds that have been waiting for a fire to give them life. Nature teaches us, in the words of Parker J. Palmer, to embrace "brokenness as an integral part of life" and "use devastation as a seedbed for new life." Devastation creates life in every cycle. It is unable to do otherwise.

As I thought about the decimated forest, my mind drifted back to the last moments I had with Hal yesterday. He was lying back in his recliner, a device that allows him to drift back and recline with the push of a button so that he doesn't have to transfer in and out of his wheelchair so often. Another small pleasure that Hal appreciates and enjoys.

When I said goodbye to Hal yesterday, he was drifting off comfortably in his easy-chair, preparing for his afternoon rest. He had a peaceful smile on his face. I took his hand and gazed into his heavy-lidded eyes.

It's been a long journey for all of us, I thought.

I kneeled beside him and took his hand in mine. I could not keep back the tears. An unexplainable power surrounded us and I was overcome by the moment. Brother to brother, and now, friend to friend. I have experienced the presence of a divine power in these precious times with Hal. I have learned to care and to live in a way I would never have imagined possible. This experience is a beautiful gift that he has given me on his journey. His life as a physician helped heal others. Now, as he is dying, his healing presence continues.

With immense gratitude and grief, I leaned forward and kissed Hal, realizing as my cheek pressed against his cheek that I missed some whiskers when I shaved him a few hours before.

"I love you, bro," I uttered.

His words were slurred, but I understood them completely. "Love you too, Dave."

He smiled as I squeezed his hand. I stood up, took in his swollen face and puffy eyes that were now closed, and walked quietly out of the room.

"Do your little bit of good where you are; it's those little bits of good, put together, that overwhelm the world," advises Desmond Tutu. It's important to take these words to heart. In the end, it may be everything we have.

## Breathings of the heart

As I look up from my writing, I again read the words sitting on my desk—sent to me by my dear daughter Hayley, a consummate encourager—composed by the romantic poet William Wordsworth. "Fill your paper with the breathings of your heart." Wordsworth wrote this profoundly beautiful line in a letter to his wife Mary. In full, it reads, "Write to me frequently and the longest possible; never mind whether you have facts or no to communicate; fill your paper with the breathings of your heart."

At the time he wrote the letter—April 1812—William had been traveling extensively throughout Great Britain, visiting various colleagues and family members. William and Mary had five children under the age of nine, and their youngest, Catharine—barely three years old—suffered from a serious illness. Catharine would die from convulsions a month later. So these lines are not a youthful proclamation, but an expression of a husband and wife's long knowledge of each other, a love letter colored by the daily burdens of their conjugal life together.

I take these words as a reminder of how complicated life can be, that even in the midst of distance and difficulties, it's possible to find the courage to speak about what is truly important and meaningful. These words remind me that, at some point in our lives, we can decide to set aside what we think the world expects of us, and be guided by the promptings of the heart. This book, the "breathings of my heart," has been such a journey.

## Something that we truly care about

In August 1921, a cave was rediscovered high up on the wall of a small canyon in northern Utah. Later that year, the subsequent discovery of another cave in the same area renewed a great interest in caves and caving.

Local citizens approached the U.S. Forest Service, which had responsibility for the land where the caves were located, and asked when tours of the caves would begin. The Forest Service responded that there was no extra money and therefore there would be no tours, but they agreed to place a gate on the entrance and secure it with a lock.

One group of local citizens was not pleased with their answer and took it upon themselves to form the Timpanogos Cave Committee. Soon afterward, they returned to the Forest Service with a plan of their own. The committee would raise the money required, build a trail up the canyon wall, install lights in the cave, and conduct tours. The Forest Service did not have to do anything but say "yes." The Forest Service agreed on one condition: if the committee ever made a profit, the extra money would be reinvested in making further improvements to the area.

With an agreement in place, the committee spent the winter of 1921–1922 building a precipitous mile-long trail to reach the cave entrance that was 1200 feet above the canyon floor. While the trail to the cave was being built, electrical wires were run to the cave entrance, and lights and wiring were installed inside the cave. The committee opened the site to the public in 1922.

That same year, the Timpanogos Cave was declared a National Monument. During the ensuing twenty-five years, even while responsibility for the cave was being transferred to the National Park Service, the committee continued operations. The committee remained true to their word and reinvested profits into improving the area. Tunnels were blasted to provide access to two other caves. The trail was rerouted and rebuilt to provide access to newly opened areas. Restrooms and other visitor facilities were constructed.

More than ninety years later, the legacy of the dedication of this small group of committee members still remains because they fell in love with an idea and made it happen.

The brief history of this magnificent National Monument was told by our guide, Royce Shelley, in a family trip to the cave. Royce is a schoolteacher and spends his summers conducting tours through the caves. His passion and love for these sacred caverns is compelling. Around every bend in the cave is a new adventure. Royce cares deeply about these caves and tells story after story about stalagmites and stalactites and the magic and history that can be found in each of their special formations. His soul is alive on these tours. His love for his work touches people daily, perhaps even more than the beauty of the caves themselves.

At the end of a tour, while visitors' eyes adjust from the darkness of the caverns as we emerge into the light, Royce continues to share his passion and love for these magnificent caves. After a moment of silence, he offers, in a quiet and unwavering declaration, a challenge for all who have been fortunate enough to be on the tour:

> Most of us will never discover a cave, but each of us has an opportunity to discover something that we truly care about, something that we love. It might be music, mathematics, art, dance, languages, science, athletics, neighborhood parks, or a million other things. Just as our lives are better today because of the Timpanogos Cave Committee, the challenge is for us to use our energies and talents so that one hundred years from now, life will be better for people and for this planet because we were here.

Discover a cause beyond your own self-interest, something to care about that makes a difference. And may you also, on your journey, find some*one* you care about. Caring is an expression of the human spirit that gets to the heart of leadership and life. Caring makes you a better person. It awakens and inspires you to be all you can be. Caring is what makes the world a place worth living. Caring is everything.

# The Footprints of a Great Physician Leader

# Dr. Hal Irvine

Carol Rowntree, Glenn Kowalsky, Diana Kleinloog and Colleen Bailey

*Sundre Roundup*, March 29, 2016

There is a well-worn path on the hospital grounds that leads from the home of Dr. Hal Irvine to the front door of the Sundre Hospital and Care Centre.

Irvine selflessly walked those 150 steps countless times over his 31 years of service to this community as a rural family physician and anesthetist. He is deeply honored that the Sundre Palliative Care Association will be dedicating the newly renovated palliative care suite at the hospital in his name in recognition of his exemplary service to this community. This project was made possible by the generous donation from Peak Theatre Players. Spearheaded by Neil Embleton, all proceeds from the recent Calendar Girls play were donated to this tribute, as were the sales of the calendar created by the cast, Heidi Overguard, photographer and Bill Lough, Peaks Printing.

Irvine's love of rural medicine and this community has been apparent in so many ways. He thrived on the variety of work in rural practice—from clinic to emergency shifts, delivering babies to palliative care. He truly valued continuity of care and the long-term relationships he developed with his patients, families and co-workers. His selfless dedication to this community was apparent by his provision of a solo epidural service to laboring moms over his years in practice.

One of the many things that made him special was his commitment to promoting a strong team. Irvine, who completed his undergraduate medical degree at the University of Calgary in 1977, pioneered weekly rounds for physicians, nurses, physiotherapy, pharmacy, respiratory therapy, home care and mental health to get together to coordinate the best care for the patients of this community. Diana Kleinloog, one of the nurses who worked by his side for 30 years, described him as "focused, approachable, and inspired excellence from all." He was always available to his colleagues to help with challenging cases; he would be by their side within minutes—day or night—without complaint.

Irvine, who was raised in Red Deer and finished high school in Lacombe, inspired many medical students to follow in his footsteps in rural medicine. To him, family medicine was not a job—it was a calling and a profession he took pride in. Dr. Carol Rowntree was one of his first medical students in Sundre in 1984 and has been privileged to be his friend and colleague for the past 26 years. Many other local physicians over the years also trained in Sundre as medical students as well as family medicine residents and they were inspired by Irvine. Among them were Michelle Warren, Chris Barnsdale, Tim Souster and Rob Warren. Irvine was much more than a skilled teacher. To many, such as Dr. Glenn Kowalsky, he was also a cherished mentor. His commitment to lifelong learning placed him in high demand as an instructor for teaching airway management and procedural sedation to practicing physicians and nurses. His contributions to rural medical education were recognized last year when a special award called the Hal Irvine Community Focus Award was created in his honor by the University of Calgary.

Irvine and his wife Dianne moved to Sundre in 1982 and raised their three children—Sarah, Bronwyn, and Brody—in the community. Despite his busy practice and family life, he contributed to the community in so many ways and he always made time for the arts.

For six years he was president of the Sundre and District Allied Arts Society, a volunteer job that entailed chairing meetings and managing the operations of the Sundre Arts Centre. He was an active member of the local photography club and for years Irvine was the official photographer for Peak Theatre Players. He took portraits of cast members for programs and publicity, and could be found before each show carefully hanging portraits in the lobby.

He always had an interest in acting and it wasn't long before he auditioned for his first play. He was subsequently involved in several plays with Sundre's local theatre group, Peak Theatre Players. Acting was a fun outlet for him. He was involved in such notable roles as a Buddhist golfer, a lecherous coachman, a developmentally handicapped man, a ghost and a salesman peddling leather-bound week-at-a-glance organizers. After this last role, his patients, friends and even a policeman who pulled him over kept asking to buy one!

Irvine also had a passion for motorcycling and surprised many of his students when the seemingly sedate and mild-mannered country doctor would invite them to ride with him on his Yamaha FJR to his weekly Tuesday morning anesthesia shifts in Olds.

His contributions to medical leadership were also many. He contributed his time and expertise to many organizations such as the Society of Rural Physicians of Canada and chaired the Rural GP Anesthesia Committee. In 1988, he was the president of the Alberta College of Family Physicians. He was chief of staff and later became the facility medical director for the Sundre hospital for 30 years. He won numerous awards for his significant contributions to both rural medicine and anesthesia, including Clinician of the Year by the David Thompson Health Region medical staff as well as the Rural Preceptor of the Year award from the University of Calgary in 2003. In 2009, the Society of Rural Physicians of Canada awarded him with a Fellowship of Rural and Remote Medicine.

Among his other notable achievements are earning his certification in family medicine in 1979 after completing residency training at Queen's University in Kingston, Ont., as well as becoming an associate member of the Royal Australian College of General Practitioners when he did a six-month practice exchange to Victoria, Australia in 1999.

While in Vancouver in November 2013, to be recognized by his peers as Alberta Family Physician of the Year by the College of Family Physicians, Irvine was diagnosed with a brain tumor and his plans for retirement and spending time were sadly cut short. His three grandchildren bring him much joy and he continues to be honored by the generous love and support shown by this community as he and his family deal with his illness.

The dedication of the palliative care suite at the Sundre hospital will be an ongoing reminder of the gratitude of this community to Dr. Hal Irvine, for his exceptional contributions as a physician and community member.

# Appendix A

## Making Caring in the Workplace Real

Here are five ways to show caring on a team. You will find that when you care, you not only succeed; you succeed together. You create a workplace worth working in. This list was inspired by my fellow consultant and friend, John Liston, who knows from first-hand experience how to build a successful team.

**Hire caring people.** Not long ago, I was in a Marriott Hotel in San Francisco where we had great customer service for the entire weekend. When I was checking out, I asked the clerk what training she was given to give such good service. After thinking about it for a few moments she replied, "You can't train someone to be nice. What we do here is hire nice people and train them how to use the computer." While you don't always get to choose your employees, a caring leader, when they do have the choice, takes the time to know both the skills and attitudes needed in the culture of the organization, and takes their time to get the right fit.

**Create an environment for people to be their best.** When are you at your best? Typically, it is when you are focused, and not worried about mistakes or about failing. In John Liston's words, "When we win, we party; when we lose, we ponder." This means it's okay to make mistakes, as long as you learn from them. See the best in people. *Fit* people, don't *fix* people. Find their strengths and build on those strengths. Find a place where people can take their gifts, their passion, and their talents and make a contribution. It takes coaching, mentoring, and, most importantly, time. When you create these environments, people "chose to" come to them; they don't feel they "have to."

**Understand the *why* (the reason) before the *what* or the *how*.** At the 1963 Washington D.C. Civil Rights March, Martin Luther King, Jr. did not stand up with a "strategic plan." Martin Luther King, Jr. had a dream. He gave people a reason. What's vital in building a team—as well as building a life—is to not confuse the means with the ends. People simply aren't going to be accountable if they aren't motivated. If they aren't accountable, it's because they don't have enough *reason* to be accountable. A vision is what gives people a reason to get on board. John uses the vehicle of sport to teach character. Character is the *why*. Character is the goal. Sport is the means to that goal. Some people get confused and think sport is about winning. Professional sport may be, but all other sports are about character. Winning is a by-product. It works the same in business.

**Execute with precision.** John is a master of accountability cultures. He understands that you have to inspire people, and then you have to link that inspiration to clearly defined outcomes and a precise way to get there. This is where John is tough. He models his own values. He cares about people and has a precise, results-driven process for creating an environment for people to hold themselves accountable—to themselves and to each other.

**Celebrate success.** In John's words, "You have to know what success is, know how to get there, and know how to celebrate it when you've achieved it." You have to know what constitutes success and shine a light on it. Tell the story. Acknowledge people. Catch them being successful. It's important to care and to connect. Celebration can be big or it can be small, but most importantly it has to be meaningful.

If you are a positional leader of a team, what kind of environment are you creating on your team? You have a responsibility to not only care, but to *show* that you care about those on your team. Here is a list of questions you might ask yourself to assess whether your team members know you care. You can *say* you care, but here are some ways that you can make caring in the workplace real:

- How clear am I about the personal values and goals of each member of my team, and how do these align with the work each person is doing?
- Do people know *why* they are doing the work they are doing, that is, how their contribution fits into a larger purpose? Do I encourage people on my team to pause and clarify the value and impact of a new project or assignment before diving in to get it done?
- What am I doing that puts unnecessary stress on people and puts them into a crisis mode?
- How much of my week is spent connecting with people, listening to what's going on in their life and their work, and expressing genuine recognition and acknowledgement?
- Do I have high standards and expectations that are both clear and achievable for everyone? Do people feel that my commitment to support them is balanced with my expectations of them?
- Do my direct reports feel that I serve them, or do they feel they have to please me in order to call themselves successful?
- Are there reports, processes, or systems that are outdated and no longer necessary but are taking up people's time?
- How am I creating a safe environment where people can challenge or change the way we do things in order to deliver the expected results? Do people feel safe to make mistakes and safe to learn from those mistakes?
- How much do people on my team actually know me? Do they know why I work here? Do they know what my personal vision and values are? Do they know why I took on this leadership role? Do they know what inspires me? Do they know what scares me?

I learned from Dr. Stephen R. Covey in one of his seminars that, "anything less than a conscious commitment to the important is an unconscious commitment to the unimportant." If you find yourself too busy to intentionally go out of your way to show people that you care about them, then you are too busy. At least, you are too busy doing unimportant things! What caring leaders have taught me is that caring, in leadership and in life, means action. Sure you can use email or other indirect communication, but a note on an employee's desk or a direct apology or a meaningful conversation that leads to change and that makes work better for an employee are what really count. You have to carve out the time and take the action.

# Appendix B
## Putting Caring Into Action

### How do you care when you don't feel like it?

This stuff about caring is all well and good, but how do you go about caring when it gets hard, or when you simply don't feel like caring?

- How do you care when you are dressed up like Goofy and you've been walking around the Disney grounds all day answering dumb questions and being poked at and getting thrown up on, in a hundred-degree heat, and you are paid to create an experience for your guests that leave them feeling that this was the "happiest place on earth?"
- How do you care in those moments when, as a parent of a child with autism, you go day after day trying desperately to connect when you get nothing back?
- How do you care, as an exhausted health care professional, when you are working with patients who don't respect themselves enough to care about you, who are unappreciative or unresponsive?
- How do you care about a group of employees who couldn't care less about their job?
- How do you care about a spouse from whom you have drifted apart?

There are no easy answers to these questions. Hopefully, you will find it helpful to reflect on this list of a few simple strategies:

**Accept your humanity.** It's inhuman to expect anyone, including yourself, to feel like caring all the time. Not feeling particularly caring at times is all part of the human experience of caring. With caring comes the necessity of forgiving yourself with kindness, periodic bouts of detachment, and accompanying guilt in the caring process.

**Get perspective.** Look at your situation from a bigger picture. Disney employees tolerate the heat and demands from their guests by reminding themselves of the bigger picture, of the vital role they serve in creating a remarkable experience for the guests. They can overlook their self-centered desires by realizing that demanding guests simply want to be connected and have a good experience.

**Recognize the value of duty.** Duty can be a joy when we make a decision to not necessarily do what's comfortable, but instead do what's right. Doing the *right* thing, not necessarily the *easy* thing, is what gives a person self-respect at the end of the day.

**Don't wait until you feel like it.** Waiting to care until you feel like caring is like waiting to exercise until you feel like exercising. It simply won't happen, at least not consistently. Usually, you have to roll up your sleeves and get to work. Usually, the feelings of wellbeing and self-worth come later, following right action. Discomfort is a part of all caring, including self-care. Feeling good about the whole thing is an *outcome*, not a prerequisite. Often, through the act of caring, enjoyment will come after the actions you take.

**Don't take it personally.** People have all kinds of reasons for lashing out at a customer service representative or a colleague at work. People bring their marriage problems, life stresses, and personal issues into the stores where they shop, the amusement parks where they come to enjoy themselves, the restaurants where they dine, and the workplaces that employ them. From time to time, we all get caught up in the fray of other people's problems. While no one should tolerate abusive or disrespectful behavior from anyone, you can reach out with friendliness and care to unfriendly and hard-to-care about people when you imagine that you are only seeing the tip of their life's iceberg. It helps to open a caring heart and not take it all personally.

**Take the high ground.** When you respect yourself enough you won't let anyone disrespect you. Caring doesn't mean you are in any way obligated to tolerate disrespectful behavior. You don't have to let anyone drag you down, and you don't want to get involved in ill-mannered arguments. A leader I have high regard for told me once, "Never argue with an idiot because they will bring you down to their level and beat you with experience." Live on the foundation of good principles, even if the people around you don't appreciate it. Do the right thing, because the right thing will make things right inside of you. Caring and self-respect can't be separated.

**Accept that you don't have to like people in order to care about them.** Sometimes we are asked to care about people that are simply not likeable. For whatever reason, patients or customers or family members or people within our communities are belligerent, rude, cold, and are not receptive to our caring. Sometimes you have to love people even though you don't like them. You can do this by attending to their humanity and to where they have been damaged or wounded in their past. It's important, in these cases, to not take it personally so you can open your heart. You can always find something you love about another person if you listen carefully and look hard enough.

**Practice showing up and letting go of the results.** It can be liberating when you give yourself permission to not carry the burden of the results of your caring. As a caring person or professional, your job is often just to be present for someone and to be with them. What they do with this is their choice. Your commitment to care may never compensate for the unhappiness your customer or patient came in with. While the act of caring can go a long way, for many there's only so far it can go.

**Keep a sense of humor.** Usually the best indicator of the effectiveness of your caring is how much you enjoy the process. Let go of trying to get it all right, and instead find ways of enjoying the whole experience. Good friends who grant you perspective, time away from caring, and a lightness of heart can provide you with a way to sustain your sanity in the arduous work of caring.

# Appendix C

## Becoming Real: A Journey to Authenticity

Caring, I have discovered, requires some self-awareness. To understand what this means, it's helpful to look at the evolution of your life in terms of these stages:

The first stage is about *living in the world*. Stage One is about learning to survive. As children, we learn the rules for getting along, the importance of listening to our teachers and our parents, and being sensible. This first stage continues into adulthood as we look for work or declare a major in college. Here, we learn to satisfy our instructors and do whatever it takes to survive the post-secondary experience. When we get a job we learn to please the boss and take care of the customer. Hollywood and the media heavily influence us in this stage, as billboards and commercials dictate what to buy, what to drive, what to wear, how to define success, and what gives us pleasure. We define ourselves by our titles, our possessions, our achievements, or the number of "likes" we get on Facebook.

We succeed in this first stage by learning to be accountable and finding ways to be useful in the world. We learn to show up on time. We learn how to be responsible adults. But if we aren't careful, we run the risk of taking a job that we hate but that pays well, and then spending all our earned cash on "toys" to cheer us up as a reward for being miserable at work.

The second stage is about *coming into awareness*. It begins when we discover a feeling of incongruence between what we bring to the world and what the world gives back. It's like being lost. Emptiness is a telling sign, a sense that something is missing. Or we begin to realize just how smothered we are by the tyranny of urgencies we allow to be imposed upon us by others. Stage Two is about resisting the tendency to continue at the same high velocity, through the same incessant busyness. It's about stopping, slowing down, and paying attention. We decide, "that's enough." At this point, we have to sort out what it takes to step away from the world and get our bearings.

Stage Two heralds a time of turning inward—away from what culture expects—to connect with a deeper, more sustaining voice that guides and affirms us. "Human resources are like natural resources," says author and international advisor on education Ken Robinson. "They're often buried deep. You have to go looking for them, they're not just lying around on the surface. You have to create the circumstances where they show themselves."

The voice of our authentic, essential self isn't discovered through the senses, or by what brings us immediate gratification or what the world values. It is realized, instead, through finding a deeper voice inside us that comes from below the surface of our emotions, our thoughts, and our day-to-day awareness. It begins to move us away from following the crowd.

The author and activist Parker J. Palmer reminds us that this emerging realization does not have to reach a conclusion, or necessarily leave us with concrete plans. "Measuring the value of inner dialogue by its practical outcomes is like measuring the value of a friendship by the number of problems that are solved when friends get together. Conversation among friends has its own rewards: in the presence of our friends, we have the simple joy of feeling at ease, at home, trusted, and able to trust."

What's important is to pay attention when we are called into this second stage. Like heeding the voice of a dear friend, if we ignore what they have to say, they'll either stop saying it, or they'll become urgent and perhaps even aggressive in order to convey their message.

In the third stage, we emerge into the *path of authenticity*. We take our essential, authentic self and bring it back into the world in a way that serves both society and the soul. In Stage Three, we begin to respond to the promptings of the inner voice. When we honor our inner voice with simple attention and action, it firmly engages us in a life-giving dialogue with the soul. It also offers us a life truly worth living.

Attend to the authentic self, not to fix, but simply to cultivate a sense of your identity and worth that allows you to feel at home wherever you are. Caring from this authentic place is effortless. It flows naturally. There is nothing to fix and no one to straighten out. You can be there merely as a presence, as caring flows through you. When caring comes from this place of overflow, it gives life, and it sustains and nourishes you rather than depleting, draining, or exhausting you. It comes from a sense of being enough. The connections welded together by authentic caregivers are not in their methods but in their hearts.

"We cannot cure the world of sorrows, but we can choose to live in joy," said Joseph Campbell. "When we talk about settling the world's problems, we are barking up the wrong tree. The world is perfect. It's a mess. It has always been a mess. We are not going to change it. Our job is to straighten out our own lives."

If you are interested in looking more deeply into the authentic journey and connecting with your authentic self, you may find my book *Becoming Real: Journey to Authenticity* of some value. While I have no formula, here are some guideposts to consider:

**We are not our roles.** Connecting to the authentic self in the work of caring requires seeing the difference between one's self and one's role. Parents who have an understanding of this know that when their teenager slams the door in their face when they have just said no to them, their fifteen-year-old is working on the task of separation. The parents may not be happy with the teen's behavior, but they know better than to take it personally. Their child is not so much angry at them as at the role they play as parents. A similar thing happens with caring. When you are connected to your authentic self, you don't define yourself by the outcomes expected in your role. Instead, the caregiving role is a vehicle to express your caring, rather than a definition of who you are. Differentiating the two enables you to care with a little more lightness.

**Solitude and silence are our friends.** Our lives get hectic. We can become so busy putting out the fires around us that we lack time to kindle the fires of our own imaginations. All too often, we react to the stresses of daily life, rather than responding to our deeper desires. When we stop and pay attention to these deeper yearnings, we see we are no longer living our own lives, but rather, in this harried and frantic world, our lives are taking the living out of us. It's a little too much like being on a boat where the oarsmen are all pulling with great enthusiasm in different directions and, in their frenzy, have stopped listening to each other.

It can be difficult to find that voice within you with the myriad demands our culture calls you to do and how it tells you to live and says what your life should look like.

What would it take to begin—and keep—a daily practice of meditation, prayer, or simple silence? It's important to make space and take time in your life to look within and listen to the voice inside you. Listening to yourself requires a place where you can hear something besides your thoughts about what the world expects of you. It helps to be able to distinguish that voice from all those other voices that clamor for your attention. It requires a sanctuary of some kind, a place where you can sit still and actually get away from the frenetic demands of the world, a place to restore your spiritual resources.

**Seek a connection to nature.** Sitting at the seashore, walking in the woods or in a pasture, taking a stroll through an urban park, putting your feet on the ground, even having a plant in your office or on your balcony, are all ways to connect with the natural world. Get outside once in a while. Experience the immense and simple beauty around you. It helps to make a connection to what matters in life. There's an interconnection between the natural world and the soul. Connecting to nature binds you to a deeper stream, a deeper voice, a deeper knowing.

**Take up journaling.** How do people maintain an adequate level of self-examination, self-reflection, and self-acceptance in order to stay connected to their inner life? Some choose to write, making it daily practice, even for a few minutes at the beginning or end of each day. Using pen and paper takes you away from the usual cerebral approach to life and connects you to a deeper sense of yourself. Buy a journal that you feel drawn to. Get a good pen that you like the feel of. Spend a little time each day in quiet reflection.

**Find a confidant.** Preserve those connections with people who care about you. "A confidant can provide a holding environment for someone who is busy holding everybody else," writes leadership guru Ronald A. Heifetz. Confidants can help you put yourself back together again at the end of the day. They come in the form of friends, spouses, lovers, and close colleagues, people who are close to you, who provide support and perspective. You can always tell a confidant by the way you feel when you're around them: a sigh of relief, your body relaxing, your lungs expanding, your heart beating stronger.

As a conduit to looking ever more deeply into your life, confidants can be coaches, therapists, mentors, and teachers—caring guides who help you step back from the situations where you care, and help you understand what has happened and what is happening. These confidants might ask you questions like, "What's going on here? What's the stress about? What can be learned from this mistake? What's your part of the problem, what is theirs, and what might you choose to let go of?"

Caring without a confidant is like struggling through the Canadian winter without a winter coat.

**Embrace the breakdowns.** You may hop off that speeding train and set out to seek an authentic life with a yearning for magical self-revelation. But what you get are periods of change where one stage dies and the next grows out of it, leading to a more fulfilled life. These series of evolving stages initiate us into ever deeper levels of authentic connections, tempering us in times of hardship when we are severely challenged. Stages or cycles can evolve naturally, or be provoked by an unexpected, dramatic defining moment: accident, illness, divorce, the death of a loved one, a loss of a career, or a destructive event in our surroundings.

Some, on this journey, find a special attraction to facing the difficulties since it is only by coming to grips with adversity that we realize our inner resources and capabilities. We are able, with support, to step back from the hell and wreckage in front of us and find a way to say, "Aha. This is what I need."

Any disaster we can survive and learn from can lead to an improvement in our character. Looking back on my life, I see that the moments that seemed like great failures and left wreckage in their wake were often the defining moments that shaped the life I have now. As my father, who suffered from disabling depression, used to say, "Every break *down* is an opportunity for a break *through*."

**Awaken to your life's purpose.** *Ikigai* is a Japanese concept meaning "a reason for being." Everyone, according to the Japanese, has an Ikigai. In Japan the word is widely used to describe a healthy passion for something that makes life worth living to the fullest. Ikigai seeks the answer to three essential questions: What do you love? What are you good at? What does the world need?

Finding your Ikigai requires a deep and often lengthy search of self. As humans, we yearn for a sense of purpose. Caring is both a compassionate and a consuming commitment. Those who care need inspiration and energy. Clarifying and preserving a sense of purpose helps us take our setbacks and failures in stride with greater ease. It inspires us to get up early, go the extra mile for someone, and care with focus and perseverance. It also guides us to know when to let go and know our own limits, to know when we've cared enough.

It takes time to unearth the gifts we possess, to match them with our life instructions, and discover a reason for being. It takes time to shut out the tales we've been told, sometimes our whole lives, about someone else's directions and edicts. When we discover and open our instructions, we should step back and examine them, perhaps with doubt, perhaps with delight, but certainly with awe and gratitude.

# Appendix D

## Character Inventory

There is no real achievement that can be separated from right living.

A job title, the letters behind our name, the size of our office, or the size of our financial statement, while perhaps worthy goals to pursue, are not true measures of the value of a human life. A more accurate appraisal of the worth of a person are the virtues of strong character: courage, humility, reliability, honesty, integrity, perseverance, prudence, unselfishness, and compassion. Being a person of character means caring enough to make the shift from being the best *in* the world to being the best *for* the world. It means striving not for what we can *get,* but what we can *give,* to seek not what we can *possess* or even what we can *do,* but for who and how we can *be.* To attract others, we must be attractive.

As an act of caring, pause every once in a while and take an inventory of your character:

- How are you doing in areas such as courage, humility, reliability, honesty, integrity, perseverance, prudence, unselfishness, and compassion?
- Are you one person in public and another in private?
- Do you focus as much on what kind of a person you *are* in the world as on what you want to *achieve* in the world?

Like a business that takes regular stock of its inventory, this is a fact-finding process. There can be blind spots to seeing yourself, so get feedback from the most important people in your life. Being a good person precedes being a good leader in any capacity.

Here's a list of actions that demonstrate strength of character. See how you measure up with this list, or take the time to write your own list.

**Let go of what you want.** Prudence is the common sense to live with what you can do without. Prudence is the ability to find joy in what is here. Every so often, it's good to surrender something that you want, but don't need. In a world that confuses wants with needs, debt continues to rise as character continues to erode. Practice living below your means, not getting everything you want, and find freedom in enjoying what you have.

**Do something difficult every day.** "Do the hard stuff first," my mother used to say. The earlier in the day you get the difficult work done, the better you'll feel about yourself, and the rest of your day will improve. Whether it's having a difficult conversation, getting some exercise, or taking a risk, character is built on the foundation of overcoming the natural tendency to take the course of least resistance.

**Clean up after yourself.** Something eats away at your character when you leave your messes for someone else to look after. If you want a taste of character, next time you walk through a park, pick up the garbage you find.

**Look beyond yourself.** Character means choosing service over self-interest. Character grows in the soil of concern for others and the commitment to act on that concern. We can all find ways to make life better for someone less fortunate than ourselves.

**Spend less than you earn.** This may be one of the best character habits you can develop. Spending less than you earn, whether it's on your home, your car, or the stuff you buy, is another version of prudence. The space you create in your life by doing so will give you freedom, renewed worth, and contentment that money will never buy.

**Practice gratitude.** Gratitude is integral to strong character. Gratitude is the antidote to entitlement—the contaminator of character. Be an appreciator, rather than a depreciator, of everything that shows up in your life, including opportunities disguised as problems. What you appreciate, appreciates.

# Appendix E
## Getting the Ball of Human Goodness Rolling

### Something we bring to others

Practicing goodness was instilled in me from a very early age. My parents taught me, just by the way they lived their lives, that goodness and generosity are important, that my word is my bond, and that my integrity is more important than making a good impression. They also taught me that goodness isn't something I should seek for recognition, but something that I bring to others.

Goodness doesn't require money or position. Anyone can make choices that improve the lives of others and do good for them. Goodness is not about the personal gain we get from our acts of kindness, but a genuine desire to give something back to the world.

Here are strategies to get the ball of human goodness rolling in the world around you:

**Claim full citizenship.** "Citizenship starts with the right questions," Peter Block, American author and speaker in the areas of community building and civic engagement, tells us. The question, "How do we get *those* people to change?" distracts us from choosing who we want to become and exercising accountability for creating our own world. "*How* is the wrong question," Block says.

Conversely, "What is my contribution to the problem I am concerned about?" Or "What courage is required of me right now?" are questions that remedy helplessness. Instead of "how" questions that stop you in your tracks, think of honestly asking yourself what role you actually play in the creation of a situation that frustrates you. Then the world changes around you. As Peter Block says, "the answer to how is *yes*!"

The right decisions are also required for full citizenship. Citizenship affirms that you have a responsibility for creating the world you live in, and a responsibility to do your part to change it. Far too often, we deny the fact that—through our perceptions and our choices—we are actually creating the culture that we so enjoy complaining about. Rather than being *held* accountable, make a courageous decision to choose to *be* accountable. Whatever you want *from* the world, bring that *to* the world. This is the essence of caring citizenship.

Deciding that you have co-created the world around you—and therefore you're the one to step in to heal it—is the ultimate act of accountability. To have any hope of changing the world, take the courage to bring your true and full self to the world. Citizenship lies at the heart of self-respect, goodness, and caring.

**Be loyal in people's absence.** Assassinating people's characters and gossiping are also excuses for not taking responsibility. It's a lot easier to criticize than it is to create. It's a lot easier to complain than to be courageous. It's a sign of insecurity and a lack of character to condemn another when you are not in their presence. To speak highly of someone in their absence, to find their strengths, even in the midst of human weakness, and express those strengths publically, to be loyal to the people around you, is the road best traveled. Having the courage to be loyal in people's absence is a sign of human goodness. It comes back, once again, to citizenship. As my good friends who live in Maritime Canada will tell you, "If you must speak badly of someone, don't speak it, but write it—in the sand, at the water's edge, near the waves."

Frustrations with other people are part of our human experience. Challenges in relationships arise because our greatest teachers are often the people who frustrate us the most. Raising teenagers taught me a lot about letting go. Learning to work with demanding and what I'd interpreted at the time to be controlling bosses, colleagues, and clients taught me to be clearer and more courageous in my communications. Learning to work with a variety of personalities different than mine teaches me to be more adaptable and to expand my repertoire of responses.

Human goodness is a belief in people's positive intent. It's easy to develop in your own mind a storyline about another's motivation. When you assume that there could be a good reason why a person did something that seems hurtful or foolish, it opens the door to both learning and an enriched relationship. It takes mindfulness to stop judging others by looking carefully, with empathy, at their intent. People's motives can be good even when their behaviors seem hurtful or stupid. If you pause long enough to ask them what they intended, there is another benefit—you can develop a better relationship. Working together will get easier.

**Do the right thing.** When fifteen-year-old Malala Yousafzai was thrust into the international limelight, she was lying in a hospital bed with a bullet wound to her head. The previous summer, she had been featured in a *New York Times* documentary advocating for girls' rights to education in her native Swat Valley, a mountainous region of northwest Pakistan. Her advocacy had begun a few years earlier, when at the age of 11 she first wrote a blog, under a pseudonym, for the BBC website. She was a mere schoolgirl challenging a military regime, but the Taliban deemed her enough of a threat that they wanted to kill her.

Malala Yousafzai survived being shot and has since become a global advocate for the universal right to education. In 2014, her bravery and determination earned her a Nobel Peace Prize. In her memoir *I Am Malala*, she says, "I told myself, Malala, you have already faced death. This is your second life. Don't be afraid—if you are afraid, you can't move forward."

We take universal education for granted in North America. By rights, no person should be refused to be taught in school for their gender, their cultural background, their religion, or any other aspect of their identity. Yet this is what Yousafzai and her sisters have faced and continue to face. So she stood up and put her life on the line for what she believed, for what she knew was right.

In an age of inconceivable speed and high expectations for success, it is easy to take shortcuts and compromise our ethical standards. Every day, every one of us will have, or already has had, temptations to cheat and be dishonest. I learned from the business icon Ron Mannix, recipient of numerous distinguished business leadership and philanthropic awards including the Order of Canada, the Alberta Order of Excellence, and an Honorary Doctorate of Law Degree, to guide your business and your life with one simple question: "What is the right thing to do?"

"There are incredible pressures on normally ethical people to set those ethics aside when under these pressures," Ron Mannix says. "From that standpoint, unless there's some counter balance to all this change and stress, then we'll end up living in a world that will follow into total chaos. In our lives and in our careers, each and every one of us will have or has already been tempted. We're all tempted each and every day, and every one of us will have the opportunity to cheat, manipulate, or hurt other people."

While ethical honesty is undoubtedly an expression of human goodness, living honestly also means living from your heart instead of reacting to the world by simply giving people what you think they want. It means doing the right thing. "Everybody can contribute in order to get the job done the very best way they can," adds Mannix.

Live honestly, do the right thing, and you will live honorably. This kind of caring will lead to a good life with the reward of inner peace and self-respect.

**Live anonymously.** Living anonymously means doing something nice for someone without being found out or seeking acknowledgement. It's about practicing random acts of kindness. With insecurity comes the aspiration to be famous. Today, I'd rather be anonymous.

Here are a few ideas to live anonymously:

- Plug someone's expired parking meter.
- Become an organ donor.
- Donate to a worthy cause.
- Give a busker some money.
- Pick up garbage in your community park.
- Clean up after yourself and recycle.
- Turn off the lights when you leave an empty room.
- Shovel snow off your neighbor's sidewalk.
- Do more than you get paid for.
- Walk slowly behind a slow walker.
- Give your seat up on the bus or subway.
- Hold the door open for someone.
- Let someone in ahead of you in traffic.
- Thank a police officer, firefighter, or military personnel.
- Come home in a good mood—even if you're in a bad one.
- Tell the flight attendant, as you walk off the airplane, they did a good job.
- Call the cashier by the name on their nametag.

- Start conversations. Talk with people you know, talk with people you don't know, talk with people you never talk to.
- Say thank you.
- Add your own ideas to this list and go out in the world, anonymously.

**Live fully.** George Bernard Shaw, the Irish playwright and co-founder of the London School of Economics, wrote in the dedicatory prologue to *Man and Superman*, "This is the true joy in life, the being used for a purpose recognized by yourself as a mighty one; the being thoroughly worn out before you are thrown on the scrap heap; the being a force of Nature instead of a feverish selfish little clod of ailments and grievances complaining that the world will not devote itself to making you happy."

It is said that the difference between what we do and what we are capable of doing would suffice to solve most of the world's problems. There is great power in discovering what we care about. Don't ask, "What is wrong?" Instead ask, "What is possible?"

It's individuation that makes it possible for us to fully participate in our communities. When we sacrifice our honest self for the sake of others, it is not belonging; it is conformity. If we compromise the gift of who we are, the world is poorer for it.

"Don't ask yourself what the world needs," wrote Howard Thurman, theologian, Baptist minister, and civil rights leader. "Ask yourself what makes you come alive and then go do that. Because what the world needs is people who have come alive." Thurman was the author of twenty books of ethics and cultural criticism, a proponent of nonviolence and peaceful advocacy, and his works deeply influenced the civil rights leader

Martin Luther King, Jr. The courage to care about others has the same origin as the courage to live life fully.

To be fully yourself, and to be human, is to be a part of a community.

**Be steady.** On June 12, 1964, Nelson Mandela was found guilty of four charges of conspiracy against the South African government and sentenced to life imprisonment. On Robben Island, where he would spend eighteen of his twenty-seven prison years, he was allowed one visitor per year for a maximum of thirty minutes, and to write and receive one letter every six months. In the small cell Mandela was confined to, the floor was his bed, he had a bucket for a toilet, and he spent his days doing involuntary hard labor in a quarry.

Nelson Mandela had many teachers in his life, but he believed the greatest of them all was prison. "Prison," writes his biographer Richard Stengel, "taught him self-control, discipline, and focus—the things he considers essential to leadership—and it taught him how to be a full human being."

It was in prison that Nelson Mandela learned to counter cruel inhumanity, senseless discrimination, and unjust violence—with fearless composure. It was in prison that he learned the art of calm reason and the power of courageous forgiveness. Through his forgiving presence, Nelson Mandela not only transformed his African country, he became one of the world's great moral and political leaders.

The greatest gift of goodness you can offer the world is your own wellbeing. When you are at peace with yourself, the world around you looks better. "Live and let live" is an approach to life that I aspire to. We live longer and more happily when we stop trying to rearrange other peoples' lives. Bringing goodness to others starts with being good and forgiving to yourself. Having a healthy sense of leisure, boundaries around your time, communities that support you, and sanctuaries to get away from the demands of the world, are all ways to maintain your inner strength in order to continue to bring goodness to others.

To be a good human, we each need a place of stability and consistency amidst the confusion and commotion of life. The poet William Stafford expresses this inner place of steadiness in "The Way It Is."

> There's a thread you follow. It goes among
> things that change. But it doesn't change.
> People wonder about what you are pursuing.
> You have to explain about the thread.
> But it is hard for others to see.
> While you hold it you can't get lost.
> Tragedies happen; people get hurt
> or die; and you suffer and get old.
> Nothing you do can stop time's unfolding.
> You don't ever let go of the thread.

Although greatness is a goal worth pursuing, if it costs you integrity, health, relationships, or the quality of your life, goodness may very well be a better aspiration. The quality of an individual life has little to do with longevity and everything to do with how a life is lived.

# Appendix F

## Honoring the Shadow: Shining a Light on the Hidden Aspects of Yourself

Socrates felt "the unexamined life is not worth living." Examining ourselves and honoring the shadow aspect of ourselves requires some intentional action. Because shadow work is about making the unconscious conscious, it takes some concerted time for personal reflection as well as working with a trusted guide. Below is a suggested process I have adapted from my work with Geoff Bellman. All of Geoff's books contain worthwhile material to help you work with the shadowy aspects of yourself. I specifically recommend *Your Signature Path: Gaining New Perspectives On Life and Work.*

By integrating and working with these strategies, you can begin to heal from the shadows that have been holding you back or even hurting yourself and others, and open yourself to a fuller range of caring.

You can approach the following strategies with a sense of adventure and lightness:

**Pay attention to new information.** Think about when you recently got a new awareness about yourself that was uncomfortable. For example, a boss gave you some feedback that was radically different than how you see yourself. Or you received some criticism from a friend. Or you found yourself reacting to a difficult situation in your life in an uncharacteristic way. Or you begin noticing a pattern in relationships that keeps cycling back to keep you somehow stuck. A new awareness can suggest a starting point, an opening. Learning about the shadow begins by turning toward what is uncomfortable and being open to what you see.

**Open a clean page in your journal.** Head the page with any of these phrases:

> "What I am afraid of is …"
> "What I am ashamed of is …"
> "What I am embarrassed about is …"
> "What I am uncomfortable having others know about me is …"

**Fill the page.** Let go and write everything you think of that might fit under the headings that you have identified. For example, if you start with, "What I am afraid of is …" you might write the following: snakes, spiders, heights, the dark, terrorists, etc. Just keep writing. Don't worry about whether or not you are getting it "right." Nobody but you is going to see this list. Try to fill the page with things as well as events: cancer, drowning, airplanes, closed spaces, elevators, pollutants, etc. When you run out of the "easier" fears, move to the more complicated one: having difficult conversations with family members, standing up to your boss, writing a book, public speaking, etc.

**Make the link.** Identify your top five things or events that are especially fearful (or embarrassing or shameful or uncomfortable) to you. Now see if you can look back and write about where in your life you may have first met these. For example, I have a fear of closed spaces. In specific circumstances, I am very claustrophobic. My earliest memory of this is being in an oxygen tent when I was in a hospital at age four, recovering from meningitis.

I am also afraid, at times, to speak my truth and ask for what I want. My earliest memory of this is when I was eight years old, standing and watching my parents fight and being afraid to say anything for fear they would turn their anger on me.

My obsessive need for order, as a way of feeling safe, can keep me up late sorting the inbox in my emails, organizing my files, and adhering too tightly to the disciplines in my life. This can prevent me from the messiness of creative work or relaxing and enjoying my life. As a young child, I learned that amidst the unpredictability and chaos in my family, I could create an illusion of safety by going into my bedroom, alone, and organizing my stuff.

This exercise is intended to encourage discovery. Notice your emotions as you explore these aspects of yourself. Are there feelings of excitement? Discomfort? Anxiety? Discovery? What is happening to you as you explore these areas? How open are you to discover these? Capture any new realizations.

**Notice any inclination to back away.** Without judgment, note if you have any thoughts like, "This is a waste of time!" or "Enough!" or "I don't like doing this!" or "I've gone far enough. I quit!" Before you quit, notice what your usual response is to resistance. Do you usually cave in to your resistance when you are up against it? Noticing how you either back away or move toward that which is uncomfortable can be a clue for working with your shadowy aspects. Pay attention where your mind goes. Use your reflective self to observe what you do instead of bringing even a small part of yourself out into the light. Your shadow lies in that which makes you uncomfortable, so moving toward discomfort is a path to the shadow.

**Name the shadow.** Give a name to the shadowy side of yourself. Once things are named, you can begin to work with them. In an Alcoholics Anonymous meeting, you hear people declare, "My name is ___ and I am an alcoholic." This doesn't mean that alcoholism is the total identity of these recovering individuals. What it means is that they are honest with themselves. Name the shadowy side of yourself. Admit that you have a problem and are willing to do something about it.

**Work with the body.** Your body can be a good guide, and your emotions will take you there. Practice slowing down, stopping, and listening to what is happening inside you. Notice where your body is expressing emotions. Your shoulders? Your stomach? Your chest? Name them. Journal about them. Share them. Be a student of your emotions. Listen to what they are attempting to teach you.

When I feel anxious, I usually feel it in my chest. My breathing gets shallow. I also get sweaty palms. When I stop and pay attention, I can remind myself things like, "I am not eight years old." "These are not my parents." "I'm safe." "I can handle the risk," etc. Then, I can counter the emotions with appropriate and helpful strategies rather than staying in my old patterns.

**Learn about it.** Get as much insight as you can. Research it. Read books on the subject. Take courses on what you are struggling with. Follow the thinking and guidance of others who have walked before you. "Be a student of your condition," is a useful motto, as long as you don't label yourself and let the shadow define you. Bring curiosity and inquisitiveness to the work rather than judgment or denial.

**Seek out a guide.** Ask for help. While contemplation and self-reflection are vital to this process, you cannot work with the shadowy side alone. Just as the eye cannot see itself, we need a mirror to help us. Find allies or confidants or a guide to help you. They can be a therapist, a twelve-step recovery group or other support group, a coach, or a mentor. The important thing is that they have some experience with what you are facing and can offer a supportive, accepting, accountable space to heal. They are people who can help get the shadow out of your head and into the sunlight. Sunlight is the best disinfectant.

A word of caution: the people you are hurting with your hidden side are generally the people who can't help you much.

While they may be able to support you, it's important to reach out for help beyond your immediate circle of family or close friends.

**Artify it.** Sometimes you can connect with your shadow indirectly using music, sculpture, painting, film, dance, poetry, literature, or drawing. Creative channels can expand the human experience and dissolve the power of the shadow. William Blake engaged his shadow side through three disciplines: painting, music, and language. He illuminated his own poems and set them to music. It's what I call *artifying* your life.

**Help others.** Helping others through your experience can be healing. Once you have faced your dark side and have realized that within this wound is your most important gift, you can use your gift to help restore others who have the same shadow. When you have "been there so you know how it feels"—in grief, sorrow, despair, trauma, or terror—you can offer others the courage, wisdom, and compassion that you gained from your experience.

**Reflect on what you learned.** Jot down some of the insights you gained from doing this exercise, however grand or humble they might be.

Visiting the edges of your shadow side requires moving intentionally toward that which is uncomfortable. Discomfort is an indicator that you are moving into unfamiliar terrain, that you are on the verge of some new growth. Care enough about yourself to trust yourself to go as far as you are ready now. Just know that life energy and power can be freed in the discovery and acceptance of these hidden aspects of yourself.

# Appendix G

## Strengthening Your Caring Response

Consider these ten caring practices for strengthening your caring response:

**Greet each morning with intention.** Greet each day with an intention to be caring. Thích Nhất Hạnh, the Vietnamese Buddhist monk and teacher, has this morning caring meditation. "Waking up this morning, I smile. Twenty-four brand new hours are before me. I vow to live fully in each moment and to look at all beings with eyes of compassion."

**Remember to pause.** Caring means living life more slowly. Volunteer, or look after a child, or hang out with a friend when there is nothing to accomplish, no goals to be achieved, and just the prospect of the pure experience of being together. Make it a habit to pause and refocus your attention on caring during the day. Make caring become a part of your life. As the Dalai Lama says, "This is my simple religion. There is no need for temples; no need for complicated philosophy. Our own brain, our own heart is our temple; the philosophy is kindness."

**Focus on commonalities.** We live in a world that builds up walls and fences and prisons. We separate ourselves from those we mistrust or feel afraid of. We focus on difference—in gender, in race, in age, in responses to a personality test. While boundaries are, at times, obviously appropriate, those who know empathy and compassion make a habit of looking for what we have in common. We all breathe the same air. We all need food, shelter, and love. We are all imperfect human beings. We all have a heart and a belly button. During the day when you feel irritated or want to punch someone in the nose, stop and say these words:

- Just like me, this person is doing the best they can …
- Just like me, this person is imperfect …
- Just like me, this person has been hurt in their life …
- Just like me, this person could use some caring …

**Be aware of suffering.** Consciousness is being able to notice what is happening around you, along with a capacity to pay attention and to realize what you are feeling and thinking, and then using that information to make choices that will guide your actions.

When suffering results from the actions of another, the impulsive response is to either retaliate or recoil. While the impulsive response might, by chance, be helpful, it usually causes further suffering either to us or the other person. Consciousness means you imagine the suffering of the human being who caused you to suffer. When another person makes you suffer, it is because they themselves are suffering within, and their suffering is spilling over to you. They do not need your punishment, just as you do not need to punish yourself. They need help. Between every impulse and every action lies a space for thoughtful choice. Let caring guide your response to suffering.

**See the good in others.** It was in reading Nelson Mandela's biography that I was inspired to make it a habit of seeing the good in others. Mandela, apparently, saw almost everyone as virtuous—until proven otherwise. He believed that seeing the good in other people improved the chances that they would reveal their better self.

His biographer, Richard Stengel, wrote that Mandela rarely had a bad word to say about anyone. It wasn't that he didn't see the dark side of people; it was that he was unwilling to see *only* that. He saw the human behind the bluster. He chose to see the good in others for two reasons: it was instinctual, and he believed that seeing the good in others might actually make them better.

This approach gets to the heart of Mandela's belief of what makes us all human. He assumed that we are better people than how we behave. Our motives are not as cruel as our actions. No one is born prejudiced or racist. Mandela believed that no one is evil at heart. Evil is something instilled or taught to people by circumstances, their environment, or their upbringing.

**Assume a positive intent.** Some time ago, I had a plant in a pot below a bookshelf. As it grew, it grew toward the light around the shelf. The stem at the point of the shelf looked horribly crooked. But the "crookedness" really wasn't crooked. It wasn't imperfect or wrong; it was the plant's phototropic impulse, an attempt to reach the light in a way that it was able—by clinging and climbing along the shelf surface.

I have learned that life and relationships work better when we care enough to assume positive intent—that people are doing the best they can with where they are and what they have. A controlling boss is a person who may be insecure and is trying to find a level of security. An aggressive child may be seeking a way to belong. A withdrawn spouse may be hurt and doesn't know a better way to respond.

Focusing on positive intent doesn't abdicate personal responsibility or avoid consequences for choices. What it does is transform judgment into caring.

**Practice acts of kindness.** Practice doing something small each day to help make life better for others. A smile, a kind word, a word of encouragement, or a few minutes of listening to another can make an important difference. Once you are good at this, find a way to make it your daily practice to focus on ways to bring a little support and reassurance to others.

There is a law in the universe. Buddhists call it karma, but I call it the law of the echo. Whatever you give out to the world will eventually come back. If you want more caring in the world, bring more caring to the world. It may not come back right away, but it *will* come back.

**Open your heart.** Caring comes from your heart, not your head. Adopt a dog. Coach a child's sports team. Visit your grandparents. Volunteer at a homeless shelter. Visit a sick friend or family member. Plant a garden. Cry. Stop thinking so much. Be vulnerable. Open your heart.

**Take a moment to reflect.** At end of the day before you go to bed, reflect on your day. Think about the people you met today and the people you talked to. Reflect on how you treated those you interacted with. Think about your goal to be caring toward others. How well did you do? What could you do better? What did you learn?

**Make haste slowly.** *Festina lente* are words that Emperor Augustus once spoke. It's a saying our financial advisor uses frequently in our conversations. It means "make haste slowly." Learning to be caring is not a sprint. It isn't a race at all. It's a journey, but with no real destination. What it is, is a method of travel. There is no hurry to get anywhere.

Patience is perhaps the most important aspect on this journey. Practice patience with yourself and patience with others. Think about caring, and then try caring your way into caring. I've learned that what you focus on is what grows. If you focus on your imperfections, your imperfections will grow. If you focus on the goodness inside of you and inside the people you interact with, the goodness within and the goodness around you will grow. When it comes to developing anything worthwhile, *direction* is more important than *velocity*.

# Appendix H

## Sticking With an Exercise Program

"You can't get somebody else to do your push-ups for you," said the great business philosopher, Jim Rohn. There are many benefits to exercise when it is done in a way that balances health with fitness. I have ten simple rules for finding and sticking with an exercise program that will keep you healthy:

**Keep it consistent.** It's better to walk around the block every day than it is to walk a mile once a month. If you walk around the block every day, you'll soon find yourself increasing this distance—gradually, of course.

**Move your body.** Get out and walk. Swim. Hike. Ride your bike to work. Find a yoga teacher. Take a golf lesson. Use this as a time to connect with yourself. Find out what you love about moving your body and what you don't like. But move it.

**Cause no harm.** *Ahinsa* is a Sanskrit word meaning "compassion" and "not to injure." It's an approach worth incorporating into exercise and all areas of your life. "Cause no harm" is a cardinal rule of all exercise. I try not to have too many "shoulds" in my vocabulary, but I do have one here. You should never do exercise that causes harm to yourself. Exercise consistently, and learn the difference between good pain and bad pain. But if in doubt, back off. Less is always more when it comes to exercise. Just be sure that less does not equal none.

**Find what is right for you.** Find an exercise program that is enjoyable. Get out and experience some nature. Although it may not be too enjoyable when you begin an exercise regime, if it is the kind of exercise that is right for you, the effects will be enjoyable—either during or afterward. Find an exercise program that is right for your body and your temperament. Above all, follow your own instinct. You won't stick with something that isn't right for you.

**Be sociable in it.** Find a friend to exercise with, or get a good trainer or health care advisor that you trust to support you and hold you accountable. A good friend or coach will keep you moving. Plus, you get that extra boost of bonding with someone while you work out.

**Track your energy.** Exercise is meant to increase your energy, not decrease it. You may start out feeling low on energy and unmotivated, but generally your energy will increase when you stick with it. Exercise is meant to leave you feeling refreshed and rejuvenated, not exhausted.

**Just do it.** Nike has it right. When you exercise, learn to rise above those thoughts that tell you all the reasons why you don't want to be exercising—and just do it. Whether you are going to the gym or the yoga studio or for a neighborhood walk, practice planting your feet on the floor and getting out the door. Plan a camping or kayak trip, join a softball team, plant trees with a stream-keepers project, walk each morning with a friend. Healthy people get it done. Most exercise is as good for our minds as it is for our bodies. If you exercise first thing in the morning, it will be mind over mattress. In the evening, it will be mind over television. Just do it. And how do you "just do it?" What stands in the way of most people is just getting started. This is where a friend, a mentor, an accountability buddy who will support you and hold you to your promises, or a fitness coach if you can afford one, can help get you going.

**Don't compare yourself to anyone.** Don't turn exercise into a fashion show or a popularity contest. Exercise, like all self-care, is for you and no one else. There is no "best" kind of exercise. While exercise that improves cardiovascular health and increases strength, flexibility, and mental wellbeing is generally recommended, the best kind of exercise is the kind you do!

**Stretch.** Stretching—both literally and figuratively—is a necessary part of life. Physically, a good program of stretching emphasizes all parts of the body, coordinates with breathing and helps you relax. Stretching leads to expansion and flexibility in personal growth. A young plant is tender and pliant. An older one is stiff, woody, and vulnerable to breaking. Softness is thus equated with life, and hardness with death. Flexibility impacts your physical and mental health.

**Make it a journey.** A curious thing can happen when you exercise regularly, doing an activity that is right for you. It may not exactly get easier, but it becomes a part of you. You look forward to the rewards of exercise and the benefits of staying healthy. You look forward to the ease exercise affords you. You feel stronger. Your brain is more alert. Maybe you learn to love it. But even if you don't love it, you can learn to accept it. You face exercise squarely because you realize that it is okay to occasionally be uncomfortable. Just keep going. Make it a journey.

What matters most to physical health is your mental wellbeing. While it may be important to have a regular activity, a sport or exercise program, or consistent yoga practice, it is also important to find ways to unplug, to let go, to have down time, to simply rest. Many people today are in need of rest more than exercise. How is your overall sense of wellbeing? Are you enjoying your life? Are you finding meaning? Are you connected to a cause beyond yourself? Do you have a sense of belonging?

Do you have a sense of purpose? Are you conflicted about what you are doing? Or are you wholeheartedly inside your life and your work? Wellbeing emerges when you relax inside and are in harmony with yourself. It's much easier to care for others if you attend to and care for your health.

# Appendix I

## Self-Care Inventory

Change is created out of "optimal" anxiety. The purpose of this simple self-care inventory is to do just that—stimulate anxiety, but without immobilizing you. This is not an inventory that assesses every area of your life or who you are as a person. It is a simple inventory that will help you identify your current level of self-care in six key areas. It is meant to help you see any disparity between where you are and where you want to be in relation to self-care. It is designed to help you focus on your needs and identify areas where change is called for.

Your self-care system may be in better or worse shape at different points in your life. There may be times when you need to get lost in the forest in order to find a new path. Here are a few guideposts and clues to help you get the most from the inventory.

- Being honest with yourself is not easy, but to make changes in your life requires a clear inventory of where you are today. In some respects, this inventory will test how rigorously honest you are with yourself. The more rigorously self-honest you are in answering these questions, the more you will gain from the experience. You don't need to "look good" or impress anybody. There is no requirement to share your scores with anyone. It's for you only.

- Many people say they would answer many of the questions differently depending on whether it is in relation to their work or in their personal life. If you feel there would be a big difference, you may want to take the test twice—once in the context of your work, and once in the context of your personal life. This is okay, but if you see a large disparity between the two, it's an opportunity to reflect on what that means.

- Some of these questions will bring confusion and anxiety. Just as there are no perfect answers, this is not a perfect test. If the answer to a question isn't clear, just relax and do the best you can.
- As you go through this inventory, you may see many areas in your current self-care system that could use a change. Rather than overhauling too much right now, focus on *one or two* areas that could use work in the next six to twelve months. Remember, it is better to be successful at one small change, than to fail at trying to overhaul too many things!
- If you don't know the answer to any of the questions below, count your score a zero on that point.

## A Self-Care Inventory

### Physical health

This area is where you examine the physical aspects of your life—how you are nurturing your body and taking care of your health.

| Almost Never | Occasionally | About Half Of The Time | Fairly Often | Almost Always |
|---|---|---|---|---|
| 1 | 2 | 3 | 4 | 5 |

1  2  3  4  5  I get seven to eight hours of sleep most nights.

1  2  3  4  5  I consistently exercise at least three times a week, for at least 20 minutes.

1  2  3  4  5  I am a non-smoker.

1  2  3  4  5  My body is a weight that is right for me.

1  2  3  4  5  I have a healthy, well balanced diet.

Total: _____

## Mental wellbeing

This area examines how your mind is supporting your self-care system, and some of the choices you make for having a strong mental attitude and firm mind in your life and work.

| Almost Never | Occasionally | About Half Of The Time | Fairly Often | Almost Always |
|---|---|---|---|---|
| 1 | 2 | 3 | 4 | 5 |

1 2 3 4 5 I am optimistic about my life and my future.

1 2 3 4 5 Joy and gratitude come easily to me, and I do things that bring me joy.

1 2 3 4 5 I am free of worry about people, places, and things that I have no control over.

1 2 3 4 5 I am able to move from self-criticism to self-acceptance easily (i.e., I treat myself with the same respect and compassion I would a best friend.)

1 2 3 4 5 I am able to deal with fear, guilt, and insecurity in a constructive way.

Total: _____

## Managing demands and personal agency

This area deals with how you clarify the most important areas in your life that need attention, and how you manage the demands from others.

| Almost Never | Occasionally | About Half Of The Time | Fairly Often | Almost Always |
|---|---|---|---|---|
| 1 | 2 | 3 | 4 | 5 |

1 2 3 4 5 I am clear about the essential elements that matter most in my life.

1 2 3 4 5 I attend to my core values on a regular basis.

1 2 3 4 5 I have clear boundaries, when necessary, around the expectations of others.

| Almost Never | Occasionally | About Half Of The Time | Fairly Often | Almost Always |
|:---:|:---:|:---:|:---:|:---:|
| 1 | 2 | 3 | 4 | 5 |

1 2 3 4 5   I am satisfied with the way I handle demands in my life.

1 2 3 4 5   I have little in my life that needs cleaning up (household clutter, destructive relationships, addictions, unmanageable debts, etc.)

Total: _____

## Spiritual health and inner wellbeing

Spiritual wellbeing is about tapping into a power beyond ourselves to give guidance, support, and clarity on the self-care journey. Spiritual health is about finding inner peace, independent of the roles, successes, and failures of life.

| Almost Never | Occasionally | About Half Of The Time | Fairly Often | Almost Always |
|:---:|:---:|:---:|:---:|:---:|
| 1 | 2 | 3 | 4 | 5 |

1 2 3 4 5   I get strength from my religious and/or spiritual beliefs, where I find peace in the midst of chaos.

1 2 3 4 5   I take quiet time for myself during the day for strength and perspective from within.

1 2 3 4 5   I have a level of acceptance of my imperfections (self-compassion) and have the strength to let go of my fears and uncertainty.

1 2 3 4 5   Having the courage and faith to believe in what I cannot see gives me strength in my life.

1 2 3 4 5   I have a community that supports my spiritual beliefs.

Total: _____

## Supportive relationships

This area examines the quality of supportive relationships in your life, people who support you and hold you accountable to take care of yourself, and help guide you to your own truth.

| Almost Never | Occasionally | About Half Of The Time | Fairly Often | Almost Always |
|:---:|:---:|:---:|:---:|:---:|
| 1 | 2 | 3 | 4 | 5 |

1  2  3  4  5  I give and receive affection regularly.

1  2  3  4  5  I have at least one relative within an hour's drive on whom I can rely.

1  2  3  4  5  I have a network of friends on whom I can—and do—depend.

1  2  3  4  5  I have at least one friend that I confide in about personal matters, and I meet with them regularly.

1  2  3  4  5  I am able to speak openly about my feelings when angry or worried.

Total: _____

## Meaning

This area speaks to the level of satisfaction and fulfillment you are getting from your life and your work right now, that makes the caring in your life meaningful.

| Almost Never | Occasionally | About Half Of The Time | Fairly Often | Almost Always |
|:---:|:---:|:---:|:---:|:---:|
| 1 | 2 | 3 | 4 | 5 |

1  2  3  4  5  I enjoy getting out of bed most days, and look forward to the day.

1  2  3  4  5  I have a sense of purpose in my life.

| Almost Never | Occasionally | About Half Of The Time | Fairly Often | Almost Always |
|:---:|:---:|:---:|:---:|:---:|
| 1 | 2 | 3 | 4 | 5 |

1 2 3 4 5 If I suddenly received an inheritance of $1 million, my life wouldn't change much.

1 2 3 4 5 I stand up for what I believe in.

1 2 3 4 5 I express my unique talents, strengths, passions, and dreams on a daily basis.

Total: _____

**Grand Total (Add Up All Six Categories):** _____

**Scores can range from 30 to 150.** While I personally wouldn't put a great deal of stock in the actual scores, I would encourage you to use the tallies as a rough indicator of where you are today.

120+      This score indicates personal wellbeing and serenity at this stage in your life. You have a good self-care system in place. You may identify an area that needs some "fine-tuning," but remember to take time to appreciate your current lifestyle, choices, and habits in the area of self-care. You may also want to reflect on areas of self-care that need attention but did not get addressed in this inventory. *Note:* If you scored in this range, you may also be an obsessive compulsive person who could benefit by lightening up and perhaps putting less emphasis on discipline and structure.

91-119      You have some areas in your life with a good system of self-care. Some areas also need focus and new habits. Take a close look at one or two areas that need attention now, and focus on them.

50-90     This score would indicate that you are strug-
          gling and could use some assistance in develop-
          ing a stronger self-care system. Look seriously
          at the area(s) in your life that need attention
          now. You may need to establish a structure to
          enhance your life through more discipline and
          consistency.

Below 50  You are likely experiencing some challenges in
          the area of self-care. Take time to determine if
          these difficulties are stemming from a current
          change in your life, and if so, ask how you can
          create some structure in your life to take bet-
          ter care of yourself in this challenging time.
          You will need to pay serious attention to some
          immediate action toward self-care, in order
          to rekindle your personal vitality. Appreciate
          yourself for being so rigorously honest with
          yourself. This is the first step to growth.

Regardless of your score, here is a short list of actions to get you
started on the next chapter of your self-care journey.

- Take time to do a more thoughtful inventory—paying particular attention to the scores that were lowest. Review any
  blocks that may be getting in your way of creating a self-care
  system that serves you best. Also, be sure to take time to acknowledge the *strengths* of your current self-care system.
- Reflect on the score that you gave yourself in this inventory.
  Ask whether the assessment fits for you. Does this score reflect
  how you are currently taking care of yourself? Take your self-
  care seriously by having a good honest look at yourself.
- Be sure to give yourself some credit for the areas in your life
  where you are attending to yourself with care!
- Pick one area in your life that needs some focused attention to
  self-care, and develop a plan for working in this area using the
  "Taking Action" process outlined below.

The following specific actions may also help you develop your self-care system.

- Create a "sanctuary," a place or time for you to get away from the demands of others to be still and listen to the voice within. This could be a physical space, a room in your house, and/or a time during the day or week that you can unplug from technology, distractions, and demands, and just to be with yourself.
- Connect with a support system to help support and renew you, give you a fresh perspective, and help hold you accountable to work with the area that you are focusing on. This could be a trusted friend, therapist, coach, mentor, trainer at a local gym, massage therapist, a religious community, social club, or a support or recovery group.
- Search for a confidant, a person with whom you can share your innermost thoughts, feelings, dreams, and challenges.
- Sign up for a class that will help you with self-care, such as yoga, Tai Chi, mindfulness meditation, developing your faith, or relaxation.
- Remember, start small and be consistent. It's better to walk even five minutes every day than an hour a month.
- Do a "clean-up" in your life to make room for something new (e.g., de-clutter your house, get rid of anything that is not bringing you joy, let go of any relationships that are not life-giving, donate clothes to charity that you haven't worn in years, have a garage sale, or give away those old self-help books you no longer need.)
- If self-compassion is an area you would like to develop (a particularly big one for me), a useful tool can be found on Dr. Neff's Web site: www.self-compassion.org. You may also find Brené Brown's book, *The Gifts of Imperfection*, to be a valuable tool.

## Taking Action

Take an honest look at each of the six following areas and do a quick analysis. Where are you and where do you want to be? Which areas show a gap between current reality and your vision? Start with one area that you are committed to work on. Which areas are going well? Acknowledge your progress in these areas.

Note: seek out an "accountability partner," a trusted friend or advisor who will support you and help keep you accountable.

**Physical health**
Current reality                                          A vision


**Mental wellbeing**
Current reality                                          A vision


**Managing demands and personal agency**
Current reality                                          A vision


**Spiritual health and inner wellbeing**
Current reality                                          A vision


**Supportive relationships**
Current reality                                          A vision


**Meaning**
Current reality                                          A vision

# Acknowledgements

Friends have I with the world before me,
Sun above and the wind behind me,
Life and laughter, double-blessed am I.

Brooks Tower

After writing my initial draft, I sent a copy of the manuscript to my accountant and good friend, Rick Elliott. After he read it, we sat together one spring afternoon sipping tea and discussing the project. He didn't criticize my writing. Instead, he challenged me to enlist a community to help write this book. Deciding that day that I'm not alone on this writing journey changed my whole outlook as I began to engage with a community of supporters. Over the past three years, I have experienced the blessings of a caring group of people who have been behind me all the way. I am blessed beyond measure to have so many of you in my life. I truly could not have done it without you.

First and foremost, I want to thank my dear brother Hal, to whom this book is dedicated, as well as Hal's loving family: Dianne, Sarah, Bronwyn, and Brody. Were it not for your permission to publish these vulnerable moments with your life partner and father, this book would not have been published.

Thank you to Val Sarsons, the most caring of all caregivers who could possibly have been entrusted to look after Hal. Our appreciation for you cannot be expressed with mere words.

My dear sister Kate Harling's fingerprint is on the soul of this book. The hours of talking through the content and philosophy in these pages, along with the conversations, endless support, encouragement, inspiration, and insights made the book better and me a better person. I could not have walked the journey with this project or with Hal without her by my side.

Dr. Ron Mitchell, a lifelong friend and Professor of Entrepreneurship at the Rawls College of Business at Texas Tech University inspired a vision of what a book on caring could be.

Laurie Hutchinson put a human touch on the whole endeavor and kept reminding me to "teach not with long explanations but with stories!" While I couldn't resist the explanations and the lists, Laurie helped me see the power of narrative. Her generosity and caring made this all possible.

Dr. Peter Nieman, one of my accountability partners, inspired me to move forward with this endeavor. His caring, enthusiastic, and optimistic presence has been a blessing to me all along the way.

I am deeply indebted to those who contributed their stories in these pages. Every story, whether credited directly or anonymously, was invaluable to the heart of this book.

I am grateful beyond words to the people who carefully took the time to read drafts at various stages of development and offered thoughtful comments, suggestions, and insights. These include Dean Beaudry, Geoff Bellman, Don Campbell, Jim Carfrae, Pat Copping, Michael Dangelmaier, Larry Dick, Rick Elliott, Warren Harbeck, Margaret Juergens, Dale Kelly, Gerry Labossiere, Larry Malazdrewicz, Michael Meloche, Glenn Lott, Stuart Peterson, Murray Phillips, Denise Summers, Mark Szabo, and Ian West.

Many other individuals played important parts in this journey:

Barry Kaufman, who inspired me with his most courageous and deeply moving story of the two years that he and his father spent together looking into the face of death.

Susan Levin, whose lifelong friendship and encouragement with this project has been an inspiration to me.

George Masselam, who, through his caring and loyal presence, has helped me integrate the principles in this book into every aspect of my life.

Amelia Curran, for taking the time from her busy tour to sing for Hal and leave such a caring imprint on all of us.

My editor, Elaine Morin, who believed in and put her whole caring heart in this project right from the start.

Many caring leaders and individuals that I have had the privilege to work with and learn from over the years have deeply and profoundly impacted me in my work and in my life. Every one had a part in inspiring me to take on this caring project.

My daughters Mellissa, Hayley, and Chandra's wise and caring presence in my life truly makes me a better person. When I first started to write this book, my motive was simply to leave you a legacy about caring. You bring unspeakable joy to my life.

And of course, my wife, Val. I want to thank you for your love that sustains me, your endless support, and your skillful editing. Without the gift of your caring heart in my life, none of this would be possible.

# Editor's Note

One fall day, I received an email from the program director at the creative writing school where I teach. "This guy is looking for you," she wrote. In her message, I learned that an author by the name of David Irvine was searching for an editor and writing collaborator, and that a pair of my students had recommended me to him.

That's one version of the story. But really, I'd prefer to say it was serendipity that brought me to this project. Without knowing it, David and I had connections. We had met some years before at a weekend training camp that David and my husband Scott were attending. In our downstairs library, we still have the copy of David's book *Simple Living in a Complex World* he gave to Scott at the time. I remember reading it. The message was candid, inspiring, and timely. I was in the process of leaving my job as an engineer and was casting about for a new career. We had two small children at home, and I was battling fatigue and a running injury. His was one of many profound books I would read during that period, books that would help me forge a new direction.

And now our paths had crossed again. David set about quizzing me, plying me with interview questions. Finally, he asked, "Is this the kind of work you would be passionate about? Could you honestly get your heart into this project?"

How to respond? I knew I was up to the task of editing a book, but these last questions seemed to ask something more of me. This wasn't about the manuscript. It was about our relationship. He wanted to know if I was ready to go the distance.

"I don't do projects unless I care about them. My heart is already in it," I wrote back. I guess this was the right answer, because a few days later David wrote to tell me I was his editor.

Another connection surfaced, days later, when I was chatting about David's project with my husband. "Didn't you work with his brother? Didn't you do a rotation with Dr. Hal?"

The light went on. "He's that Dr. Hal? Well, yes. I did," Scott said.

It wasn't exactly a surprise that Scott had worked with Dr. Hal Irvine. Scores of University of Calgary medical students had done their rural medicine rotations with him and had benefited from his knowledge. Being a rural doc, Hal's skills were broad and self-sufficient. He had even trained in anesthesiology. He had a way of making the residents feel at home, and even loaned out his mother Joyce Irvine's old house to accommodate them.

Another day, I recalled yet another connection. I remembered having spoken to Dr. Hal one time over the phone, after my daughter Maria showed up at his clinic. She was attending a nearby summer camp and was maybe nine years old.

One of the counselors had brought Maria in after a tick got embedded in her scalp. With gentle calmness, Dr. Hal phoned me to explain that the tiny insect had burrowed under her scalp. He'd had to remove the tick surgically, but things had gone okay. There was no sign of an infection. Hal reassured me that everything had gone well, and that Maria could return to camp if she wanted. I was touched that a physician would take the time to patiently go through all these details with me. Even more, Dr. Hal's caring helped Maria learn a little lesson in independence. I could have easily driven out to "rescue" her. Instead, Maria returned to camp, and she gained some of the self-reliance that camp life is supposed to teach. Plus, she learned to trust in the kindness of others.

There are a few passages in the book I had more influence in shaping, including "The Gift of Adversity," "Allowing for Hope" and "A Radical Notion." Throughout my editing, I have sought the lightest touch possible. Working on this project has been a pleasure and a privilege, a true project of the heart.

I can't wait for the book to go on its own journey with readers.

Elaine Morin, Editor

# Select Bibliography

Bellman, Geoffrey M., *Your Signature Path: Gaining New Perspectives on Life and Work*, Berrett-Koehler Publishers, 1996

Block, Peter, *The Answer to How is Yes: Acting on What Matters*, Berrett-Koehler Publisher, 2003

Bly, Robert, *A Little Book on the Human Shadow*, HarperOne, 1988

Brown, Brené, *Daring Greatly: How the Courage to Be Vulnerable Transforms the Way We Live, Love, Parent, and Lead*, Avery, 2012

Brown, Brené, *The Gifts of Imperfection: Let Go of Who You Think You're Supposed to Be and Embrace Who You Are*, Hazelden, 2010

Cade, Valerie, *Bully Free at Work: What You Can Do to Stop Workplace Bullying Now!*, Performance Curve International Publishing, 2008

Covey, Stephen R., *The 7 Habits of Highly Effective People: Powerful Lessons in Personal Change*, Simon Schuster Limited, 1990

Dass, Ram and Paul Gorman, *How Can I Help? Stories and Reflections on Service*, Knopf, 1985

De Pree, Max, *Leadership is an Art*, Crown Business, The Crown Publishing Group, 2004

Faulder, Liane, *The Long Walk Home: Paul Franklin's Journey from Afghanistan*, Brindle & Glass, 2007

Frankl, Viktor E., *Man's Search for Meaning*, Beacon Press, 1959

Heifetz, Ronald A., *Leadership Without Easy Answers*, Harvard University Press, 1998

Irvine, David, *Becoming Real: Journey to Authenticity*, DC Press, 2003

Irvine, David and Jim Reger, *The Authentic Leader: It's About Presence, Not Position*, DC Press, 2003

Kalanithi, Paul with Abraham Verghese, *When Breath Becomes Air*, Random House, 2016

Kielburger, Craig and Marc Kielburger, *Me to We: Finding Meaning in a Material World*, John Wiley & Sons Canada, Limited, 2007

Lang, Dale, *Jason Has Been Shot!*, Castle Quay Books, 2009

Maté, Gabor, *When the Body Says No*, Wiley, 2011

Nieman, Dr. Peter, *Moving Forward: The Power of Consistent Choices in Everyday Life*, Balboa Press, 2015

Osbon, Diane, *A Joseph Campbell Companion: Reflections on the Art of Living*, Harper Perennial, 1995

Palmer, Parker J., *The Courage to Teach: Exploring the Inner Landscape of a Teacher's Life*, Jossey-Bass, 2007

Pink, Daniel H., *Drive: The Surprising Truth About What Motivates Us*, Riverhead, 2010

Robinson, Ken, *Finding Your Element: How to Discover Your Talents and Passions and Transform Your Life*, Penguin Books, 2014

Savory, Allan, The Savory Institute, http://www.savoryinstitue.com. Allan Savory is a Zimbabwean ecologist, farmer, soldier, exile, environmentalist, international consultant, and president and co-founder of The Savory Institute. He originated holistic management, a systems approach to managing resources.

Simmons, Philip, *Learning to Fall: The Blessings of an Imperfect Life*, Bantam, 2003

Stengel, Richard, *Mandela's Way: Fifteen Lessons on Life, Love, and Courage*, Crown Archetype, 2010

Vaillant, George E., *Spiritual Evolution: How We Are Wired for Faith, Hope, and Love*, Broadway Books, New York, 2009

# About the Author

David Irvine, the Leader's Navigator™, is a sought-after speaker, author, and trusted leadership advisor. His work has contributed to the building of accountable, vital, and engaged organizations across North America. As one of Canada's most respected voices on leadership, organizational culture, and personal development, David has dedicated his life to making the world a more authentic, accountable, caring place to work and live.

In addition to this book, David is the bestselling author of *Becoming Real: Journey to Authenticity*; *Authentic Leadership: It's About Presence, Not Position*; and *Bridges of Trust: Making Accountability Authentic*. He presents to corporations, governments, professional associations, and education and health care organizations.

A former family therapist, David Irvine, MSW, now speaks, facilitates workshops, and advises leaders at all levels of organizations and in all walks of life. Each year, thousands of people attend David's inspiring and thought-provoking programs on authentic leadership, accountability, caring, and cultural alignment.

David lives with his wife and family in the foothills of the Rocky Mountains near Cochrane, Alberta, Canada.

Contact us for a list of David Irvine's keynote presentations, workshops, retreats, coaching opportunities, books, and audio programs.

Phone: 1-866-621-7008
Email: info@davidirvine.com
Website: www.davidirvine.com
 @DavidJIrvine
 David Irvine & Associates
 David Irvine